THRICE-TOLD TALES

Married Couples Tell Their Stories

... here is to your healthy relationships,

Best wishes,

WNIC "The Love Doctor"

(Dr. Terri Orbuch)

THRICE-TOLD TALES

Married Couples Tell Their Stories

Diane Holmberg
Acadia University

Terri L. Orbuch
Oakland University and University of Michigan

Joseph Veroff
University of Michigan

 LAWRENCE ERLBAUM ASSOCIATES, PUBLISHERS
2004   Mahwah, New Jersey   London

Lawrence Erlbaum Associates, Inc., Publishers
10 Industrial Avenue
Mahwah, NJ 07430

Cover design by Kathryn Houghtaling Lacey

Library of Congress Cataloging-in-Publication Data

Holmberg, Diane.
Thrice-told tales : married couples tell their stories / Diane
Holmberg, Terri L. Orbuch, Joseph Veroff
    p. cm.
Includes bibliographical references and index.
ISBN 0-8058-4099-0 (c.: alk. paper)
ISBN 0-8058-4100-8 (pbk. : alk. Paper)
1. Marriage—United States—Longitudinal studies 2. Nar-
ration (Rhetoric)—Psychological aspects.   I. Orbuch,
Terri.   II. Veroff, Joseph, 1929-   III. Title.

HQ536.H638 2003
306.81'0973—dc21   2003049232
                                              CIP

Books published by Lawrence Erlbaum Associates are printed on
acid-free paper, and their bindings are chosen for strength and
durability.

Printed in the United States of America
10 9 8 7 6 5 4 3 2 1

To Libby Douvan
Colleague, mentor, friend,
whose spirit inspires us

Contents

Preface

Even before we had the opportunity to work on narratives from the Early Years of Marriage (EYM) project, the study on which this book is based, we three authors had been intrigued with what people reveal about themselves and their worlds when they tell us stories about their experiences. Diane had studied how married couples reconstructed the ups and downs of daily life with their spouses. Terri had studied the accounts that men and women gave about sexual assaults they had experienced. Joe had studied how people projected their own feelings of affiliation and power into stories they told about pictures of people unknown to them. Thus, when the EYM project came along, affording us the chance to consider how married couples tell the story of their relationship from the time they first met until the present and anticipated future, not just when they were newlyweds, but also in the third and seventh years of their marriage, it was like manna from heaven—a narrative researcher's dream come true.

A reasonably representative sample of 344 couples, some African-American, some White, all in their first marriages, told us their stories in their first year of marriage. Naturally, progressively fewer did the same in the third and seventh years, primarily because many marriages broke up in the interim. This book is mostly about the 144 couples who stayed married and bravely told us their stories in all 3 years of the study.

From these 144 couples, we assumed we could glean information about the meaning of marriage that we could not get from direct questioning. That assumption was supported. The narratives were subtle but powerful vehicles for the couples' thoughts and feelings that they could not speak of easily in response to a forced-choice question or a rating scale. From our couples, we also assumed that we could discover new insights about narratives in general, and that assumption was also supported. We were able to show how narratives change over time, being affected not only by how much time has elapsed since the event, but also by changes in the couples' feelings about their relationship. We also uncovered new insights about how gender and ethnicity can affect the nature of a narrative.

Although we consider this book to be essentially a research report about how we gathered the manna from heaven that was the EYM, we wrote it not only for other researchers but also for readers who may not be committed researchers themselves. With the current academic battles about the value of quantitative versus qualitative research, we stand off on the sidelines. This research certainly is qualitative. We allowed our couples to tell us, in their own terms, what their experiences were like. And yet, this research is also highly quantitative. We used systematic ways of coding that depend on high coding reliability, reconstructed qualities coded into systematic variables, and put these variables to systematic statistical analyses. Nevertheless, we tried not to overwhelm our discussion with the fine points of statistical analyses. These analyses are reported in the tables that appear at the end of each chapter for those who like to see numbers in their research. However, we hope that those not well versed in quantitative analyses can follow our presentations in each chapter with interest.

Much has been discussed in the social sciences about the value of narrative research as a fresh way to collect data. And yet, many fledgling researchers who decide to get narratives from a group of people of interest to them find that when they listen to the tapes collected from the project, they are perplexed as to what to do next. How do you go about extracting the themes of a narrative? How do you then analyze what you do extract? Should you describe the themes of a narrative or use these narrative themes to predict other psychological outcomes? We hope this book can be of assistance to people who have such questions about the steps to follow in narrative research. This book is not a manual for how to do narrative research, but we hope the story we tell about our research and how it unfolded can offer some insights to budding researchers about the process of conducting narrative research.

ACKNOWLEDGMENTS

Many people are part of the story of the research project reported in this book. Needless to say, without the couples who let us hear their stories, we would have little to report but our own musings. To the husbands and wives who told us their stories, we give our heartfelt thanks. We also want to give special thanks to the numerous EYM interviewers, in each of the 3 years, who spent countless hours gathering the couples' stories. We're also grateful for the financial support provided by the National Institute of Mental Health (MH Grant 41253) and the Social Sciences and Humanities Research Council of Canada (SSHRC Grant 410-98-1214).

Two other researchers were part of the EYM project from the inception, Elizabeth Douvan and Shirley Hatchett. They both moved on to other things, and to our great sorrow, Libby Douvan passed away recently. Still, their wise advice and insights permeate our work. Toni Antonucci and Hiroko Akiyama also gave us thoughtful advice. Many Survey Research Center field interviewers were dedicated colleagues in the overwhelming task of collecting couples' stories. Graduate assistants and postdoctoral students helped set up codes and persisted as the seemingly endless coding and check-coding processes occurred: Linda Acitelli, Letha Chadiha, Lindsay Custer, Sandra Eyster, Betsy Francis-Conolley, Doug Leber, Janet Malley, Charlea McNeal, Jean Oggins, Robert Ortega, Lynne Sutherland, Amy Young, and many undergraduate volunteers and research assistants. Some of the same assistants who helped us in coding went on to work out ideas for publication: Letha Chadiha, Doug Leber, Robert Ortega, and Lynne Sutherland. We borrow many of their ideas in this book.

Still other individuals have been valuable contributors to preparation of the book. Halimah Hassan has been an overworked, careful data manager and analyst. Jennifer Pringle and Anita Scott devoted many hours to labeling and documenting the dataset. Tessah Woodman worked carefully at formatting and copyediting the manuscript. Lisa Byrd also assisted in manuscript preparation. Although not technically part of the project, our spouses were critical to our progress. Diane's husband, Mark Young, Terri's husband, Stuart Jankelovitz, and Joe's wife, Jody Veroff, heard us out, provided encouragement and new insights, and put up with our deadlines when we made outrageous demands for time away from the family.

Thank you to all.

—*Diane Holmberg*
Terri L. Orbuch
Joseph Veroff

Chapter 1

Introduction

The elderly savor telling the stories of their lives. With the perspective they have about their shrinking future, they often turn to reminiscing about the past as a special pleasure for their ongoing lives. They tell, or want to tell, stories about both the dramatic and everyday events of their former selves. These reminiscences can be merely internal conversations with themselves, but sometimes, with great joy, they are performances for eager audiences, especially for loved ones who have shared their lives in some way, or for young people who are hungry to discover the personal side of earlier times.

Rarely do young people themselves get to tell their stories when they are still young. After all, their lives are still ahead of them. Present time is preoccupying. Who would listen to their stories, and what difference would they make, anyway?

This book is about an opportunity we gave to young married couples to tell the stories of their lives together, not just once, but at three different times to three different people. These are *thrice-told tales*. The couples quickly warmed up to the task and were as willing as the elderly to reminisce when given a chance to do so. They seemed to enjoy the opportunity. From them, we learned of the kind of meaning they were making of their married lives—past, present, and future—at three different times. From them, we learned much about the changing nature of narratives as they are told and retold. From them, we also learned about the changing nature of marriage as couples go from newlyweds to veteran married couples. This book is about what we have learned.

The decision to use a narrative method to collect information from newlywed couples was not merely to bring some unexpected pleasure into their lives. Rather, it evolved from the scientific expectation that this method would uncover information about newlyweds that would be unavailable through other techniques. We wanted to learn about marriage, but through the voices of married spouses. The study in which the narrative method was embedded was designed to use as many different ways as possible of assessing marital qualities and marital experiences in 373 newlywed couples, in order to understand their relationships and to predict their marital quality and stability over time. We expected that what we would learn from having couples tell the stories of their relationship from their initial meeting until their current lives would be different from what they said in response to direct questions about those lives. In narratives, we believed that couples would reveal their hopes and concerns, their ways of interacting, their feelings and evaluations about themselves and each other in a much different light. We hoped their stories would be an indirect path to finding out about them, and would reflect their less guarded feelings and their less consciously considered ways of presenting themselves.

Not that the direct pathways are useless. We profitably used many. Much information becomes available by examining answers to questions like "Taking things altogether, how would you describe your marriage? Would you say your marriage is very happy, a little happier than average, just about average, or not too happy?" Or, in answers to questions like "What things about your marriage are not quite as nice as you would like them to be?" These types of questions have certainly given us and other researchers a great deal of important information, and yet they do not necessarily get at the meaningful flow of experiences that a couple can reveal in a story. When combined with standard survey research questions, we predicted that the narrative method would offer an enriched set of explanatory factors for understanding the quality of marriage.

And indeed it did. Veroff, Sutherland, Chadiha, and Ortega (1993) showed that assessments made from the narrative technique predict marital quality over time in ways different from parallel direct assessments. These researchers also found that certain ways of assessing marital experiences through narratives have no counterpart in possible direct questions; of course, some direct questions target particular factors in the couples' lives better than any narrative assessments possibly could. Thus, there is plenty of room for both methodologies in this study, or in any study of marriage over time. Indeed, we would argue that there is plenty of room for both methodologies in the study of any close interpersonal relationship.

In this book, we concentrate primarily on the narrative method. From time to time, we will make use of the more direct questions as well. By and large, however, this book reflects the particular discoveries that emerge in using a narrative method to do systematic social research. We have become advocates of this method, and we wish to convince the reader that this method has a profound usefulness for conducting important research.

Although it is easy enough to ask people to tell the story of their experience with respect to anything important in their lives, it is another thing altogether to use what they tell you to do carefully analyzed research. Many a researcher has started with hours of tapes containing people's accounts of their interesting lives, of their experiences with a given problem or a given transition in their development, or of their experience with any issue that is of focal concern to the researcher. Indeed, these tapes often give the researcher an immersion in the participants' experience that ignites speculations and new insights. But that same researcher often becomes immobilized by questions about what to do next to turn these speculations and insights into systematic analyses. We hope that the procedures we followed, and the techniques we developed to perform systematic research using narrative techniques, are useful for others pursuing research questions with narratives, not only on the topic of marriage, but also on many other social phenomena.

So, let our story begin.

Chapter 2

A Narrative Approach
to Relationships

As adults, we tell stories about our lives and our relationships to others around us. Sometimes others prompt us for these stories, perhaps by asking us how we first met our spouse or best friend. Other times, we spontaneously decide to tell others a story about our experiences. We also might notice that those around us tend to present their lives in story form. At the dinner table, families swap stories about interesting things that happened to them during the day. At high school reunions, groups of friends gather to revisit the stories of the "good old days," and catch up on tales of what has happened to their classmates in the intervening years.

Intuitively, we understand the importance of the story form when people think about their lives. Stories allow us to search for meaning or understanding about events, relationships, and other people. They help us make sense of our daily experiences, sometimes for our own benefit, and sometimes for the benefit of those we select as our audience. Since the late 1980s, social scientists have begun collecting and interpreting the stories individuals tell about their lives and relationships (Bruner, 1986; Gergen & Gergen, 1987; Harvey, Weber, & Orbuch, 1990; Lieblich, Tuval-Maschiach, & Zilber, 1998; Maines, 1993; Orbuch, 1997). This *narrative approach*, in which scholars investigate participants' stories told in their own words, has become an important part of the social sciences. This chapter describes how that happened, and how the use of narratives and related concepts in the social sciences has developed over time. We discuss the types of processes narratives represent or illuminate, and what functions narratives serve for individuals and for couples. In so doing, we clarify why we think the narrative approach is especially useful for gaining a better understanding of marriage and marital processes over time.

A BRIEF HISTORY OF NARRATIVES
AND OTHER NARRATIVE-LIKE CONCEPTS

Theories and research on narratives and other related concepts have flourished in the 1990s. It has been an innovative, refreshing approach because social scientists using narratives have turned directly to the voices of individuals for insight and information about social experiences. Strictly quantitative researchers strongly emphasize obtaining objective, reliable, quantifiable measures of the constructs they are investigating. Emphasis on understanding what an experience really means from the perspective of the respondent takes a distant second place to the need to obtain standardized, quantifiably reliable measures. Today, many researchers have reversed that order of emphasis. Careful methods and procedures that ensure reliability are still crucial, but the primary focus of their scientific concern is to understand the meaning of important life experiences from the perspective of an individual.

Although the narrative approach has only recently been accepted in the social sciences as a legitimate methodology, other related constructs have a somewhat longer history. We review these related constructs next.

Attributions. First, early work on narratives developed in close connection with work on attributional processes. Early attribution theory focused on the explanations individuals generate to help them integrate and explain events and people around them. Fritz Heider (1958/1983) described individuals as "naive psychologists," who regularly search for explanations and understandings of one another's behavior. According to Heider, individuals spontaneously form simple causal theories about themselves, their experiences, and others around them. When we see someone behave in a particular way, especially if that behavior is somewhat unexpected, we immediately and automatically ask ourselves the question "why did that happen?"

Consider an ordinary experience in the life of a young woman, Jenna. If Jenna's new date, Greg, is very late picking her up, she spontaneously begins to wonder why, and forms theories to explain his behavior. She might attribute his lateness to something internal to him ("he seems pretty unreliable") or to some external cause ("I guess he got tied up in traffic"). Forming these theories helps people understand their social world, gives them a sense of consistency and coherence, and allows them to predict future behavior. For example, if Jenna attributes Greg's lateness to unreliability, it helps her form a clearer impression of his personality, and might affect her expectations of his future behavior (e.g., she may decide not to count on him to deliver an important message for her). Such an attribution may have a negative impact on Jenna's feelings about this new relationship and could contribute to a decision not to pursue the relationship further. Notice that the mere observation of Greg's lateness tells us little about the potential impact on his relationship with Jenna. Only by understanding what conclusions Jenna draws from this behavior are we able to predict whether Greg's lateness will have a negative impact on the relationship. By taking Jenna's perspective and determining what Greg's lateness means to her, we can understand their developing relationship more clearly than had we simply focused on the objective facts of each partner's behavior.

Later, in the late 1970s, many attribution theorists began to find single-sentence explanations or attributions inadequate. These researchers broadened their focus from single statements of causality to more inclusive, account-like processes. They observed that when people are asked "why did that happen?" they in fact often give rich and elaborate stories, rather than merely simple and direct statements. For example, if Jenna and Greg have been together many years, and Greg is late getting home, Jenna's attributions might run more like this: "It's Wednesday, so I bet he stopped off with George in Accounting for a quick drink at that Happy Hour again. I don't mind if he does that; I just wish he'd let me know so I wouldn't worry. But he always intends to be on time, he just gets caught up and loses track. It's not like he's unreliable—he's never once missed one of the kids' soccer practices—he just loves to socialize and sometimes doesn't pay attention when he's with his friends from work . . ."

Notice that in many real-life situations, especially with those we know well, our attributions go well beyond simple internal and external decisions. Jenna's attributions here are much more finely nuanced, attributing Greg's behavior to a complex interaction between his personality and a particular type of social situation. When faced with such complex attributions, social psychologists began to appreciate more fully the value of examining attributional processes within the context of natural stories that people tell about their lives. Simple scaled ratings, asking individuals whether a person's behavior was due to something internal or external to them, do not begin to capture the rich nuances of people's actual social understanding.

Today, many scholars continue to examine attributions and the roles attributions play in our experience, and in particular, the roles they play in people's perceptions of themselves when they are victims or survivors of harmful or traumatic events. In fact, present-day narrative scholars still see attributions as critical to the stories that people tell. However, most narrative researchers also extend the scope of their investigation to include much more. Narratives concentrate on a chain of events, in which many complex cognitive, emotional, and social or cultural reactions come into play. These reactions certainly include attributions about specific events, but also encompass other important constructs.

Accounts. The work on narratives also has strong connections to the concept of "accounts" (Harvey et al., 1990; Orbuch, 1997). In the 1980s, early work in sociology first described accounts as explanations or justifications for behaviors that were unanticipated or deviant. If we act in a way that goes against social norms or expectations, we are often motivated to give explanations, or *accounts*, to others. These accounts help us maintain our self-esteem or personal status; they also aid us in regulating our social interactions. For example, if you are driving faster than the speed limit and a police officer stops you, you are likely to seek to explain to the officer exactly why you behaved in this unacceptable fashion: "I'm so sorry, officer, I didn't see the speed limit sign" or "I feel awful—I was just trying to get home to see my children and didn't realize I was going so fast." These are attributions, explanations for why you acted in a particular fashion, but they are a specific type of attributional account. They are given when you know you have done something that others might judge negatively. They serve to present your actions in the best possible light.

According to Scott and Lyman (1968), accounts fall into two general categories: *justifications,* in which one accepts the responsibility for an action in question ("I should have watched more carefully for the speed limit sign"), and *excuses,* in which one denies responsibility for that action ("My speedometer said I was only doing 55 mph"). Scott and Lyman suggested that the primary motivation for such accounts is to protect self-esteem or social status.

Such thinking dates back to Goffman's (1959, 1971) classic work on how the self is presented to others in potentially blameworthy situations. Goffman suggested that whenever people commit an offense, they receive powerful societal demands to account for it. As social animals, when we know we have violated the expected norms we must seek to explain, excuse, or justify our actions. Only then can we protect our positive feelings about ourselves and the positive regard of those around us. Such a process is part of the routine we learn that guides our interactions with others in situations wherever there is a question of why we do what we do.

Accounts as Storylike Constructions. More recent work on accounts has broadened their focus and function to include not only justifications and excuses, but also other storylike constructions. This more recent work places far less emphasis on the use of accounts to justify unexpected or disrupted social interaction. It is not only when we know we have violated social norms that we are drawn to explain our behavior to ourselves and others. More broadly, almost any complex, stressful situation can lead people experiencing it to search for understandings, meanings, and explanations. For example, Robert Weiss, in his book *Marital Separation* (1975), interviewed married people who were in the process of separation. Weiss found that in telling their stories, people gave complex accounts that helped them explain to themselves and to others exactly why the separation had occurred. Weiss suggested that these storylike explanations helped individuals deal with the stress and distress they experienced during the break-up period.

Since Weiss, other researchers have also examined storylike accounts by asking individuals to explain or interpret other stressful events. Harvey et al. (1990) sought accounts of sexual assault, whereas Pennebaker and Harber (1993) asked people for their accounts of experiencing an earthquake. Individuals do not simply accept such stressful events at face value. They actively attempt to understand why such difficult events happened, even when there is no need to justify their own behavior. By building up a story of the causes of such stressful events, individuals may develop a sense of closure or control. We do not want to feel like helpless victims of powerful negative events. By constructing an understanding of why these events happened, individuals may begin to believe they can avoid such events in the future or that the experience has made them stronger. Such a sense of psychological control can be a powerful source of healing in the face of stress.

A handful of researchers found that individuals develop complex storylike accounts even for relatively positive events. For example, Surra, Batchelder, and Hughes (1995) have done analyses of stories of how couples became romantically entwined in their courtships. Developing a relationship is certainly not as stressful as surviving an earthquake; however, it is a complex event, not fully under either individual's control, that has profound consequences for their ongoing well-being. Under such circumstances, individuals may seek to review and understand the reasons why they are together, especially because such understanding helps them decide whether they should remain together in the future.

Narratives.   The narratives we examine in this book are similar to the accounts studied by Surra et al. (1995). In them, couples reflect on how they began their life together, what their life is like now, and how they perceive their future. Although accounts may not involve telling one's story to others, often remaining at the level of private reflections or diary records, narratives are storylike constructions that are told to others in an oral format. Despite this distinction, the concepts of narratives and accounts tend to be used and interpreted interchangeably in the wider literature.

Both narratives and storylike accounts, then, are stories individuals tell, centered on complex or stressful events, that attempt to make sense of those events, either to themselves or to others. Orbuch (1997) suggested such stories provide several important benefits to those who engage in them. Narratives help give individuals: (a) a greater sense of control and understanding of their environment, (b) the ability to cope with emotionally charged and stressful events, (c) a certain sense of closure, (d) order to their daily relational experiences, and (e) a greater hope and will for the future. Orbuch argued that when we try to understand what has happened in our lives, either through private accounts or more public narratives, we tend to feel a sense of mastery of the past that helps contribute to our present well-being. Such understanding can also arouse a sense of optimism about the future.

In developing the sense of understanding a good narrative can bring, storytellers often place more value on reaching a sense of control or closure than on relaying the exact facts of an event in chronological order. The perspective conveyed to others in a narrative is subjectively constructed by the individuals telling the story, given their needs and motivations at the time, in interaction with the context and meaning of the storytelling situation. In other words, narrative researchers understand that people's stories may not always reflect reality. Others might give very different versions of the same event, and even one storyteller's narrative may change over time or when faced with different audiences. The reality of the narrative is a more subjective one, in which the act of developing a coherent story at a particular point in time and for a particular audience helps the storyteller develop a sense of meaning, understanding, and mastery over complex events. Narratives are critical psychological realities, which take on a life of their own as presented. According to Spence (1982), the stories individuals tell represent narrative truth, not historical truth.

In this emphasis on subjective rather than objective truth, the narrative approach shares much in common with *symbolic interactionism*, a theoretical framework prominent in sociology (Blumer, 1969; Cooley, 1902; Mead, 1934; S. Stryker, 1981, 1983). According to most symbolic interactionists, there is in fact no objective reality; instead, reality is constructed subjectively through interaction and meaning-making processes within groups. We understand our surroundings by learning meaning from those around us. The concept of perceiving the world "as it really is," without any form of observer perspective or bias, is meaningless. The observer cannot be separated from what is observed: Our history, prior beliefs, emotions, values, and cultural perspectives profoundly color the way we observe even the simplest events in the world around us.

For example, Maines (2001) suggested that if a tree falls in the woods and there is no one there to hear it, then symbolic interactionists would argue that it is meaningless to speak of the tree having made a noise. Only when individuals are there to interpret the soundwaves, to give meaning to that raw event, can we discuss the concept of noise. Likewise, stressful or emotional events may happen in people's lives, but we can never collect valid information on these raw events. An individual's subjective perspective is always going to color his or her perceptions and memories of the event. Thus, the primary goal shared by both narrative researchers and symbolic interactionists is to understand people's subjective experiences and how these experiences tie into other important aspects of their lives, such as their beliefs, emotions, and personal and social interactions (Orbuch, 1997).

Concepts such as *self, identity,* and *self-presentation* are also major themes examined by both symbolic interactionists and narrative researchers. Symbolic interactionists argue that we develop our identity, our sense of self, through our interactions with other people. One way we can negotiate new identities is through the process of presenting narratives about important life events. For example, Duck (1982) gave the example of a relationship break-up. You and your partner might decide between the two of you that it is time to move on, perhaps because neither of you is ready to commit to a serious relationship at this stage. But until you publicly deliver the fact of the break-up and the accompanying story to your friends and family, they continue to treat you and your partner as a couple. Only by the process of telling your story to others do you publicly change your identity from a member of a couple to that of a single person. Narratives can help to develop and maintain various identities and can also dissolve them.

To summarize, narratives are storylike constructions told to other people, in which individuals try to summarize, explain, and make sense of stressful, complex, or emotion-laden events in their lives. Along with symbolic interactionists, narrative researchers would argue that these stories do not necessarily represent objective reality, but instead give insight into the more important subjective reality of each individual. They might change when told at different times, or to different audiences. They can help individuals understand events, justify their actions to others, and negotiate important social identities.

Such narratives are relatively easy to elicit and collect. The true challenge comes in analyzing these stories in a way that allows a systematic investigation of the meanings they may contain. There are many models of narrative analysis to which we might have turned when examining our data (Mishler, 1995). Some narrative scholars rely heavily on linguistic analyses. Their emphasis is on a precise scrutiny of how the story is told, carefully analyzing the storytellers' choice of words and particular phrasings. Zilber (1998), for example, listed a number of formal features in a life story that can be used to diagnose emotional concerns. These include repetitions of parts of the discourse or breaks in the chronology of events. In contrast, we, along with other scholars, are more focused on the overt content of the story—on what couples say, more than on how they say it. Maines (1993) spoke of three ways in which one can analyze the content of any narrative—the events, the sequence, and the plot. Like Maines, we believe that it is the last element, the plot, which best conveys and represents meaning through narration. The plot connects the beliefs, emotions, and behaviors together. A plot gives structure or coherence to possibly random events. Thus, the plot plays an important role in our analyses. Do our couples present their story as a dramatic series of ups and downs? Do they present it as a quietly positive sequence, one in which their relationship slowly and steadily gets better? Or is their plot a more negative one, in which the thrilling beginnings of the courtship period are slowly fading away into the monotony of a daily routine?

In addition to the overall plot, we also explore the particular themes or issues that may emerge as the story progresses. Some themes or issues might be prominent in the best relationships; others may serve as warning signals of a relationship in trouble. We also examine the affects that emerge while couples tell their story. Affects can consist of feelings or emotions (joy, sorrow, anger, jealousy) or wants or needs (wanting, hoping, wishing, desiring). Will couples' stories be cool descriptions of the events of their lives together? Or will their stories be filled with these warmer feelings and emotions? In summary, we are looking for meanings expressed in couples' narratives by examining their overall plots, the more specific themes or issues that may emerge in relating these plots, and the affects described or catalogued in the process of exploring these themes. The details of how we coded these aspects of the narrative are described in chapter 3. Meanwhile, let us turn to examining how these plots, themes, and affects might be shaped by the context in which the narrative emerges.

NARRATIVES: A PATHWAY TO MEANING

Many narrative scholars emphasize the meaning and understanding that narratives bring to an individual or couple. Bruner (1990) suggested that the quest for meaning is fundamental to human nature, that the very selves and lives we construct in story form are the outcomes of the process of meaning construction. Like others (Frankl, 1963; Harvey et al., 1990), we also believe people are driven to search for meaning in all aspects of their daily and social lives. The marital context is no exception. How do individuals and couples come to make sense out of their emerging relationship? In this section, we explore three sources of information couples might turn to in building an understanding of their relationship as they tell narratives about their lives. First, they may turn to information provided about relationships and marriage in their culture or subculture. Popular media, religious teaching, and peers in their cultural or ethnic group pass on information about what marriages should be and how husbands and wives should treat each other. Consciously or unconsciously, these expectations may color married couples' stories. Second, couples can develop meaning at an interpersonal level. Over time, they can develop beliefs and expectations, through talking to each other or simply by living their lives together, about what their relationship means to them. This shared belief system and sense of what makes a good or bad relationship for them can also influence the stories couples choose to share with others. Third, the two individuals comprising the couple will have their own personal beliefs and issues. These may include beliefs about marriage and relationships. They may also include personal styles and preferences (e.g., degree of extraversion) that would shape any story they choose to tell, not just a marriage story. All three levels, *cultural, interpersonal,* and *personal,* can serve as sources of meaning that affect the stories couples tell.

Two important themes emerge in our discussion of these three levels of meaning. The first is that the interplay between these sources of meanings and the meaning constructed within the narrative is bidirectional. Most obviously, the narratives couples choose to tell are shaped by the three different levels we outlined. For example, at the cultural level, a public emphasis on harmony within a relationship might lead couples to tell stories that emphasize their compatibility and de-emphasize conflict. At the interpersonal level, a strong and happy relationship may elicit more positive or optimistic themes; problems and distress at the interpersonal level may result in a story holding more negative or conflictual information. At the personal level, a strong belief in egalitarianism might lead to a story emphasizing the couple as equal partners.

More subtly, however, the stories couples choose to tell, and the meanings that they make in the process of constructing their narrative, can in turn shape their culture, their interpersonal well-being, or their personal beliefs. Consider the following examples: If more women become economically self-sufficient despite traditional norms against it, they may choose their life partners for noneconomic reasons. The stories they tell might come to reflect those new realities, and as a result, the traditional cultural emphasis on the roles of women as homemakers and men as breadwinners will be weakened. Thus, individual beliefs and meanings can indirectly shape the culture. Likewise, telling stories emphasizing positive and optimistic aspects of a relationship may not only reflect solid well-being at the interpersonal level, it may also contribute to it. And stories emphasizing the couple as equal partners can reinforce and solidify a personal belief in egalitarianism, as well as reflect it. Thus, the stories couples tell are shaped by their cultural, interpersonal, and personal worlds, but those stories can in turn affect and influence those worlds. Thus, as Bruner (1990) suggested, the selves, lives, and worlds we construct during the process of meaning construction can act as shapers of future meaning as well.

A second important theme, suggested by the first, is that the meaning constructed in couples' narratives is by no means static. As mentioned earlier, narratives tend to reflect narrative truth rather than historical truth. Over time and across audiences, the meanings couples construct change and evolve as they learn from their cultures, develop their relationship at an interpersonal level, or change their beliefs at a personal level. All these changes are reflected in the stories couples construct. Their stories change and evolve over time, as do the meanings reflected in those stories.

Cultural Meaning. Popular culture is full of messages regarding how relationships and marriages should work. Romantic comedies at the movies or in sitcoms portray the ongoing quest for Mr. or Ms. Right. Popular magazines give simple 10-item quizzes to help readers determine if their relationship is right for them. Books such as *The Relationship Cure* (J. M. Gottman, 2002) and *The Good Marriage* (Wallerstein & Blakeslee, 1996) define good and bad marriages and reassure readers that relationships in trouble can be rescued. Even children have developed some relatively sophisticated ideas about marriage and relationships, if widespread reports available on the Internet are to be believed (*Kids & Marriage*, n.d.). Ten-year-old Alan espouses notions of the importance of similarity in relationships ("You got to find somebody who likes the same stuff. Like, if you like sports, she should like it that you like sports, and she should keep the chips and dip coming"); 10-year-old Camille has carefully considered the best age at which to marry ("Twenty-three is the best age, because you know the person forever").

These examples suggest that our culture is constantly emphasizing what factors are present in a good relationship. These cultural beliefs may or may not be true. Some, such as Alan's emphasis on couple similarity as conducive to well-being, do find support in the research literature (e.g., Plechaty, 1987). Other beliefs, just as firmly held, may not hold up to careful scrutiny. For example, many people believe that marriages become steadily better over time, as spouses learn how to compromise and adapt their lives to each other. Unfortunately, empirical evidence based on national statistics suggests that this view is overly optimistic: Marital quality declines steadily after the first few years of marriage and does not begin to increase again until the 25th year, on average. Only after 35 years of marriage is average marital quality higher than in the first few years (Orbuch, House, Mero, & Webster, 1996).

Whether these cultural myths about marriage are true or false is almost beside the point. If people believe them to be true, these myths will shape how they think about marriage, and most crucially from our perspective, how they talk about marriage. Cultural beliefs and expectations about what is expected and appropriate in a marriage are therefore expected to shape couples' stories. Such reliance on culturally provided meanings may well be more prominent in the early years of marriage. Those who have less experience with the married state may turn to cultural norms for information about how a relationship "should be," turning to the world around them for "acceptable" relationship stories. As a relationship progresses, partners may develop the confidence to realize that every marriage is different. Cultural meanings may lose their significance and importance and couples' own interpersonal and personal meanings may come to the forefront. Following such an argument, we might suggest that the relationship stories presented in Year 1 of the couple's marriage (and of our study) would show less variability in themes and content than do the stories those same couples present in Year 7. Over time, the individual flavor of each couple's unique story may emerge.

That is one possible way that couples' narratives might change over time. Other patterns of change are also possible, however. For example, couples' stories may actually adhere more and more to cultural expectations over time. In a classic study, Bartlett (1932) had participants read unusual stories that did not fall into the usual narrative conventions of our culture. He then examined how these stories changed over time, whether it was in repeated remembering by a single individual over time or through the transmission of the story across multiple individuals. Bartlett found that the stories consistently changed over time to more closely fit the cultural norms and expectations of what stories should be like.

Similar processes could work in our study as well. There certainly are basic norms and expectations for how a courtship, wedding, and marriage should progress. Consider a wedding, for example. A multimillion-dollar industry surrounds the process of planning for a wedding. Certain expectations are nurtured. The bride, often with the support of her family, takes the lead in planning the event. Family and friends are invited for a celebration. There is normally at least a best man and a maid of honor. There is generally some gathering after the service, often a reception with food, music, and dancing. The bride and groom leave the reception and go off on their own. A honeymoon normally follows.

These general expectations of what happens at a wedding, and in what order, may come to form a standard cultural script (Ginsburg, 1988). If this script is followed in telling a wedding story, communication is facilitated, because both the speaker and listener know what to expect next. Over time, with telling and retelling, couples' stories may come to more closely approximate such cultural scripts than when they were first told, just as Bartlett's (1932) participants' stories more closely approximated the standard cultural story form over time. Telling the expected story is easier, and couples may consciously shape their narrative to fit expectations.

Such shaping may also be less conscious. We argued elsewhere (Holmberg & Veroff, 1996) that over time, as the precise details of early relationship events fade, couples may unknowingly draw on these scripts to help them fill in gaps in their memories. Thus, whether due to consciously shaping a "good" story, or unconsciously fleshing out a half-forgotten story, couples' narratives may come to more closely approximate the expected cultural script over time. Note that this perspective would lead us to expect that stories are more variable in Year 1 across the sample, but become more similar by Year 7, quite the opposite of our speculations just mentioned. Few studies have collected narratives across time like ours has; this wealth of data can help us to sort out such conflicting hypotheses. Chapter 5 examines how narratives change across time; chapter 6 focuses more specifically on the issues surrounding memory reconstruction.

Subcultural Meaning. Thus far, we have spoken of popular culture quite broadly. Certainly, all individuals living in North America today are exposed, to some extent, to the same movies, books, magazines, talk shows, and other carriers of the common culture. Yet we should also be aware that North American society is composed of many subcultures. Prominent in our study is the fact that half of our couples are African-American and the other half are White. Both groups partake of mainstream culture, certainly, but there are subtle differences in their cultural surroundings. They may differ somewhat in the books, magazines, movies, and TV shows they favor. They may tend to belong to different religious groups. Importantly, we get our cultural beliefs not only from the mass media or organized groups, but also from informally observing important others in our social worlds—our parents, siblings, friends, and neighbors. In a less than fully integrated society such as ours, members of each ethnic group tend to develop their ideas of relationships and marriage primarily by observing other individuals from their own ethnic group. This partial separation could well lead to distinct conceptions of what marriage means arising within each group. As few studies to date have compared African-American and White relationships, we do not know the extent to which these two groups are similar or different in the meanings they ascribe to marriage, parenthood, or changes in relationships over time. In chapter 10, we compare and contrast the narratives of our White and African-American couples to see whether their stories tend to be similar (perhaps inspired by the broader cultural context) or different (perhaps informed by their more local subcultural experiences).

Interpersonal Meaning. Although expectations fostered at the cultural and subcultural levels definitely can help shape couples' relationship stories, they are certainly not the sole shapers of narratives. Couples are well aware that although their marriage stories share much in common with those of others in their cultural or subcultural group, each of their stories is also to some extent unique. No one else has a relationship, or a relationship history, precisely like theirs. Such awareness of their uniqueness may be especially apparent when their stories do not fit neatly into the usual cultural script. For example, the stereotypical relationship progression might include dating, engagement, wedding, honeymoon, establishing a marital home, and eventually having children, in that order. Some couples violate this standard progression, however, perhaps by skipping a stage (e.g., dispensing with the honeymoon to save money for the wedding), or by rearranging the usual order (e.g., having children together before marriage). As their story will not fit neatly into the usual societal script, they will have to develop their own sets of meanings, their own version of the marriage story.

Furthermore, the usual cultural expectations tend to dictate that, although there will be occasional disagreements, the establishment of a good relationship basically progresses relatively smoothly from one stage to the next. What about couples who face major setbacks or difficulties in the establishment of their relationship, those who must deal with breakups and reunions, those who must work their way through infidelities, those who must cope with unplanned pregnancies, or heartbreaking miscarriages? Such couples may be forced to search for new meanings to help them understand or control such unplanned events. Such meanings may have special value for the couple because they serve as a mechanism for coping, influencing the psychological well-being of the couple or individual involved (see Orbuch, 1997; Orbuch & Eyster, 1997, under review; Orbuch, Veroff, & Holmberg, 1993).

Thus, couples often do not settle for the standard cultural or subcultural story, but add their own variations and elaborations to the usual script. Importantly, in narratives such as ours, told by a couple together, the members of the couple cannot each build up their own separate version of how their relationship works. As Berger and Kellner (1964) pointed out, couples need to work together first construct a joint meaning by amalgamating the two partners' views and styles. Only then can this joint meaning be easily presented to others. There are different ways this joint meaning may emerge. For example, one analysis from our dataset (Orbuch & Eyster, under review) examined the narratives our couples told of the birth of their first child. These stories were told by each spouse individually and then by the couple together. In constructing the joint narrative, the spouses had to work together to come up with one consistent story, although initially they might each have had slightly different perspectives. In some cases, the couples seemed to meet halfway (e.g., if she said the pregnancy was planned, and he said it was not, in the joint story it came across as sort of vaguely planned). In other cases, one partner would defer to the other's point of view (e.g., if he said he was highly involved in the birth process and she did not, then in the joint story his high involvement would be mentioned). By compromising and by deferring to each other's point of view, couples can construct a joint narrative that truly represents the experiences of the couple as a unit, not just of either individual separately.

Couples' narratives can thus come to reflect the interpersonal meanings that they build up in their lives together. One important aspect of such interpersonal meanings is their overall level of well-being or satisfaction. We believe that the stories told by happy couples differ in many ways from those told by unhappy couples. Their overall level of satisfaction and ability to cope with the difficulties of forging a life together might shape their narratives—the overall trend of the plots they devise, the feelings or needs they discuss in the context of their story, or the way they build up the story in a collaborative or conflictful fashion.

Perhaps more controversially, we also believe that the narratives they shape can, in turn, affect their overall level of satisfaction or well-being. Such a view is not without precedent. For example, there is a school of psychotherapy that advocates sharing narratives to help individuals better understand their lives, relationships, and difficulties with each. Narrative therapists draw out life stories from their clients, looking for omissions or for troublesome perspectives in the way a tale is told (see White & Epston, 1990). The therapist and client then work together to shape the stories, seeking to construct a "preferred" reality. The assumption is that by encouraging clients to look for new perspectives on their life stories, narrative therapists can help those clients deal with their demons and the challenges of their lives. Similar approaches are common in family therapy, where the goal is to help families regulate and manage relationships. Family therapists again often elicit stories about the relationship from their clients, and seek to help clients shape those stories as a means of helping their clients cope with difficulties and tackle new challenges. Research by Pennebaker and his colleagues (e.g., Pennebaker & Seagal, 1999) also found that when people told stories about critical or traumatic events in their lives, their physical and mental health improved considerably.

Likewise, we believe that when couples air their joys and challenges to each other, shaping a common perspective on their life together, it may predict or determine their subsequent adjustment and emotional functioning within their relationship. This is the basic framework we took when we examined the themes, styles of presentation, and interactive qualities of the courtship stories couples told in Year 1 of their marriage to see whether these qualities were predictive of marital well-being in Year 3 of their marriage (Orbuch et al., 1993). In fact, we did find that the specific types of courtship stories couples told in Year 1 (e.g., who initiated, type of tension, flow of the story) were predictive of their self-reported marital happiness 2 years later. Thus, happier couples tell happier stories, but also, those who tell more positive stories become happier couples over time. Life shapes narrative, and narrative may shape life.

We can also see life shaping narrative when we examine how couples' stories change over time as their relationship changes. In one study (Holmberg & Holmes, 1994), we compared the narratives of two sets of couples who were equally happy in Year 1; by Year 3, however, half of the couples had remained quite happy, whereas the other half had shown a sharp decline in marital satisfaction. Although both groups' narratives were similar in Year 1, by Year 3 those in the less happy group were telling more negative stories. Intriguingly, it was not only their current life which was presented in a less favorable light. The negative tone also spilled back to the beginning of the relationship, leading to more negative courtship stories, for instance, where initially all had been well. The meanings couples make in their narratives are by no means static; they shift and change as the couple's life circumstances shift and change. Here we see clear instances of changes in couples' interpersonal meanings, specifically their marital well-being, predicting changes in narratives. We suspect the path can run in the other direction as well: Those who let current negative feelings in their relationship affect their memories of the past, allowing themselves to forget all the positive circumstances which brought them together in the first place, may continue their drop in marital well-being over time, perhaps even leading to divorce. Those who hold on to the memories of once being happy may be inspired to work harder to regain those feelings, leading to narratives predicting and shaping well-being over time. Couples' lives and narratives can move in a constant interplay, each reflecting and shaping the other. Such memory reconstruction issues are investigated in chapters 6 and 7.

Personal Meaning.   Although the couple must work together to come up with their narrative, making it to a great extent a joint construction, there are still two separate individuals involved. Whenever there are individuals involved, their personal styles, preferences, motivations, and needs are going to shape their behavior. Thus, narratives can also be shaped and influenced by each individual storyteller's personal style and quest for meaning, above and beyond influences at the couple level.

First of all, individuals are not uniformly elaborate in their narrative styles. Some people are born storytellers, happy to elaborate on their stories in great detail. Others are more reticent, sticking to only the most basic facts and not endeavoring to expand on or investigate the themes that might arise. Such differences in narrative style might arise for any number of reasons: cultural or family background and emphasis on storytelling, general verbal abilities, degree of comfort with abstract thought, degree of extraversion, and so forth. For whatever reason, we notice when listening to the narratives that some individuals' stories are lively and full of detail, allowing the listener to clearly picture the events described; others' stories are relatively bland recitations of who met whom, when, and under what circumstances.

Such stylistic differences may become even more apparent when repeated stories over time are available, as we have in our dataset. Some individuals, perhaps those with a high need for order, might try to "smooth out" their stories over time, removing any awkward or uncomfortable sections. They may engage in "leveling," to borrow a classic term from the perceptual and cognitive processing literature (Krech & Crutchfield, 1948), tending to forget, gloss over, or ignore any unexpected events. For these people, last-minute problems with the wedding planning, for example, might be downplayed in their initial stories, and disappear altogether by Year 7, as the need to present an orderly and organized sequence of events makes itself felt. Other individuals, however, perhaps those with a less strong need for order, might instead engage in "sharpening" (Krech & Crutchfield, 1948), seizing on the unexpected events, elaborating on them for the amusement of self, partner, and audience, perhaps even exaggerating the incident over time until it becomes a signature anecdote. No two people tell a story the same way, and our participants' individual approaches might become ever more apparent as time goes on.

Personal meanings may also shape our participants' narratives through their goals for self-presentation. Harvey, Hendrick, and Tucker (1988) noted that it is not only factors within an individual, or only factors within an audience, but also interactions between the narrator and the audience which can affect how incidents are recalled and presented. In our stories, we present a certain image of ourselves, of the kind of person we would like others to believe us to be. We might censor certain ideas or themes and augment others in a desire to shape the reactions of the people to whom we tell the story. And again, these meanings need not stay stable over time. For example, we found in one study (Holmberg & Veroff, 1996) that those individuals who placed more emphasis on egalitarianism in their relationship over time also showed changes in their narratives, emphasizing the degree to which the wedding was jointly planned. We shape our narratives to present ourselves as the kinds of people we wish to be. And, we also argue, by presenting ourselves as the kinds of people we wish to be, we come to shape our thoughts, beliefs, and even actions—eventually becoming those kinds of people in reality. Again, life shapes narrative and narrative shapes life.

SUMMARY

There is a solid history to the use of narratives and other related concepts in the social sciences. Many believe that narratives are at the core of our existence and at the heart of all social behavior. They help shape our lives and at the same time represent the meaning we attach to our lives. Recent work has used the narrative methodology to examine individuals' experiences in relationships. We use this methodology in this book to learn about marriage, by having married couples tell the story of their relationship from the time they first met until the present, and with regard to the future. This we had them do not just when they were first married, but again in the third year of their marriages and then again in the seventh year. We expect these "thrice-told tales" to be revealing of the way couples think about themselves, each other and their relationship, and to illuminate how these processes may shift over time.

Here are the words of one young couple, discussing their lives around the time they first met:

H: Well, my life before I met my wife was rather boring, dull, and lifeless (laughing). I was over the hill in terms of dating and experience away from home. I went to school, did my work and went home.

W: Me, I didn't like him at all when we first met. I just thought he was really ugly. But then we became friends. Then we went for walks. Went to church together. We got to be pretty good friends. We found that we had a good rapport with each other. We could talk about anything. I felt like I could tell him anything, you know. I decided I didn't think he was yucky anymore.

The warmth and affection between these two individuals comes across in their teasing descriptions, and in the way they describe the transformation of their lives and their feelings as they grew closer. Just these few sentences give us insight into their relationship, how they feel about each other, and what they value in their life together. It is our hope that by examining a series of such stories in our research project, we will gain insight into what marriage means to young couples starting out. By examining how couples tell their stories, including how those stories might change over time, we may also cast new light on the nature of the narrative process. Let us now turn to the specifics of our study, to learn the details of who our couples were and how we analyzed their stories.

Chapter 3

The Early Years
of Marriage Project

The goal of the Early Years of Marriage (EYM) project from the beginning was to understand the factors that contribute to the positive development of marital relationships in the early years. At the same time, we were aware that these processes might possibly be different in African-American couples as compared to White couples. Given the high rates of divorce in the United States, we were interested in discovering what aspects of an early relationship predict later marital stability and happiness. Many researchers have proposed explanations for what keeps marriages together and happy (Karney & Bradbury, 1995; Orbuch, House, Mero, & Webster, 1996). One type of explanation focuses on how a couple interacts with each other for such matters as maximizing positive feelings (Cartensen, Gottman, & Levenson, 1995; Huston & Chorost, 1994), reducing conflicts (Markman, 1991), avoiding maladaptive attributions (Bradbury & Fincham, 1992), and integrating work and family roles (Tallman & Riley, 1995). Another type of explanation concentrates on several objective social conditions such as changes in family composition with the addition of children, the couple's economic viability, and their embeddedness in social support networks (Orbuch, Veroff, Hassan, & Horrocks, 2002). The EYM project was open to both types of explanations and therefore gathered information over the first 7 years of marriage with an eclectic array of measures.

THE PROCEDURE

Because we wanted to track the development of couples' marriages over time, our participants were interviewed on multiple occasions. The first interview took place just a few months after their marriage, at a time when

21

most couples are firmly in the glow of the honeymoon period. We then re-turned to interview them in Years 2, 3, 4, and 7 of their marriage.

The interviews in Years 1, 3, and 7 were the most extensive. We knew many factors could potentially predict couples' marital well-being and sta-bility, and we wanted to tap into as many of these factors as possible. Profes-sional interviewers from the University of Michigan's Survey Research Cen-ter separately interviewed each member of each couple in 1- to 1½-hour standardized sessions in the couple's home. The interviewers were all fe-male and their racial background was matched to that of the participant be-ing interviewed.

In these individual interviews, respondents answered a wide variety of questions tapping into virtually every aspect of their married life. Most of the questions were closed-ended, requiring participants to choose an an-swer from a scale, but some were open-ended, allowing respondents to an-swer in their own words. Participants described their feelings about their marriages, their views of their spouses' personalities, their approaches to conflict, their divisions of household responsibilities, their experiences with and philosophies of childrearing, their leisure-time activities, their work lives, their social support networks, and many other aspects of their daily experiences. In Years 2 and 4, participants completed a much-ab-breviated version of this interview over the telephone. We were mostly in-terested in keeping in touch with the respondents, obtaining an assessment of their current levels of marital well-being, and identifying instances of di-vorce or separation.

Interviewing members of the couple individually was important. They might feel less constrained about revealing slightly negative aspects of their partner or relationship when interviewed alone than they would when to-gether. However, there is also important information to be gleaned from observing how couples interact. Accordingly, all couples were also asked to participate in a couple interview, again in their own home.

Couples completed a number of short tasks such as answering questions about a recent disagreement, negotiating the importance of certain "rules for marriage," and agreeing on and describing some particularly pleasant aspects of their life together. A final component of the couple interview consisted of obtaining their joint narrative about their relationship. As these narratives are the main focus of this book, we describe the procedures for obtaining them in detail.

THE NARRATIVES

In obtaining the couple narratives, as much as possible we wanted to let the couples tell the story in their own words, in any way that felt most natural to them. Because we believed the way they chose to tell the story would be as revealing as what they chose to say, we tried to leave the task as open as possible. Accordingly, couples in the first year were told:

> Today I'm going to ask you to do something different—tell the story of your relationship from the beginning, up to now, and into the future. There's no right or wrong way to tell the story. Just tell it as it naturally comes to both of you right now. I'm talking to both of you together and want the two of you to tell me in your own words the story of your relationship. I have no set questions to ask you. I just want you to tell me about your lives together as if it were a story with a beginning, a middle, and how things will look in the future. There is no right or wrong way to tell your story. Just tell me in any way that is most comfortable. It's something that couples really enjoy doing. Each of you can talk and I hope to hear from both of you. You can agree about the story; you can disagree—any way that seems comfortable for you.

Initial pilot testing suggested that we could not simply leave the instructions there, however. Couples were sometimes uncertain as to how to approach the task when it was left completely open-ended, or would skip over some stages of the relationship altogether. Accordingly, we decided to provide a rough guideline for couples to follow when telling their story.

The interviewer said, "To help you think of your story, we'll use this guide," and showed couples the storyline sheet reproduced in Fig. 3.1. As can be seen in the figure, the couple was asked to describe how they met, how they got interested in one another, becoming a couple, planning to get

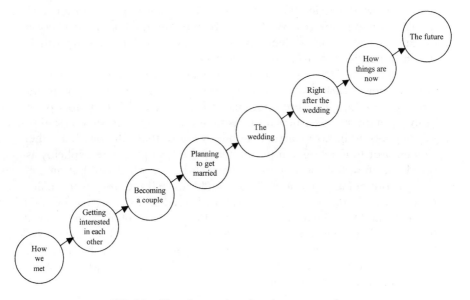

FIG. 3.1.   Narrative storyboard as shown to couples.

married, the wedding itself, what life was like right after the wedding, what life was like now, and what they thought married life would be like in the future. The storyline sheet served to give couples a general idea of what topics to cover and helped them to remember all the important stages of the relationship. By using this technique, we did tend to promote a story with a linear, chronological shape. We acknowledge that spontaneous stories are not always linear; however, the linear, chronological story is a common form in our culture. In addition, it was the best frame for an interviewer to use to ensure coverage of a "complete" story, and to guarantee comparability of standardized interviewing. Furthermore, it facilitated later access to particular sections of the story during coding procedures.

To get couples started, the interviewer said, "Everyone seems to come up with an interesting story, ways in which their story is different from others. Just tell it as it happened to both of you. To get you started, why don't each of you tell me what your life was like just before the two of you met?" She then called on the wife first for a brief story, then the husband. After these introductions, the interviewer said, "Now, let's hear the story of your relationship. How did it all begin? Let's start the story here. How did you two meet?" The interviewer then placed a marker on the circle stating how they met.

From that point on, the interviewer made her presence known as little as possible. If couples had difficulty coming up with anything to say for a particular part of the story, interviewers were provided with specific probes they could use, such as "Did you go on a honeymoon?" for "what life was like after the wedding" or "Tell me the kinds of things you do during the week" for "what married life is like now." For the most part, however, such intervention was unnecessary. With the help of the storyboard, the majority of couples readily worked their way through their relationship story with little further assistance from the interviewer.

In Years 3 and 7, the procedure was virtually identical. There was a different interviewer each time, so couples were not repeating the story to the same person. Couples were reminded that they had told their story previously. To minimize pressures for consistency, however, interviewers said we were interested in how married couples' views of their life together either change over time or remain pretty steady. The couples were explicitly assured that they did not have to remember what they had said last time or worry about being repetitious. They should just tell the story as it seemed most natural to them now. One additional storyline category was inserted for Year 3 and Year 7 narratives, with "the first few years of marriage" placed between "what life was like after the wedding" and "what life is like now." Otherwise, the narratives proceeded much as in the first year. Because couples were experienced with the procedure, they tended to require even less intervention from the interviewer than in Year 1.

THE SAMPLE

Now that we have an overview of the study, let us examine who actually participated. In the EYM study, our goal was to get a broad overview of couples' experiences in the early years of marriage. Accordingly, we wished to use a large and diverse sample. Some previous programs of research on married couples have relied either on clinical samples of couples seeking marital counseling (e.g., J. Gottman, Markman, & Notarius, 1977) or on volunteers recruited through advertising (e.g., J. M. Gottman & Levenson, 1992). A clinical sample is likely to be experiencing many more marital problems than the average, whereas the recruited volunteers may have among them many who feel especially secure about their marriage or are especially eager to get advice about problems in their marriage. To get a more representative sample, we turned to marriage licenses, which provide a complete list of all the couples preparing for marriage in a given area. We then approached a representative sample of all these couples to ask them to take part in the study, rather than waiting for them to approach us.

The area we selected for study was Wayne County, Michigan. This area was obviously desirable for its proximity to our research base at the University of Michigan. However, Wayne County is also a good location for other reasons. First, the communities it contains are very diverse, ranging from poor inner-city neighborhoods in downtown Detroit to posh suburban enclaves such as Grosse Pointe. Also, Wayne County has a sizable African-American population. Most of the work on marriages to date has focused on White, middle-class relationships (see Bradbury, 1998); one of our goals in the EYM study was to broaden our perspective and investigate how African-American marriages might be similar to, or different from, the usual White population. Thus, Wayne County allowed us to look at individuals from all walks of life, from wealthy to poor, and to compare the experiences of African-American and White couples. It is, however, essentially an urban sample.

We obtained names and contact information for every couple who had applied for marriage licenses in April through June of 1986 in Wayne County, MI. We applied several selection criteria to the full sample. To be eligible for participation in our study, both partners had to be either White (non-Hispanic) or African-American, and matched in their racial background. Other ethnicities (Asian, Hispanic, Native American) are less common in the Wayne County area, and we would not have obtained sufficient numbers to allow adequate statistical comparisons. Mixed-ethnicity marriages are also relatively rare, and no doubt bring their own issues and challenges. We elected to exclude this group as well, although they would make for fascinating research.

We also restricted our sample to include only couples where both partners were entering their first marriage. Again, the challenges of entering a second or subsequent marriage, negotiating relationships with ex-spouses and potentially forming blended families, are important issues that should be and are being studied by other researchers (e.g., Braithwaite, Olson, Golish, Soukup, & Turman, 2001). The issues may be very different from those that arise in negotiating one's first marriage, however, and again we elected to simplify our lives somewhat by focusing exclusively on first marriages.

Finally, we restricted our sample to those couples where the wife was 35 years old or younger. One of the issues we wished to explore was how the transition to parenthood might affect a marriage; we therefore restricted ourselves to couples where the wife was young enough to allow the possibility of childbearing during the course of the 7-year study. As the husband's age is less relevant to the possibility of childbearing, no restriction was placed on his age.

Once we had narrowed down our group in this fashion, we contacted all the remaining African-American couples on our list. As the White list was longer, we randomly selected a subset of all White couples comparable in size to the African-American group, and contacted those couples. Potential participants were contacted by both phone and letter. The study was described to them in general terms (saying we were interested in studying what makes for lasting marriages) and their participation was invited. For their participation, they were to be paid $25 a couple in Year 1 and again in subsequent years. In all, 373 couples, 199 African-American and 174 White, agreed to take part in the study, representing a response rate of 66%. Although this rate may seem somewhat low, it must be remembered that both members of a couple had to agree to participate before that couple could be part of our study sample. If individual partners had been allowed to take part, our participation rate would have been 80% or more.

Our final sample is certainly broader and more representative than most volunteer samples, and therefore more likely to generalize to marriages as a whole. However, the sample still has its limitations. Those who agreed to participate when contacted might differ in many ways (e.g., more satisfied, more trusting of authorities, more reliable) than those who did not. Our sample does not speak to the experiences of much older couples, of those in their second marriage, of Asian or Hispanic couples. It may or may not generalize to the experiences of those in rural areas, to those in other regions of the United States, or to couples in other Western countries. Thus, although we have a broad and diverse sample that should give us good insights into many aspects of the early years of marriage, we must always keep in mind that this one group's experiences do not necessarily reflect everyone's.

Although 373 couples took part in the larger study in Year 1, we obtained usable narratives from only 344 of them. In some cases, participants completed their individual interviews but later were unable or unwilling to schedule the couple interview; coordinating both of their schedules plus the interviewer's was at times too challenging, especially when both partners worked shifts. In other cases, mechanical problems were at fault, when a malfunctioning tape recorder rendered a couple's narrative inaudible. Finally, at times real life intervened. The interviewer did her best to find a quiet place free of distractions for the couple to tell their story in peace. These interviews were conducted in couples' homes, however, which as many young couples can appreciate, are not always havens of peace and quiet. In a few instances, there were so many distractions from children squabbling in the background, the telephone and doorbell ringing, or so much background noise from music blaring or *Jeopardy* being listened to at top volume that the coders were unable to make out enough of the narrative to complete their coding tasks. These types of problems intervened more frequently for our African-American respondents. We obtained usable narratives from 97% of all White couples in Year 1, but only 88% of all African-American couples.

So, who were these 344 couples for whom we had usable narratives in the first year of the study? At the end of chapter 3 appears Table 3.1, which shows demographic and background information on these participants. Most couples were fairly young (wife most often age 20 to 24, husband 25 to 29), moderately educated (high school degree or some college being most common), with relatively modest incomes (more than half <$30,000 per year). The husband generally earned more; he most often worked as a skilled ("craft") or semi-skilled ("operative") factory worker, whereas the wife most often worked at a clerical job (e.g., secretary). Participants were overwhelmingly Christian. They were divided between those who attended religious services on a regular basis and those who attended seldom or never. The wives were more religiously observant than the husbands. The majority of couples rented their dwelling, although some owned a house, and a few lived with parents. Perhaps surprisingly, more than half had lived together before they married, although usually not for very long. In the most surprising finding, 40% of couples entered marriage with children, either their own or from previous relationships. Although more than half of couples lived in the traditional newlywed state, with just the two of them together, a large number did not experience their first year of marriage that way. A full 45% shared their home with others, usually their children, but sometimes with other adults as well.

As in any longitudinal study, our sample also changed over time. Couples divorced, or moved away from the area. Despite our best efforts, we lost track of some who moved frequently within the area, generally leaving no forwarding address. Just a handful of couples declined to participate in the study in later years. In total, we were left with 282 couples in Year 3, and 171 couples in Year 7. Again, due to the sorts of difficulties outlined previously, we did not always obtain a usable narrative from all who participated in the larger study. Table 3.3 displays the number of narratives obtained in each year or combination of years. As can be seen, longitudinal data are not always neat and clean; participants come and go at various times and for various reasons.

To impose some order on this chaos, most of our analyses focus on one of two groups: either the full sample of 344 participants, described in Table 3.1, or the subset of 144 respondents for whom we had usable narratives in all 3 years, described in Table 3.2.[1] This smaller group may differ from the original sample in many ways. This group was a relatively stable lot: They stayed together, and stayed in one place, or at least in the same general area, for 7 years. They may have been a relatively satisfied group with little to hide because they allowed strangers to ask personal questions about their relationship, not just once, but multiple times over the years.

Comparison of the two groups in Tables 3.1 and 3.2 suggests that the couples for whom narratives were obtained in all 3 years were slightly older and better educated, with slightly higher incomes than the full sample. A larger proportion of couples were White. They were somewhat more likely to be professionals and less likely to work in service occupations or be unemployed. They were somewhat more likely to be Catholic and slightly less likely to attend religious services seldom or never. They were slightly more likely to own their own homes. Finally, they were considerably less likely to have lived together before marriage, or to have entered into the marriage with children. Fully 68% of the subsample who provided narratives in all 3 years lived in the traditional couple-only household in Year 1, compared to only 55% of the full sample. In summary, this subsample seems to be somewhat more affluent and more traditional than the full sample.

So far, we have a basic overview of the EYM study and its participants. Next, let us turn to a more in-depth examination of the narratives themselves.

CODING OF RELATIONSHIP NARRATIVES

The establishment of reliable codes for the stories was largely an inductive process. We and our staff listened to countless tapes to perceive what the

[1]Some reduction from these *N*s will be noted, depending on patterns of missing data in some analyses. For example, more narratives were coded with the thematic coding than with the affective or interaction coding (see next section for details of coding schemes). Barely audible tapes might still be adequate to obtain the gist of the narrative, which is enough for thematic coding, but not the microlevel details needed for affective and interaction coding.

couples were trying to tell us about their lives. We had no a priori categorizations in mind, only that we should attend to issues the couples focused on, to feelings the couples were expressing about their lives, and to the different styles of interacting that came through as they told their stories. Over time, the specific categories emerged. We tried out many categories that were eventually discarded because we could not reliably code them. It was largely an empirical, rather than a theoretical, process.

Before proceeding to a description of the coding schemes applied to the narratives, let's look at a verbatim excerpt from one couple's story, to provide a feel for how these tales actually progressed. To facilitate the task of examining some narratives in depth, we selected 20 couples (10 White, 10 African-American), varying in income levels and marital satisfaction, and transcribed their narratives in each of the 3 years. We found that more than 300 stories were too many to explore intimately; 20 is a much more manageable number. By reading these couples' stories again and again, we have obtained a good feel for their experiences. They are the source of most of the quotes used throughout the book to illustrate the points made by analysis of the full sample. We hope that you get to know some of these couples throughout this book, as we feel we do. Naturally, all names, dates, and other identifying information have been changed to protect their identities. We have "cleaned up" the quotes just slightly, by removing excess "ums," "likes," or "you knows," when they began to detract from the flow of the narrative. Otherwise, the excerpts are presented exactly as the couples related them.

To begin, let us look at an excerpt from the Year 1 narrative of Mike and Alison. Mike is 28, Alison 24. Both are high school graduates. They live alone in a rented apartment. Our excerpt begins with Mike describing how they met:

M: Um, we met . . . Actually, we knew each other before we actually met . . .

A: That's where the baseball games come in. He coached the baseball team that my friends were in, so I knew him through that.

M: But we didn't really know each other as far as we didn't really talk together or anything like that. It was just she knew who I was and I knew who she was. But, we went to a Halloween party about two months after the baseball season ended, or a month afterwards, and um, we kinda hit it off that night.

A: Yeah. The party was really boring. We left the party, him and a friend of his and me and my sister and two of our friends. We left the party and crashed a . . . What was it? The Holiday Inn Class Reunion or something?

M: Class reunion at the Holiday Inn. We, we were gonna go to the bar at the Holiday Inn and, there was a class reunion for [School], Class of [Year] or something or other, and we were all dressed up, and it was a Halloween party and we were all dressed up. She didn't really even know what I looked like.

A: I had no idea. He was dressed like a clown.

M: But I told her I was gonna call her the next day, and I did, and we started going out then.

A: (giggles)

M: She didn't think I was gonna call her.

A: Uh uh.

A little later, the couple talk about their uncertainty about developing a serious dating relationship:

A: I didn't really wanna go out with him, though (giggling). I was having fun.

M: She was going to the bars a lot.

A: (Inaudible) fun.

M: I didn't know what I wanted, cause I was actually supposed to be going with somebody else.

A: And I didn't find that out till a couple months later (giggles).

M: So after that night, I went away on a business trip. The place I work for sent me to school, training school. And, then, we called each other a lot and I was still going out with that other girl. So I called her too, and I was tied between—I didn't know what I wanted to do. The other girl, you know, that the times weren't going too good with her and I met Alison, and you know. She seemed really, really nice. So I decided I wanted to go out with Alison instead.

A: Yeah, I think that's what did it, when you went away. I missed him. I said something's wrong. I never missed anybody before (chuckles).

M: I was gone for about two weeks and, um, I really . . . It was really weird, cause we've only known each other for about two weeks.

A: No. It was about a month.

M: Well, the 28th to the 16th, or 13th, right. The 28th of October till the 13th of November, we've known each other that long and that's when I went away.

Slightly later, the two discuss their feelings about getting married:

M: Everything seemed to be going really well and I wanted to get married a little bit sooner than she did. She talked me into waiting.

A: A lot sooner.

M: Yeah.

A: I did (chuckles). Three years sooner.

M: Yeah. We actually talked about getting married. Well, we both talked about it, but I was a little . . .

A: Yeah.

M: . . . bit more serious about it. She was more realistic about it.

A: He wanted to get . . . We met or started going out in October. He wanted to get married in May.

Interviewer: Oh really?

A: The following May. Uh uh (giggling), too soon!

M: We ended up getting married two years after that.

A: No, three.

As can be seen even in these brief excerpts, the narratives contain a great deal of information, at several different levels of abstraction. At the broadest level, we can look at the general themes or ideas conveyed—even in this brief passage, for example, a recurrent theme seems to be that Alison was not prepared to commit to the relationship as soon as Mike was.

At a slightly more microlevel of analysis, we could also examine the important feelings and emotions conveyed in the passage. For example, we learn about Mike's feelings of ambivalence or uncertainty, when he was unsure whether he wanted to pursue a relationship with Alison or continue with the woman he was dating at the time. We also learn about Alison's feelings of missing Mike when he was away, signaling to her that this was a potentially important relationship.

Finally, at the most specific level, it is intriguing to look not only at what the couple is saying, but also at exactly how they are going about saying it. Notice how the two build on each other during the story of their first date, taking turns and adding more detail to weave a more complete story. Mostly, they seem to be working well together to build the tale—laughing, joking, and largely agreeing on the basic details. They do have some slight disagreements, however, mostly when Alison corrects Mike about the timing of events.

It is clear that a great deal of information can be gleaned from the narratives, and at several different levels. We chose to focus on three particular types of analysis for the couple narratives. The first is *thematic coding*, which looks at the narrative as a whole and asks what are the major issues, sources of conflict, and storytelling approaches. The second is *affect coding*, which focuses on the feelings and needs expressed by the couple while telling the story. The third is *interaction coding*, which looks at couples' interruptions and turn-taking during the storytelling process, and asks whether, for the most part, they are supporting each other's stories or are in conflict, at each step of the tale.

Each of these three systems was coded by a different set of graduate and undergraduate coders, with occasional overlap across the sets. The coding procedure was similar for each. Once the coding schemes had been developed by the primary researchers, a graduate student would be thoroughly trained in each system. This student would then take responsibility for training other students in the coding procedures, and for maintaining an updated coding manual incorporating any additional rules decided on during the coding process. Full examples of the coding manuals for each system are included in this book's appendixes; those desiring more information on any coding categories beyond that provided in this chapter should consult these manuals.

As required, a batch of coders were trained by the graduate student for that system. Coding manuals were reviewed, then the group listened to tapes together and discussed appropriate codes. Coders then practiced coding tapes individually until they consistently reached agreement of 80% or more in each coding category. Coders then began actual coding, with no individual coding any of the tapes on which he or she had practiced. As coding progressed, a random 10% of all tapes for the thematic coding or a random 10% of all pages of coding for the affect and interaction systems was selected by the graduate student supervisor for check-coding. These tapes, or segments of tapes, were rated by a second coder, and inter-rater reliability was calculated. Check-coding rotated, so each coder served as a check-coder for each of the other members of the group at some point. Disagreements were discussed in a weekly meeting of all coders, occasionally leading to clarifications of coding rules, which were then incorporated into the coding manual. If a coder showed a consistent misunderstanding of a coding rule or failed to show adequate reliability in one or more categories, he or she was given refresher training, including additional practice tapes if necessary, then asked to recode all tapes since the problem arose. In cases where the overall level of reliability was acceptable, with only occasional legitimate disagreements about the application of categories, the coding decisions of the primary coder were always retained. Using this method, the inter-rater reliability scores remained at a consistent level of 80% or more in all categories throughout the long period of coding.

Let us now investigate each of the three coding systems in more detail. We present the complete coding schemes briefly, although we do not use every category in this book. We do this so that readers can have an overview of what is entailed when systematic analyses of narratives are proposed.

Thematic Coding. For the thematic coding, the coders first listened to the entire couple narrative and selected up to two major themes or issues that predominated in the story. These issues were selected from a list of 17 (see Appendix A) and included themes such as finances, religion/church, personal loss, or growth and development in couple relations.

In Mike and Alison's case, the major themes of the entire narrative were finances and couple/family relations. Although these issues do not emerge in the section of the story quoted, they become important later on. In describing what life was like right after the wedding, both discussed how they found it a somewhat difficult adjustment moving from their family homes, "big families with dogs, big houses, you know, lot of noise in it" to a small apartment with only the two of them. In the "current life" and "future" sections, the couple spent some time describing their goals of paying down their credit cards and avoiding expensive entertainment so they can save their money, "win the lotto, buy a great big old farmhouse, some horses . . . and three golden retrievers."

The coders then reviewed each section of the narrative (courtship story, wedding story, etc.), and coded that section on several dimensions. Some questions related to the style of storytelling. For example, coders rated how dramatic the content of the story was. Dramatic content included tales of surprising changes or overcoming negative obstacles. Coders also noted how dramatic the storytelling style of both the wife and husband was. A dramatic style might include strong emotions, or a tale told with liveliness, enthusiasm, or animation.

In our example, neither the story nor the storytellers were rated as particularly dramatic. Although Mike and Alison told their tale well, they also told it in a fairly straightforward fashion. The few couples who were rated as highly dramatic in style tended to virtually re-enact scenes from their relationship, complete with dialogue and voices, or engaged in a teasing banter full of good-hearted contradictions and protestations over what did or did not happen.

Coders also indicated how much the husband and wife collaborated on telling the story, how much conflict there was between the partners regarding the events of that story, and how much direction the interviewer used in developing the story. Mike and Alison were coded as high in collaboration and low in conflict. The interviewer was coded as being not at all directive.

Finally, coders provided an assessment of the overall quality of storytelling in each subsection. Was the substory told as one overall integrated tale, with plot elaboration, coherence, and a clear beginning, middle, and end? Was it a set of smaller but interconnected stories? Was it a set of stories, but told only intermittently or nonlinearly, with the couple out of sync with each other or drifting from one story to the next? Or was it not an independent story at all, but merely a set of descriptions given in direct response to the interviewer's questions?

Our passage described previously was coded as a set of stories told intermittently. There were the stories of the first date, of Mike going away for a business trip, and of them disagreeing about the timing of the marriage. In between these stories, however, were sections where the couple checked with the interviewer as to whether they had provided enough detail, or engaged in general descriptions of their dating experiences ("Other than that, I mean, we just talked and stuff." "We just dated for a long, long time.").

In addition to these stylistic assessments, coders also completed a number of thematic ratings for each substory. Coders chose up to three main aspects or themes that were central to a particular substory. The list of possible aspects varied for each substory. For example, in the courtship story, some possible aspects were "Love at first sight" and "On rebound from previous relationship of one or both"; for the story of present-day life, possible aspects included "Developing multiple roles (e.g. spouse and parent)" and "Financial security/stability." Each of these aspects was coded as to whether it was primarily a concern of the husband, the wife, or both.

In our example, physical separation was coded as an important aspect for Alison because it made her realize the strength of her feelings for Mike. In addition, "general positive progression" and "would make good mates" were selected as important aspects for both. These themes emerged in slightly later sections of the narrative, where, for example, Mike mentioned "I felt really comfortable around Alison. She made me feel really relaxed. I could be myself around her," or Alison stated "We got along really good, and I don't think to this day, we had a fight, and he got along really good with my family. I get along with his family. It was like, right away, it felt like we knew each other forever." Full lists of all aspects can be found in Appendix A. These codes and all others were developed by consensus among small groups of staff and graduate students, and took more than 2 years of concentrated efforts to make them reliable.

In addition to the aspects described here, coders also noted up to three sources of tension in each substory. "Tension" did not include only overt conflicts, but rather any sense of negative obstacles, strain, or opposing forces in the narrative. Each tension was identified as to who was experiencing it: Was it between the husband and wife? Between the husband, wife, or couple and someone external? Personal tensions within the husband, wife, or both? Experienced by someone other than the husband or wife? Coders also noted the degree of each tension (causing a lot of tension vs. only some). Finally, coders also noted the cause or type of each tension. The exact categories varied somewhat depending on the substory (see Appendix A for specifics).

For example, in our excerpt, Alison was coded as experiencing "some" personal tension regarding deciding whether to get married. Mike was coded as experiencing "a lot" of inner tensions about living arrangements or conditions. (This tension actually appeared somewhat later in the narrative. Mike moved into their new apartment alone about a month before the wedding. He had always lived at home with his parents before, and found the adjustment difficult: "Well, I was here by myself for like the first month, and when I was living at home, it's just, you know. Guys are afraid to show their feelings, you know how they say. I cried my eyes out on the way here, when I moved out. . . . It's a big change.")

Finally, for some substories, coders answered specific questions such as where the couple met, who initiated the courtship, who proposed, or who planned the wedding. For example, their thematic coding shows us Mike and Alison met in a "social setting" (i.e., through the baseball team), and that Mike was the primary initiator in starting the courtship (although it is unclear who asked whom to the Halloween party, or whether they both just happened to be going, Mike was definitely the one who called Alison back the next day and pursued the relationship). The proposal was coded as unclear. Although it was definitely the case that Mike was more interested in marriage than Alison all along, whether a formal proposal ever in fact took place was not made clear (Alison: "We talked about marriage, but no big plans, you know. Someday we're gonna get married, but we didn't set dates. He set dates. I said no [giggling]. I kept saying too soon, too soon. And then it was '82, '3, '4, November of '84?" M: "Yep." A: "Was when we got engaged. So that was two years later."). The two worked together planning the wedding, a task they found fun but overly long (Interviewer: "What type of plans did you make for your wedding?" A: "Too many!" [giggling] M: "And it was fun." A: "Oh, was it really . . ." M: "It was fun, but it got, you know. After awhile, it just got to be . . ." A: "Yeah. It was never-ending.").

By scanning all these categories, thematic coding gives us a good overall picture of what the major issues or concerns of our respondents are at each stage of their story and of the styles they choose to employ in telling us these events.

Affective Coding. The second coding system focuses on the affect or emotions reported by the couple during the course of their narrative. Coders listened to the tapes and recorded every statement that mentioned a feeling or a need. Feelings were usually direct statements of preferences (e.g., liking, disliking) or affective states (e.g., happy, angry, stressed, excited), although indirect statements from which inferences of emotions could easily be made were also included (e.g., "the trip was a disaster"; "I laughed so hard"). "Needs" included statements of hoping, wanting, wishing, or intending to reach some goal state. (See Appendix B for details on identifying feeling and need statements.)

Coders made eight judgments for each affective statement they identified. First, they indicated whether the statement expressed a feeling or a need. Second, they judged the valence of the affect, whether positive, negative, neutral, or not ascertainable. Most affects were coded either positive or negative; the neutral category was reserved for negations of negative affect (e.g., "I wasn't too unhappy"). The not-ascertainable category was used only on the few occasions when it could not be determined from context if an emotion was positive or negative (e.g., surprised, only if it could not be determined from context whether the surprise was experienced as a positive or negative one).

Third, coders indicated the speaker who had made the affective statement, either the husband or the wife. Fourth, coders determined the source of the affect, or who experienced the affect, whether the husband, wife, couple, other people, or not ascertainable. In cases where the impersonal "you" was used, such as "you're really going to get mad when something like that happens," the speaker was judged to be the one experiencing the affect.

Fifth, coders indicated the object of the affect, the person or situation toward which the emotion was directed. Categories here included the husband, the wife, the relationship, some outside person/relationship/situation, or not ascertainable. In cases where it was not clear from context whether the relationship or an external situation was the object of the affect (e.g., "things are going great these days"—does "things" mean things in the relationship, or things in life in general?), the relationship category was selected.

Sixth, coders indicated at what stage in the relationship the affect was experienced: before knowing the spouse, during courtship, at the wedding, during the time immediately after the wedding (usually the honeymoon), during the first few years of marriage, during current marital life, in the future, or not ascertainable. Ongoing emotions, which probably apply across a variety of time periods (e.g., "She really enjoys her job"), were coded as occurring during current marital life.

Seventh, coders indicated if the affect arose in response to one of five topics: housing, children, work, finances, and families or family members.

The eighth coding category, and the most difficult one to judge, assessed the motivations underlying the feeling or need. The motivations could be deemed to be related to agency or self-expression (e.g., achieving goals, expressing one's identity, asserting one's own values and preferences), to being connected or related (e.g., caring about others, being involved, being loved by another), to both (e.g., expressing one's own desires, but in the context of a relationship, such as wanting a relationship to be a particular way), or to neither (e.g., feeling relaxed).

To illustrate some of these categories, let's look at two sample statements from Mike and Alison. When Mike said "I decided I wanted to go out with Alison instead," it was coded as a need because he was expressing his desires. It was positive (only negations of needs, e.g., "I don't want X," were coded as negative). Mike was coded as both the speaker and the source of this need whereas Alison was the object. None of the topic categories was applicable. The context was courtship. Finally, the motivation was both self-expression and connection (Mike stated his own desires but they were relevant to forming a relationship).

When Alison stated "I was having fun," a positive feeling was inferred. Alison was coded as both the speaker and the source. The object was "other" (i.e., her general life situation, partying, going to bars, etc.). The context was before meeting the spouse. Again, none of the topic categories was deemed applicable. The motivation was self-expression: Alison is enjoying herself pursuing her own goals and desires.

Interaction Coding. In interaction coding, the focus was more on the process of storytelling, rather than on the content of what was told. We were interested in whether participants built on each other's statements, sharing the process of telling the story in a supportive fashion, or whether they vied with each other for the floor, disagreeing with or ignoring each other in the quest to deliver their own version of events.

In this coding scheme, coders noted each time the speaker changed from husband to wife or vice versa, even if it was merely for an "umm-hmm." Every time the speaker changed, the first statement made by the new speaker was recorded, and coded as to whether the husband or wife was speaking. The period of the relationship to which the statement referred was also coded (i.e., before knowing spouse, courtship, wedding, honeymoon, first few years, current marital life, future, or not ascertainable). Finally, the first statement made by the speaker was assigned to 1 of 10 possible categories, described next (see Appendix C for details).

First, a *confirming* interaction indicated agreement with the statement the spouse had just made. It might consist of an explicit agreement (e.g., "yes," "yeah," "you're right"), direct repetition of the words just uttered by the spouse (e.g., H: "The wedding was beautiful." W: "Just beautiful."), or simply an affirming noise (e.g., "umm-hmm," "uh-huh").

A *collaborative* interaction consisted of elaborating on what the spouse had just said in a supportive manner. Collaborative sequences might consist of picking up the ideas of the partner and elaborating on, extending, or qualifying them. For example, Mike stated that he was in costume for the Halloween party, and Alison elaborated by recalling that he was dressed like a clown.

Collaboration might also consist of posing a question that furthers the story, such as when Alison said "What was it? The Holiday Inn class reunion or something?" Such questions, which served as an explicit invitation for the spouse to join in the story, were the only exception to the rule of coding only the first statement made by a speaker in each turn. These questions were coded as collaborative interactions wherever they occurred, even if they were not the first statement in a turn. Answers to questions that furthered the story were also coded as collaborative interactions, but only if they were the first statement made, as when Mike clarified by stating it was a class reunion held at the Holiday Inn.

Confirming and collaborative statements were simply one–two combinations of the aforementioned codes, when a speaker began a speaking turn by agreeing with what the spouse had just said and then immediately proceeded to continue the story. For example, Alison engaged in a "confirm and collab" when she carried on Mike's story of the party by saying "Yeah. The party was really boring."

Confirming laughter was coded whenever one partner laughed in a clearly amused reaction to what had just been said. All of Alison's laughter seemed to fall into this category. *Other laughter* was coded whenever laughter occurred that did not seem to indicate genuine amusement. The most common example was sarcastic mock laughter, made in reaction to a challenging or teasing statement by the spouse.

Continuation was coded whenever one spouse continued on with what he or she said in the previous statement with no change in storyline whatsoever in response to an interruption by the spouse. Continuation was generally coded when the interruption was so brief that no response would reasonably be expected or required, such as a simple "yeah," "uh-huh," or a laugh by the spouse. Such interruptions usually went on in the audio background, with the spouse who was talking carrying on the story without pause in the foreground, as when Alison's "Yeah" appears in the middle of Mike's statement "I was a little more serious about it [getting married]."

In contrast, a *nonresponse* was coded when the spouse made some statement that logically required a response or at least some acknowledgment from the speaker, yet the speaker ignored the spouse's statement and carried on with what he or she had been saying. None of Mike and Alison's interactions quoted here fell into this category; however, here's an example from another couple, John and Darla. Some time before, John had been speaking of how he was glad they had waited for several years, rather than getting married right away. After that, the topic of conversation changed, as Darla described the positive changes she had seen in their relationship since they were married: "Little things that he says, you know, little things that he does for me . . . I don't know. Sometimes he'll just say now 'Oh, I really like being married. I'm so glad we got married.' You know, little things like that he'll say." Rather than pick up on this theme, John returned to his earlier topic, saying "Yeah, I'm glad we waited as long as we did," and proceeded to describe how many of his friends who got married young were now divorced. John's statement was coded as nonresponsive to Darla's previous statement.

Conflict was coded when one spouse explicitly disagreed with or denied the other spouse's version of events, such as when Alison said it was a month that they'd known each other, not 2 weeks, or when she said it was 3 years later they got married, not 2. If one partner proposed a potential disagreement in the form of a question that accepted that the spouse's version might be correct (e.g., "Are you sure it was the 24th? Or was it the 25th?"), it was considered collaborative, not conflictful.

Conflict was also coded when one partner interrupted the other to make a very different point, without any consideration of what had just been said. Again, Mike and Alison did not show examples of this behavior, but John and Darla did. For example, after describing some conflict about choosing the music selections at their wedding, Darla went on to describe the wedding, talking about where it was held and saying "It wasn't a large wedding. It was . . ." John then interrupted to say "Yeah, that was the other thing," and proceeded to explain how they had also had some trouble with the guest list, with Darla and John's mother wanting to invite many more people than John wanted. John's statement was coded as a conflictful interruption.

Sometimes interruptions were simply one partner eagerly wanting to support the point made by another, such as when Alison interrupted Mike to explain that they knew each other through meeting at baseball games. Such interruptions were considered collaborative, not conflictful. Conflict was only coded when the tone was negative, as John's was, or when the interrupter seemed to be openly disagreeing or disregarding the partner's right to speak.

Lastly, a statement was coded *other* when it did not form part of the storytelling interaction, as when one partner got up to get a drink and asked the other if he or she wanted one too. Unintelligible statements were coded *NA*, not ascertainable.

Finally, it should be noted that only verbal exchanges between the husband and wife were coded in the interaction coding. Any statements made by the interviewer were not coded nor were any responses made to a question by the interviewer, no matter how long.

Now that we have an overview of the study and the sample and have seen some sample narratives and how they are coded, we turn to chapter 4, where we explore the couples' Year 1 narratives in detail.

TABLE 3.1
Year 1 Demographics on Full Sample of
344 Couples Providing a Narrative in Year 1

Couple-Level Variables

Race/Ethnicity		*Parental Status*	
White	49%	Not parents	61%
African-American	51%	Children, together only	23%
Family Income		Children, together & with others	10%
<$10,000	12%	Children, with others only	7%
$10,000–<$20,000	13%	*Household Composition*	
$20,000–$30,000	25%	Couple only	55%
>$30,000	46%	Couple & kids only	31%
Lived Together Before Marriage?		Couple & other adults only	6%
Yes	54%	Couple & kids & other adults	7%
No	46%	*Living Situation*	
If Lived Together, How Long?		Own	37%
<1 year	45%	Rent	57%
1–< 2 years	22%	Live with parents	6%
>2 years	34%		

Individual-Level Variables

	Wives	Husbands
Age		
<20	9%	2%
20–24	50%	32%
25–29	31%	44%
>30	10%	22%
Education		
<High School	14%	14%
High School	30%	33%
Some College	39%	37%
College Degree	16%	17%
Individual Income		
<$10,000	49%	16%
$10,000–<$20,000	31%	35%
$20,000–$30,000	15%	25%
>$30,000	4%	24%
Religion		
Protestant	69%	62%
Catholic	25%	26%
Other	1%	1%
None	6%	11%
How Often Attend Religious Services?		
Every week	18%	14%
Almost every week	15%	11%
Every 1 to 2 months	21%	15%
A few times a year	35%	43%
Never	12%	17%

(Continued)

TABLE 3.1
(Continued)

	Wives	Husbands
Occupation		
Professional/Technical	14%	16%
Managerial	5%	8%
Sales	3%	4%
Clerical	33%	7%
Crafts	1%	20%
Operative	1%	21%
Laborers	<1%	5%
Service	12%	13%
Not employed	31%	7%

Note. Numbers do not always sum to exactly 100% due to rounding and/or missing data.

TABLE 3.2
Year 1 Demographics on Subsample of
144 Couples Who Provided Narratives in All 3 Years

Couple-Level Variables

Race/Ethnicity		*Parental Status*	
White	64%	Not parents	73%
African-American	36%	Children, together only	15%
Family Income		Children, together & with others	8%
<$10,000	6%	Children, with others only	4%
$10,000–<$20,000	11%	*Household Composition*	
$20,000–$30,000	25%	Couple only	68%
>$30,000	54%	Couple & kids only	22%
Lived Together Before Marriage?		Couple & other adults only	5%
Yes	40%	Couple & kids & other adults	5%
No	60%	*Living Situation*	
If Lived Together, How Long?		Own	45%
<1 year	41%	Rent	51%
1–<2 years	24%	Live with parents	4%
>2 years	35%		

Individual-Level Variables

	Wives	Husbands
Age		
<20	6%	1%
20–24	49%	31%
25–29	35%	45%
>30	11%	23%
Education		
<High School	8%	6%
High School	25%	31%
Some College	42%	35%
College Degree	25%	27%

(Continued)

TABLE 3.2
(*Continued*)

	Wives	*Husbands*
Individual Income		
<$10,000	39%	9%
$10,000–<$20,000	32%	32%
$20,000–$30,000	23%	29%
>$30,000	5%	27%
Religion		
Protestant	64%	55%
Catholic	31%	32%
Other	1%	1%
None	5%	13%
How Often Attend Religious Services?		
Every week	18%	18%
Almost every week	21%	15%
Every 1 to 2 months	19%	18%
A few times a year	31%	35%
Never	10%	15%
Occupation		
Professional/Technical	20%	24%
Managerial	7%	9%
Sales	2%	4%
Clerical	33%	10%
Crafts	1%	22%
Operative	2%	21%
Laborers	0%	3%
Service	8%	6%
Not employed	27%	2%

Note. Numbers do not always sum to exactly 100% due to rounding and/or missing data.

TABLE 3.3
Number of Couples Providing a Narrative, by Year

Year Combination	*N*
Year 1 only	109
Year 3 only	4
Year 7 only	0
Years 1 and 3 only	83
Years 1 and 7 only	8
Years 3 and 7 only	2
All 3 years	144

Newlyweds' Stories

Newlyweds told us stories about their own experiences, in their own voices, with minimal prompting. What did they tell us, and how did they go about fulfilling this unusual request from a survey researcher? Here the interviewer was, a stranger in their home, asking them to give an account of their life together: how they became a couple and decided to marry, their wedding, their honeymoon, what their marriage was like in the early days, and what they see in their future. How did the couples deal with this request for revelation? How did they feel comfortable enough to share such stories with us?

In this chapter, we provide an overview of what couples' narratives looked like in the first year, a few months after they were married. In the first section, we focus on the style of the narratives, the way in which couples talk about their lives together. Do they tell integrated stories or simply describe the facts? Are their interactions collaborative or conflictful? Are the stories emotional or unemotional? In the second section, we turn to the content of the narratives, giving a glimpse of the major themes and sources of tensions in each substory.

STYLE OF NARRATIVES

Before proceeding to the actual content of the newlyweds' stories, we first depict the style in which they presented their narratives. There are, of course, multiple ways that we could characterize the style of the stories. In this section, we limit ourselves to presenting a few different indices of style that we coded. For those more quantitatively inclined, Table 4.1 summarizes the exact mean scores or percentages on which our discussion is based. We refer to that table from time to time throughout this chapter.

Quality of Storytelling.   First, what is the overall quality of storytelling by our respondents? By using the term *quality*, we do not wish to convey that there is only one right way to tell a story. People have different approaches: Some are terse, some long-winded. Some use dramatic ploys, others are more straightforward. Some couples rely on each other to fill in parts of the story, whereas others depend on one partner or the other to be the main storyteller.

Nevertheless, we can ask whether the couples' stories generally revealed them to be gripping raconteurs, telling coherent, dramatic, and inspiring tales of their life together. As the passages so far may suggest, not particularly. The tales had a certain inherent interest value for the glimpses they gave us into respondents' lives, but the dramatic quality of the stories was modest at best, according to our coders. Furthermore, we have perhaps biased the selections so far, by selecting relatively clear excerpts, and skipping over the many sections where the couples groped for their facts, or basically stated "I don't know what to say, we just dated and stuff." To give a clearer idea of what many of the stories actually sounded like, let's examine an excerpt from John and Darla, telling the story of their engagement:

J: Cause I gave you the ring and I wasn't even saving no money (laughs). To be honest. It was like, I was getting the ring in December.

D: Uh huh.

J: and . . .

D: Christmas Eve. I forget what year? What year? Okay. We got married this year. Was it last Christmas?

J: I don't know. Was it? It might have been a year later. No, it wasn't. No, it wasn't.

D: No, it wasn't.

J: No, it was after . . .

D: It was the year . . . it was . . . it was the year before that, because I said, well that year . . . it was the year before that. Okay. What was last year (chuckles)? This year is, ah . . . eight—it was '85. '84 is when you gave me the ring.

J: Oh.

D: And '85 was when I did my planning [for the wedding].

J: Okay.

D: Okay, '84 is when you gave me the ring, '85 when I did my planning.

J: Okay. That's why it took so long. Okay.

And that's the entire "story" of the proposal. After that, the couple was sidetracked and began talking about the wedding planning. In reading over the narratives, one at times wants to tell the couples "Quit worrying so much about getting the exact sequence right—just tell me what happened, what you thought, what you felt. Give me a glimpse into what it was like for you to propose, or to be proposed to!" At times couples did just that, but more often they gave a straight description of the facts of their relationship or interspersed occasional interesting stories with listings of the facts.

To quantify the overall quality of the storytelling more precisely, coders evaluated each substory on a 5-point scale, ranging from "no continuity; mere answering of questions in question–answer format" to "integrated overall story, with plot elaboration or coherence." Overall, collapsing across substories, couples obtained moderate scores on this measure, averaging 3.21 on the 5-point scale. Most couples got into the rhythm of letting a story flow; only 5% of all stories obtained the lowest score overall, indicating that couples really weren't telling any story at all, but simply responding briefly to interviewers' questions. However, couples were not particularly expert storytellers, either. Only 6% of the stories received the highest score, which was reserved for coherent stories with a beginning, middle, and end, plot development, coherence, and so forth. The most common scores were in the middle, with 31% of all substories coded as "a story or set of stories with connections," and 40% coded as "conventionalized continuity in response to questions; descriptions."

Similar findings emerged when we looked at ratings of the drama of the story content and style. Coders rated the content of each substory on its drama, using a 3-point scale (not at all dramatic, somewhat dramatic, dramatic). A dramatic story was one that contained negative obstacles, important turning points (e.g., death, pregnancy), surprising changes in events, or suspense, in that the final outcome was doubtful at times. The stories definitely tended toward the less dramatic. Collapsing across substories, the average drama rating was 1.48 out of 3, with 61% of all substories rated as "not at all dramatic," and only 9% rated as "dramatic." Although the low drama may make for less-than-gripping relationship stories, it must be remembered that it is probably a good sign for our couples. The aspects that make a dramatic story—negative obstacles to overcome, surprises, suspense about what may happen—may make for a good story, but they no doubt make for a relatively stressful relationship. Many of our couples' stories in the first year seemed to fall into the format of "We met, we liked each other, we got along well, so we decided to get married, and did, and we're quite happy about it now." Perhaps not exciting, romantic, or dramatic, but definitely harmonious and comfortable.

Even in telling a relatively mundane story, however, some individuals added drama through a lively style, animation, emotional tone, and so on.

For example, here are Angie and Chris, describing the undoubtedly common experience of getting a sunburn on a Florida honeymoon:

> A: We wanna go down to Florida and get tans, you know. We ain't gonna come back being white as a ghost (chuckles). So, we laid out and it was . . . it was so hot out, and you know, we did not tan that night. We were burnt!
>
> C: (Laughing)
>
> A: (Laughing and talking) We were walking around like, like . . . Our skins were just so tight, you know, so we ran to the store and got Noxzema, and just kept putting Noxzema on (laughing).
>
> C: Every hour, we were coating ourselves with Noxzema!
>
> A: Cause we couldn't even move we were burnt so bad (giggling). And then the next day, it's "We gotta go out in the sun! It's all gonna disappear!", you know, and then we only had a few days left. So I go, "Well, okay. We'll go out for a little bit." So we lay down for like two seconds. And I'm like "I CAN'T, Chris, it's too hot!!"
>
> A & C: (Both giggling)
>
> A: *Sunburned!*

Angie and Chris could have just said "and then we got bad sunburns," as many of our couples did. Instead, they turned it into an amusing and dramatic incident with the use of exaggeration, direct quotes, and strong positive emotion in the retelling. Such talent in storytelling was relatively rare overall, however. Coders rated the drama of each storyteller's style on a 3-point scale (not at all dramatic, somewhat dramatic, dramatic). Overall, the ratings were quite low: 1.41 out of 3 for the husbands, and only slightly higher (1.51) for the wives. Collapsing across all substories, the husband's storytelling was rated as "not at all dramatic" 64% of the time and "dramatic" only 6% of the time, whereas the wives were rated as "not at all dramatic" 57% of the time and "dramatic" only 8% of the time. The majority of the stories were more like the excerpts we saw from Mike and Alison, or John and Darla: descriptions of little incidents or of basic facts of their relationship, told in a fairly straightforward fashion.

Negotiating a Joint Narrative. Couples were given the task of telling their stories together. The interviewer explicitly stated that we wanted to hear from both of them. How well were participants able to negotiate this task of telling a joint narrative? In general, extremely well. As in the passages reviewed thus far, couples seemed adept at moving back and forth, playing off each other to tell a complete story. The narratives were not at all a series of monologues, told in turn by each partner. Instead, most couples constantly tossed the conversational ball back and forth in a well-measured duet. Listen to Angie and Chris detailing Chris's attempts to work up the nerve to ask Angie out:

A: He kept coming in there [the store where Angie worked] and buying cookies (giggles).

C: Buying anything I could just to get a chance to talk to her (giggles).

A: (Chuckles) Right, it was quite awhile, and finally he asked me out after a long, long time. I was getting impatient.

C: Yeah, I was . . . I didn't know whether or not to ask her out or not. I had gone in there, bought candy bars, bread, . . .

A: Cookies and everything.

C: Cookies.

A: (Laughing)

C: Anything just to talk to her. And I've always been shy, so finally I asked her out.

A: And that's how we met.

Note how they picked up each other's thoughts, even completed each other's sentences. Many couples went through such sequences, where they told a story as a team, sharing the conversational task at practically every step. At other times, couples took turns telling brief vignettes (see, e.g., Mike and Alison's description of the Halloween party). It was unusual, however, for one partner's turn to extend for more than 7 or 8 lines of transcript before the other partner made a contribution. For the most part, the narratives truly were jointly constructed. In fact, across all substories, fully 69% were rated as collaborative, whereas only 6% of all substories were rated as told exclusively by one partner or the other (4% exclusively by wife, 2% exclusively by husband).

The couples also showed very little conflict in their storytelling project. They had the occasional slight disagreements about timing, such as we saw in Mike and Alison's story, but remarkably few major disputes. Fresh in the newlywed glow, and no doubt aware that the interviewer was listening, overt conflict virtually never arose or was quickly smoothed over when it did. Here is about as strong as the conflict gets—in this excerpt, John disputes Darla's assessment of him:

D: John was really afraid of marriage. . . . You know, men get this mental thing—"Oh, I'm gonna get married!" And he's thinking everything's gonna end. "I gotta put everything aside," you know, but that's not the way that I wanted our marriage to be. I wanted to continue. . .

J: When?

D: Huh?

J: When was this?

D: What?

J: I ain't like that.

D: Ah, John, I'm, I'm . . . That's . . . I'm sure you . . . Ah, you were afraid of marriage.

J: When?

D: Huh? "When, when?" You never wanted to talk about it when I was ready to talk about it.

J: Oh.

D: Remember the times when I was ready to talk about marriage and you didn't, you weren't?

J: Yeah.

D: Weren't you afraid?

J: Oh, *that* was when.

D: (Chuckles).

This interchange stood out as an unusual one, in that one partner openly disputed the other's version of events. Even here, though, the disagreement was swiftly covered over, as John conceded to Darla's view and the incident ended with humor. Using the thematic coding's global assessment, across all substories, a full three fourths were coded as containing no conflict at all, and only 3% of all substories were coded as containing a lot of conflict.

Turning to the more microlevel interaction coding, a similar story emerges. When coding each change in speaker during the narrative, the collaborative code was by far the most common, comprising half of all interactions. In contrast, only 4% of all speech turns were coded as being openly conflictful. In fact, if you look at the ratio of all positive or neutral interaction codes (collaborative, confirming, confirming and collaborative, confirming laughter, continuing, other) to the more negative interaction codes (conflict, nonresponse, other laughter), the ratio is approximately 22 to 1. More than 22 times as many speech turns served to support and build on what the spouse said as served to deny or ignore the spouse's contribution. Our couples' interactions in constructing their joint narrative were quite remarkably supportive and affirming.

Affective Tone.   Couples did not openly disagree when presenting their narrative. But what was the overall emotional tone? Were the stories predominantly straight descriptions of the facts, or did they contain intriguing glimpses of couples' feelings and desires?

Overall, the narratives were somewhat emotional in tone. On average, couples completed approximately 175 separate speech turns in presenting their story and made approximately 79 affective statements. Of course, these affective statements were not uniformly distributed. Many speech turns consisted of simple laughter or confirmation, with no explicit mention of any affect. It was the longer speech turns, wherein the storytellers related the key incidents of their lives, that generally contained multiple affective statements. Here, for example, Chris explains how he is not yet ready to have children:

> C: I wanna be able to love them and I don't think I could love . . . Oh, no, I take that back. I would love a child, but I couldn't devote myself to a child. But, I'm selfish, you know, very selfish. When I get up in the morning, if I wanna be able to go play golf, I wanna be able to. I don't want somebody telling me that I can't, because I have to stay home with Junior.

In these few sentences, Chris communicates a complex set of feelings of love (or lack thereof) toward a hypothetical child, desires to pursue his own goals, reactions against restrictions of his freedom, and so forth. Our couples definitely articulated their feelings and desires throughout their narratives.

And what do these affects look like? Again, quite positive: Two thirds (66%) of all affective statements were coded as positive, compared with only 29% negative. Expressions of feelings or emotions were more common than expressions of needs or desires; 71% of all affective statements fell into the feeling category. Perhaps surprisingly, however, the couples seemed to be directing these feelings not primarily toward each other, but rather toward other people or things. A full 70% of all affective statements had "other" as the object of the affect, compared with only 9% each for the husband and the wife, and 12% for the couple. Thus, the narratives did not seem to concentrate on the feelings that the couples had for each other, although such feelings were clearly present. Rather, couples' feelings seemed to focus on the ongoing connections they must forge with the world. The couples must work to manage both the daily interactions and the long-term plans that make up the foreground and background of their life together. Their relationship story does not, and cannot, exist in a vacuum.

In a similar way, we were surprised at the motivations expressed in the newlyweds' affective statements. Recall that we had coded each affect as to whether it reflected a directly social or "connected" motivation (e.g., "I felt so close to him from the start"), or whether it reflected a more "agentic" motivation, one concerned with getting things done (e.g., "I was glad we could reserve the church for that Saturday"). We were surprised to see that the affects in these narratives dealing with a relationship were largely about achieving agentic goals. Agency was coded in a clear majority of affective statements found in the stories (62% coded as agentic, and an additional

10% coded as combining agency and connection). Only a minority of affective statements (20%) were rated as primarily concerned with connection. Perhaps we should not have been so surprised. Once again, we should realize that people telling the stories of their lives together must speak to the structure of their everyday events, many of which do not deal directly with social connections. Even if the raison d'être of the narrative is the story of a relationship, the story of the couple's interaction with the world around them must play a key role.

It should be noted, however, that the lack of focus on the couple per se, and the lack of connection motivation, make the narratives sound somewhat more individualistic than they actually were. Here is Chris describing how he and Angie were feeling just before the wedding:

> C: We knew that neither one of us wanted to have an apartment and we didn't want to have to rent. So we knew we needed a house, but the planning, it's so rough, you know. We not only worried about the house and getting the house. We got the house 3 weeks before the wedding. So not only were we worried about signing all the payments for the mortgage and everything. We were worried about money for the wedding, and how the plans for the wedding were going.

All of the emotions and desires expressed here were coded as agentic (expressing preferences and desires), and as directed toward an outside situation (the house, the mortgage, the wedding plans). Yet even in the midst of this agency, a sense of the couple working and feeling together, of "us against the world," emerges. Likewise, here is Angie describing the wedding:

> A: It went good. It went really good. We had . . . I had a nice time (chuckles). I wasn't nervous, though. Everybody's going "Oh, you're nervous, you're gonna be nervous" and all that stuff. And I thought I would be, because I'm the type that's always nervous and I'm real sensitive and stuff, and I thought I'd be really scared, but everybody's going "We can't believe how calm you are." I go "Well, I wanna get married and get it over with." That's all I wanna do, you know. I go "Just hurry up and get the wedding over with and be with Chris."

Again, most of the affective statements expressed here had an object of "other" (e.g., feelings of nervousness were directed toward the wedding ceremony), and were agentic or mixed in their motivation (e.g., "I wanna get married" expressed both self-expression and connection). Yet beneath it all, the sense of Angie wanting to be with Chris above all else is what emerges.

Thus, although couples do express many agentic feelings, directed toward other people and things, an overall sense of the two standing together and facing the world united does tend to emerge.

Gender Differences and Similarities. So far we have been describing the couple's style in relating the narrative and have not distinguished much between men's and women's approaches. Do the genders differ in the way they tell the relationship story? Overall, not much. As briefly mentioned earlier, the women were rated as slightly more dramatic in their style than the men (1.51 out of 3 overall vs. 1.41 for men). This slight advantage held across all substories, with the exception of the future (see Table 4.1). Gender differences noted in the literature support the advantage for women we found. Women tend to be somewhat higher in verbal fluency than men are (Hyde & Linn, 1988) and to have greater facility, even from a young age, at recalling and relating personal events (Reese, Haden, & Fivush, 1996). Women also tend to be slightly higher in emotional expressiveness (Brody & Hall, 1993), which was one of the criteria that coders used to assess dramatic style. It is thus not surprising that women would score slightly higher on this variable.

Women also seem to be slightly more involved than their partners are in some portions of the narrative. As noted earlier, the large majority of all narratives (69%) were coded as collaboratively or jointly told. Some, however, were in fact coded as being mostly or completely told by the husband or wife, respectively. By dividing the number of substories coded as mostly or completely told by the wife by the number told mostly or completely by the husband, we obtain a ratio reflecting the couple members' relative involvement. A score of 1.0 would indicate that the couple members were equal in their involvement; a score greater than 1.0 would indicate more narratives were dominated by the wife, whereas a score less than 1.0 would indicate more were dominated by the husband. Collapsing across all substories, the ratio was approximately 1.20, or slightly biased toward the wife. When we create the same ratio for each substory, we see that the wife predominated in the past sections of the narrative, relating the courtship, wedding, and honeymoon substories. In the present substory the two were more equal, and in the future substory the husband tended to predominate (although only slightly). See Table 4.1 for a summary of these findings.

The wives' relatively greater involvement in the past segments of the story might be explained by a slightly richer memory. Research suggests that both men and women agree that women tend to have better memory for past relationship events (Holmberg, 1998) and that women seem to demonstrate somewhat clearer, more vivid memories of relationship events (Ross & Holmberg, 1992). The reasons for this gender difference are not completely clear, although they may have to do with relationship memories' greater importance for women (Ross & Holmberg, 1992), or for their stronger connection to women's more relational self-concepts (Acitelli & Young, 1996). For whatever reason, the woman is often somewhat more the "expert" on past relationship events. It is perhaps not coincidental that most of the corrections of details we have seen involved a wife correcting her husband.

Still, these gender differences should not be exaggerated. The men were full, active participants in most narratives and seemed to remember the details of the past events fairly well. Furthermore, in terms of exactly how they went about telling the story, the two genders were remarkably similar. Men and women used affective statements with relatively equal frequency (53% of all affective statements had women as the speaker). They were described as experiencing affects equally often (34% of all affective statements had the husband as the source, 36% had the wife as the source, and 18% had the couple as the source). The genders did not seem to differ in their use of positive versus negative affects, in their use of feelings versus needs, in their motivations for affects, or in the objects of their affects.

Neither did men and women differ much in the types of statements they made, according to the interaction coding. They were virtually identical in terms of how often they used collaborative, confirming, or confirming and collaborative statements (scores representing ratios of wives' usage to husbands' being .99, .94, and .99, respectively). Wives were slightly more likely to use the conflict category (ratio of wives' to husbands' usage was 1.15), perhaps reflecting the fact that wives corrected husbands' facts slightly more often than the opposite. Men were slightly more likely to make "continuing" statements (ratio = .81), probably reflecting the fact that women are generally more likely to use verbal reinforcements such as "yeah" and "uh-huh" (Wood, 1993), which are frequently continued over.

The only sizable difference we saw was that wives were approximately twice as likely to laugh during the narratives (whether confirming laughter or other laughter) as were their husbands. Again, this difference has precedents in the literature; women are more likely to smile and laugh in social situations than are men (Hall & Halberstadt, 1994).

Overall, the women may be just slightly more involved and emotionally expressive in the narratives than the men, but the similarities between the narrative styles of the genders far outweigh their differences.

We return to the question of gender differences again toward the end of the book, in chapter 9, where we systematically analyze results across the years and include ways in which narrative characteristics are related to marital well-being differently for men and women. Some of the same conclusions we draw here about how men and women compare in their stories when newlyweds will reappear in our across-the-years analyses. Some conclusions will differ as we add the Year 3 and Year 7 stories into the mix. We should thus emphasize that the gender differences and similarities we have just reported pertain to the stories of newlyweds as they approached the narrative task in Year 1.

Comparison of Substories. We must also point out a final intriguing pattern of results that emerged when we compared the quality of the various substories that make up the larger narrative. We looked at ways in which the style of storytelling changed as couples proceeded from the story of their courtship to that of their wedding, honeymoon, present life together, and, finally, their future. A number of comparisons pointed to ways in which the quality of the courtship and wedding stories differed from that of the other substories (see Table 4.1, and examine each row across the columns for each substory).

First, we noted that the integration of the substories seemed to erode steadily over time. Couples started out fairly well in the courtship and wedding substories, with overall ratings at least above the midpoint on the 5-point scale. The modal or most common category for both the courtship and wedding substories was "a story or set of stories with connections," representing 47% of all narratives. Only a minority of responses (9% for courtship and 26% for wedding) fell into the lowest two categories, "conventionalized continuity; descriptions" or "no continuity; question-and-answer format."

The coding looked quite different for the remaining substories. For each, the modal response was now "conventionalized continuity; descriptions." This category, combined with "no continuity," now accounted for more than half of all narratives (50% for honeymoon, 61% for current married life, and 80% for the future). Couples seemed to tell stories about their courtship and wedding, but simply describe their current and future life.

Similar results emerged when we looked at other coding categories. The drama ratings for the courtship and wedding story were notably higher (approximately 1.70 out of 3) than the ratings for honeymoon and present life (approximately 1.40), whereas the future story had the lowest drama ratings of all, at 1.15. Similarly, turning to ratings of the dramatic style of both spouses we see higher ratings occurred for the courtship and wedding stories than for the remaining portions of the narrative.

Furthermore, couples devoted more of their narrative time and energy to the earlier substories of the overall relationship story. When we look at the distribution of speaking turns across categories, we see that 71% of all speaking turns and 63% of all affective statements occurred during the courtship, wedding, and honeymoon stories (wedding and honeymoon categories were combined when summarizing the affect and interaction data).

Our couples seemed to be fairly good at telling detailed, emotional, integrated and interesting stories of their courtship and wedding (and, to a

lesser extent, their honeymoon), but had more trouble with the remainder
of the narrative. One possible explanation for this pattern is a practice effect: Because the courtship and wedding events are further in the past, couples have had more opportunity to hone their tales and pick out the most
interesting parts. In addition, there may simply be more to say at this point
about those earlier experiences. After all, couples were often dating for
years, and the wedding planning generally stretched over many months. In
contrast, most of these couples had only been married for 3 to 6 months at
the time of the interview. There may simply not have been time for much to
happen yet in their married life. As Chris put it: "We've only been married
four months, so there isn't a whole lot to tell." In chapter 5, we compare
Year 1 narratives to those told in Years 3 and 7. If practice does indeed make
perfect, we should see steady improvement in all aspects of the storytelling,
with clear stories of couples' experiences in married life emerging over
time.

The more likely possibility, however, is that the courtship and wedding
stories simply fit more easily into a conventional narrative structure in our
culture. These stories have relatively clear beginnings, middles, and endings (meeting, dating, and proposing, for courtship; planning and preparation, the wedding itself, the reception, and leaving for honeymoon, for
wedding). They feature development toward relatively clear goals (engagement; the married state). Progress toward and away from these goals can be
easily assessed. They therefore fit our conceptions of stories quite well.

In contrast, honeymoons and married life consist more of a series of
events—some good, some bad, some more or less interesting, but the point
of all these events, the goal toward which they might be developing, is not
always clear. Life goes on, but it is hard to pinpoint exactly what one should
talk about. Almost all the couples at some point in the current and future
stories noted that what emerges most strongly is a basic sense of continuity.
As Mike said, "It almost seems like the only difference between being married and going out, is that we're together more." Or another husband,
Troy: "Still learning about each other, growing pains, whatever, in marriage. So that right after the wedding and how things are now—about the
same. They kinda run together." Or, as John perhaps best summed it up:
"It's already like setting a pattern, you know. You get married, you have a
kid and you try to raise it. . . . I don't plan on being no rock star or anything."

Married life continues comfortably and happily for these couples. They
may spend time in the current section talking about their jobs, how they
spend their leisure time, how they divide the household chores. In the future, they describe their general plans for buying a house, starting a new career, or having children. But these are not the events of which gripping stories are made in our culture. Under these circumstances, conventionalized

continuity and simple descriptions of events might be as much as respondents will ever be able to manage.

Summary. To summarize, couples' narratives in Year 1 were not tremendously dramatic in either content or style. They told stories about their courtship and wedding, but simply described their current and future lives. The overall affective tone was quietly positive, and although the emotions seemed to focus on outside circumstances, a sense of the couple working together as a team did emerge. The couples also worked well together in telling their stories. Both partners contributed, although the wives contributed slightly more, especially in the past sections. The stories were not spellbinding, but they did provide a heartwarming glimpse into the lives of mostly contented newlyweds.

CONTENT OF NARRATIVES

Now that we have some understanding of the basic style of the newlyweds' stories, let us turn to an examination of the actual content of their narratives. What did they tell us about the process of forming a lifelong bond with each other? Initially, we wondered whether tensions or doubts about committing to each other for life might be a common element of modern marriage narratives. After all, with the age of first marriage rising steadily and marriage rates falling somewhat (Norton & Miller, 1992), marriage today is becoming more of a voluntary step, rather than a universally expected rite of passage. With future divorce a prospect for approximately half of all couples who take their vows (Norton & Miller, 1992), it would not have been surprising to find some hesitations or worries in couples' minds about making such a major life commitment. With common optimistic biases (Taylor & Brown, 1988) firmly in hand, however, our newlywed couples showed few such worries or tensions. As we saw previously in the style analysis, harmony and lack of drama or tension chiefly characterize these Year 1 narratives.

We know the overall tone is a positive one, but what were the precise themes or issues that our couples highlighted when telling the story of how they blended their lives together? We examine each substory in turn in the following sections, but first we consider the narrative as a whole. Coders were asked to listen to the entire narrative and select up to two main issues that seemed to be central to the entire story. These overarching themes are summarized in Table 4.2 at the end of the chapter.

As might be expected in a narrative about a relationship, the most common major themes reflected quite directly on the nature of the couple's relationship with each other. In just under half of the narratives (46%), discussion of the nature of the couple's relationship formed a major issue: whether they were happy with each other, in love, good friends, communicated well (24%), whether their relationship had grown slowly or quickly (17%), or whether they had troubles with each other (4%). This thematic analysis echoes the stylistic findings. The themes predominantly focused on the couple's harmonious relationships. There was very little emphasis on the problems they encountered with each other in the course of building their life together.

In addition to these direct relationship themes, couples also emphasized issues that had an indirect effect on their relationship by permeating their daily lives. They spoke of family and friends they had to learn to connect with as a couple (36%), their work and career commitments (29%), their financial issues and concerns (16%), their housing decisions (8%), and their current or future children (13%). Again, we see that these couples' relationships do not exist in a vacuum but are fully embedded in their ongoing lives. They must learn not only to negotiate their feelings and their communications with each other inside the relationship, but also to sort out their joint position in a complex social world. Marriage often means finding new housing, coping with new children, and embarking on new jobs and finances to support these additional responsibilities. Marriage means in-laws; marriage means a trail of friends that each partner might have had alone but who can potentially become friends of both. Marriage involves a whole set of adjustments and accommodations, not just to each other, but to their now joint social world. Thus, the major issues coded often implicated the couple's relationship profoundly, even if they did not directly speak to it.

Having some perspective on the major themes dominating the narrative as a whole, let us now turn to examining each substory in turn. First, the courtship, the substory that lends itself best to a conventional narrative structure.

The Courtship.   Just as issues in the overall narrative most frequently revolved around the couples' relationship, so too did the courtship story. Coders noted up to three issues that aroused some degree of tension in the courtship narrative (recall that tension does not necessarily indicate overt conflict, but merely some sort of obstacle, strain, or sense of opposing force). In over half of all instances[1] (52%), the tension originated from within the relationship. However, these tensions were relatively minor. Only a tiny fraction (0.5%) focused on infidelity. Only a small proportion (9%) spoke of the awkwardness one partner or the other experienced in

---

[1]In cases where multiple responses could be coded for each substory, the denominator when calculating percentages is not the number of narratives, but rather the total number of responses coded.

extricating themselves from a previous relationship. Instead, couples spoke more often about deciding to get married (15%) or the nature of their premarital relationship (17%). Some also highlighted tensions that occurred due to periods of physical separation (10%), most often in an "absence makes the heart grow fonder" vein.

What other types of tension arose? Some stories focused on tensions the couples experienced with important others in their lives, such as family (12%) and friends (4%). Again, we are reminded that becoming a couple involves not just the two partners, but often an extensive social network as well. Negotiating the couple's position in this network can arouse tensions, particularly if there have been objections to their union.

Given that almost 40% of the sample entered into the marriage with children, it was quite surprising how little emphasis children received in the courtship story, emerging as a source of tension less than 1% of the time. Pregnancy was also a little-mentioned theme, arising only 2% of the time. Perhaps the cultural ideal of a courtship involving the conjoining of two individuals for reasons of love and affection precludes or overshadows any consideration of external factors, such as children, or children-to-be, that may draw them together. After all, the playground chant goes: "First comes love, then comes marriage, then comes baby in a baby carriage." Baby coming first violates the cultural scripts or norms and may therefore be glossed over at this stage of the story.

There were a handful of other types of tension mentioned in the courtship narrative that were not directly connected to the couple's relationship to each other or their friends and family. These included finances (3%), jobs (5%), education (1%), and substance abuse (< 1%). Such issues certainly can indirectly affect a couple's relationship; by and large, however, the courtship narratives seemed to revolve around direct confrontation of issues of the couple's commitment and feelings toward each other, either arising within the couple unit or in the context of their relationship with their loved ones.

In addition to examining types of tension, there is another way to explore the content of the courtship narratives: in terms of types of story plots. After all, most married couples are asked at some point "How did you two meet?" and most couples quickly develop a story that outlines the basics of when and where they met, how they became interested in each other, and how they progressed toward marriage. We developed a set of codes to capture the most common central themes or plots that seemed to emerge in these stories, such as "love at first sight," "relationship evolved out of friendship," or "on the rebound from a previous relationship of one or both."

These plots turned out to be quite diverse across our sample. No one specific theme emerged as especially prevalent. Most were coded in no more than 5% of all stories. We did find, however, that the plots could be grouped according to their affective tone. We found that positive plots were in fact the most common (39%), but negative (33%) and neutral (28%) plots were not far behind.

The positive plots follow the course of what Gergen and Gergen (1987) termed *romantic augmentation*—describing the relationship as a continuous increase in positive commitment to each other with no major hitches or setbacks along the way. These themes included such ideas as being childhood sweethearts (4%) or being friends first and gradually falling in love (8%). Other positive plots reflected the common cultural myth of a man pursuing a woman and making her his bride (8%), although a smaller number described a role reversal in which the woman pursued the man (3%). The more extreme romantic visions of "love at first sight" or of the relationship as a fulfillment of spiritual destiny were somewhat less common (4% and 1%, respectively). In fact, the single most common positive theme (10%) was simply that of "general positive progression," in which no major theme emerged other than that the whole experience was generally positive. Thus, more than one third of our couples describe their courtship progression in quite positive terms, but the stories seem to outline the gradual development of a solid relationship, rather than describing hearts and flowers and dramatic outpourings of passion.

Almost one third of the couples (28%) were even more low-key in their description of the courtship, falling into the neutral or pragmatic grouping. These couples seemed to describe the movement from acquaintance to marriage as simply a gradual, not overly emotional evolution that made sense at the time, reflecting themes such as "settling down" (3%), "next logical step" (3%), "partner would make a good mate" (6%), "partner would make a good parent" (2%), or "relationship evolved out of contact with each other" (8%). A few spoke of external pressures such as pressure from other people (2%), or deciding to get married because of pregnancy or children (4%). Mostly, however, this group seemed to describe a gradual, pragmatic intertwining of their lives which made marriage the next reasonable step.

Finally, although one third of the courtship plots fall into the negative grouping, they do not appear to be extremely negative. These stories are of the "romantic relief" type, in which some obstacle or challenge arises in the development of the courtship, which must be overcome before progress toward marriage can continue. Undoubtedly, some obstacles arise in virtually any courtship, but those are not always what is remembered and incorporated into the courtship story. These couples did place some emphasis on overcoming obstacles; however, the obstacles they described were for the most part not extreme. Common themes of negative plots included a temporary physical separation (8%), one partner or the other being on the rebound from a previous relationship (5%), and either the man (5%) or the woman (3%) pursuing the partner and encountering some initial resistance. Fewer negative plots spoke of serious individual (3%) or shared (2%) difficulties that had to be overcome; few outlined a generally stormy or turbulent relationship (2%); and few described serious obstacles or resistance from their parents (2%). Most couples in this group seemed to experience some relatively minor, temporary obstacles that were readily overcome, leaving their relationship more positive than ever. The Romeo and Juliet myth of star-crossed lovers facing any number of virtually insurmountable obstacles did not figure prominently in our couples' narratives.

Thus, most of the courtship stories could be characterized as consisting of a quietly positive, not terribly dramatic sequence in which the couple gradually spent time together and merged their lives into one. The emphasis was on shared time and interests and gradually evolving feelings, not on extremes of either positive or negative emotions. For example, here's Darla: "It was fun. . . . We went to movies, like we still do. . . . We went to concerts, cause he's in the band." Or Mike and Alison:

M: I think we have a lot in common. We like to do the same things, have a lot of fun.

A: Outdoorsy things and be around a lot of people, go to parties and go-cart tracks. Eat (giggles).

M: Yeah, of course, eat, go to the movies, be with friends. It was . . . I don't know. I felt . . . I felt really comfortable around Alison.

As we saw in the style section, such narratives may not be tremendously dramatic, but that probably is just as well as far as our participants are concerned. "May you live in interesting times" is, after all, still a curse.

Now that we have examined the overall sweep of the courtship narrative, let us look with a closer lens at some of the specific subplots that emerged. Prompted by our diagram, most couples' courtship stories followed a set progression of scenes, beginning with what life was like before they met, moving on through how they met and became interested in each other, and progressing toward the decision of whether and when to get married. Let us examine each of these subplots in turn, to see what they can reveal about the experience of courtship in urban America today.

Initially, couples were asked to open their narratives by giving a brief picture of what their lives were like immediately before they met. Most couples gave only brief, perfunctory accounts of this prespousal era. For example, Chris said: "I had graduated from high school in '82. I had a couple of jobs, and wasn't doing a lot. Mainly just working and going home and working on cars, seeing friends. I wasn't really dating anybody until I met Angie." Or Denise: "I was in school. A sophomore, and I was pledging a sorority at this time. And that was that." Couples seemed to know that the "main attraction" of the narrative would be the description of their relationship together, and wished to move on to that story as quickly as possible.

Couples next gave a description of how they met. From the interview, we learned that the most common way for couples to meet was in a social setting (21% of all couples), like Mike and Alison at a baseball game, or Troy and Denise at a sorority party. The next most common was at school (20%) like John and Darla, who had a class together in high school. Couples also met at their work (14%). Of those who met at work, 58% met at their joint workplace, 26% at the wife's workplace, and 16% at the husband's. Angie and Chris met at Angie's workplace and, as usual, have a good story to tell:

> A: Chris just worked three stores down from us. He worked at [restaurant] and I worked at [convenience store], and, this girl that was working for me, we're just standing around looking out the window, and Chris walked by, and she said "Oh, my God!" And she ran in the back, and goes "I used to go out with him." And she went in the back and starts combing her hair and everything (laughs). And then, I go "Sure, you did. Sure!" you know. I thought she was goofing around. And she goes "His name is Chris." So I opened the door and I said "Is your name Chris?" And he like turned around, 'cause he didn't know who I was. "Yeah . . ." "Okay," and I shut the door, and he just kept on walking down to the other drugstore. And then he came . . . He kept coming in there and buying cookies (giggles).

Some couples also met through their friends (11%) or family (8%) or because they lived near each other (8%), and 17% met in other public places not previously coded (e.g., grocery stores, libraries, parks). In general, there did not seem to be a single common way for couples to meet; they simply encountered each other in any number of ways through their daily activities. In urban America today, there is no clear script to follow about how to meet one's future spouse; at least, we would be hard-pressed to provide any such advice based on our couples' experiences.

In describing how they first became interested in each other, our newlyweds again followed no one set sequence. For some, there was a definite occasion they could point to when they first developed an interest, like Alison and Mike at the Halloween party, or Troy and Denise, who became interested in each other at a sorority party. For others, the relationship evolved more gradually, like Angie and Chris spending time together at the store while Chris worked up the nerve to ask Angie out, or John and Darla, who spent time together talking in class.

When it comes to formally initiating a dating relationship, most couples are still quite traditional, in that the husband is the one who initiates. The husband was coded as the initiator in 60% of all cases (41% husband initiated; 19% he initiated, wife rejected but later agreed). Quite a few women are still traditionalists like Angie, who, although she liked Chris and "was getting impatient" thinking he would never ask her out, still waited until he asked, rather than doing the asking herself.

In only 16% of the narratives was the wife coded as the primary initiator. Even when she was the primary initiator, her actions often came in the form of giving the husband an explicit prompt. For example, John and Darla got to know each other in a class they had together, but then John got transferred out of the class. At that point, Darla took the initiative, but in a roundabout way. "I gave my phone number to Charlene, and Charlene gave it to Louise and told you to call me. . . . Then you called me and that was it." In 19% of the narratives, the couples both agreed to start dating. This agreement was often rather implicit, as when they "just started seeing each other." For example, Troy described how he and Denise gradually developed a relationship after meeting at the sorority party:

> T: She was at home in Detroit and I was at school, and she came up a couple of times during the summer to visit some of her soros [sorority sisters]. One of her soros was living in my building. So we talked a little more, talked a little more. We didn't really start getting really serious until school started. . . . Um, it just kinda came natural. We didn't plan it or sit down and formally exchange rings.

Finally, in 11% of the narratives, the relationship was initiated by someone else (1% husband's family, 2% wife's family, 8% friends). Occasionally, this would take the form of explicit blind dates; more often, the family and friends would think the two might hit it off, and would simply arrange for them to meet each other at some social function with a group of other people.

The stories of meeting, getting interested in each other, and perhaps the first date generally take up the bulk of the courtship narrative. At that point, there is a gap that's generally filled with some variation on "and then we dated for awhile." As Mike said, "We just dated for a long, long time," or as Troy put it, "There for each other through the tough times, through the ups and downs." Couples did not seem to elaborate much on the exact details of the dating process. Here are Chris and Angie:

> A: We just started going out steadily again. A year later, we got engaged (laughs).
>
> C: Yeah.
>
> Interviewer: That's it?
>
> A: Yeah, that's it.

C: Yeah. Just kept going out a lot.

A: Having fun, going to shows and doing some things. He was fun to be around.

Finally, we proceed to the final courtship subplot, deciding whether and when to get married. As we have already noted, this would sometimes cause conflict or tension in the relationship, with one spouse (e.g., Mike, Darla) ready to get married long before the other (e.g., Alison, John). In fact, "deciding about getting married, including premarital jitters" was the second most common source of tension in the courtship narratives, coded 15% of the time. It is difficult to tell from the stories what the couples said or did to negotiate that tension about deciding to marry. In many cases, it simply seemed to be a matter of waiting patiently until the more reluctant partner felt ready.

Once couples had negotiated any differences of opinion and were both prepared for marriage, the time came for a proposal. The stereotypical image of the husband down on one knee with a ring did not always apply. In fact, the single most common category coded for the "proposal" is "Both agreed; couple discussed or implicit agreement" (e.g., "we talked" or "we decided to get married"). This category covered 33% of all narratives. It was also quite common to have no discussion about the proposal or to have it unclear who proposed to whom (21%). These narratives most likely also fall into the category of a general discussion or agreement between the couple that the time had come to get married. Thus, in almost half of the cases, the couple simply agreed that the time had come to marry, rather than having a formal proposal event.

When there was a formal proposal, however, with one partner explicitly asking the other, it was still much more likely that the man asked the woman, rather than the opposite. The husband proposed in 41% of all narratives (composed of "husband proposed on own initiative," 27%; "husband proposed on wife's prompting," 8%; "husband proposed on someone else's prompting," 0.6%; and "husband proposed, wife rejected but later agreed," 5%). In contrast, the wife proposed on her own initiative only 4% of the time.

A formal proposal, when it did occur, was often recalled and relayed in some detail, forming one of the key vignettes of the courtship substory. For example, here are Troy and Denise:

T: She was in school. I had graduated. . . . I was living here in Detroit and I had to go up there [to the university] on the weekends, every weekend. And one Saturday morning, I just woke up and asked her to marry me.

D: And I didn't believe it (laughing).

T: So we got engaged. Then about a month later, I woke up on another Saturday morning, say "Let's go get your ring," just kind of spur of the moment. She didn't believe that, too!

D: (Giggles)

T: But I said "Get in the car and let's go." So we came down and got her ring and she's like really in shock . . .

Angie and Chris provided a particularly memorable story. Angie had bought Chris an expensive stereo system for Christmas, but Chris told Angie he hadn't bought her anything, as he was short of money. Angie assured Chris that was fine. But then on Christmas day, Chris was just heading out the door to help his brother jump-start his car, when he told Angie her present was under the tree. Angie reported:

A: And I go, "where?" And I see one present, but it was his little sister's, and it's already opened. And I'm looking, "where?" And he's going, "It's under the tree." And he's like, all ready to shut the door, you know, to go help his brother. And I'm looking, "where?" And he goes, "It's under there." And I couldn't see nothing under there, and it was on one of those Christmas tags, those ones "To:" and "From:" And it was hanging on the Christmas tree on the bottom limb. There was a ring on it, and it says "Will you marry me, Angie?" And I saw it and I just started shaking, and he's out the door. He goes, "Well?," and I didn't say anything. He says "Well, what's the answer?" And I go, "Yeah." He goes "Okay. I'll see you in a little bit." And he shut the door and he left me there!

C: Well, I had to go to my brother!

After the discussion of the proposal, the couple generally moved quickly into discussing wedding planning.

The Wedding. The wedding substory of the narrative comprised the wedding planning, the ceremony, and any party or reception held after the ceremony. The wedding planning was often a fairly large undertaking, although 10% of couples did not discuss planning the wedding at all, and 10% gave only a brief description, not making it clear who did the planning.

Of the narratives that included a clear discussion of the wedding planning, it is heartening to know that over half were planned either by the couple working together (47%) or by the couple with the help of others (4%). Both members of the couple generally seemed to pitch in fairly cheerfully, although the multitudes of decisions they had to be made seemed to be a bit wearing. As Angie and Chris described it:

C: The plans went okay though. I wouldn't wanna plan for another one,
       though!

C and A: (Laughing)

C: I tell everybody else, if anybody ever asks me to help them, "Elope!"

A: "Elope!"

C: Yeah.

C and A: *"Elope!!"*

C: Elope. It's the easiest way!

If one partner did take primary responsibility for the wedding planning,
it still tended to be the wife. Thirty-eight percent of the narratives reported
the wife taking primary responsibility for the wedding planning, either by
herself (23%) or with the help of other friends or relatives (15%). In contrast, only 2% of the weddings were planned primarily by the husband.

Tensions did arise at times, such as when the wife tried to persuade the
husband to be more involved than he wanted to be (John: "Seems like every time she came home, she had another book, and those bride books,
they always have special things, you know, and when you get married and
what to do and how soon you gotta make your plans and all that stuff. . . .
That's made it real nerve wracking . . ."), or when the couple disagreed
about the expense, size, or details of the wedding (Denise: "So *he* thinks
that things like flowers and things that are not gonna be here for you to see
them forever, then there's no reason why. Why should you buy flowers that
are going to die? Why should we have a big wedding?"). The most common
types of tensions noted in the wedding narrative were tension regarding the
"nature of ritual, size, type of ceremony, etc." (20%), "wedding arrangements—involvement of others" (13%), and "anxiety about getting married
and other worries just before or during wedding" (25%).

However, the couple usually managed to work through these issues without major problems. In only 5% of all narratives was open disagreement expressed between the couple, whereas in 16% of the narratives the couples
compromised, and in 6% they engaged in reciprocity (each got something
he or she wanted). In fact, it was more common for the couple to have disagreements with others than between themselves; in 24% of all narratives,
some conflict between the couple or member of the couple and others was
expressed. These problems ranged from the relatively minor (Mike: "That
photographer didn't take any pictures of my side of the family at all") to the
more severe (Angie: "I was brought up Catholic, and my parents are strict
Catholics, and when I told them that I was getting married in Chris's
church, I thought they were going to disown me"). Finally, and reassuringly, the most common coding category was for there to be either no differences expressed in planning or executing the wedding (39%), or for it
to be unclear whether there were any differences or not (8%). Most cou-

ples managed to negotiate the perils of planning the wedding relatively well.

Next, couples described the actual wedding ceremony and reception, if any. We noted earlier that the details of much of the courtship period tended to be glossed over when couples told their relationship story. From what we can surmise, these day-to-day interactions are often hard to summarize, consisting of myriad subtle verbal and nonverbal interactions, gradually developing signs of trust and affection, and slowly evolving knowledge of each other's hopes and plans and dreams. This time spent learning about each other is crucial to a relationship's successful development, but it is difficult to describe to an outsider in detail.

A different picture emerged when we turned to the story of the wedding, which for all our couples took place approximately 3 to 6 months before the Year 1 interview. A wedding is a concrete, publicly observable event that can be readily described to others. Some couples did indeed take this opportunity to provide a detailed description of their day, expounding at length on the wedding arrangements, the location, the officiator, the guests, the entertainment, and the refreshments provided. Some truly seemed to enjoy sharing the details of this event held in their honor. It is interesting to see, in chapter 5, whether their descriptions remain similarly detailed in subsequent years.

We noted that couples did not seem to spend equal time describing all aspects of the wedding event, however. We suggest that the general outline of an urban wedding at the end of the 20th century has become relatively standardized, with most weddings sharing certain characteristic features (e.g., special clothes for bride and groom, attendants for each, an officiator blessing the marriage in the presence of friends and family, a party or reception afterward featuring food, drink, and music). Accordingly, some couples seemed to emphasize the uniqueness of what happened at their wedding, the special touches that set their experience apart from everyone else's.

For example, here is the kind of detail one couple, Jeff and Anna, gave as to what happened when they left the church after the wedding ceremony:

A: Instead of throwing rice or birdseed after the wedding was over, his Mom and Dad blew up balloons in the colors for the bridesmaids. They wore a lilac or lavender color, so his folks went and got balloons and had purple and white balloons all blown up with helium. And they had everyone outside on the steps and everyone held one. We didn't know that until we went to walk out. We knew they weren't going to throw rice or anything on us. And we didn't know why they wanted us to walk out, you know, after the wedding. But they kept saying "go outside, go outside." So we went out, and as soon as we walked out, everyone let go of their balloons, and it was blowing balloons up in the air.

J: That was nice.

A: That was so neat. And then they cheered. Oh, it was so nice. It was really nice. It was a surprise for me. His parents did that, which was really cute. So it saved us from getting all messy.

J: That's true, with all the birdseed. And we drove around after the wedding.

A: And took pictures of everything. We went . . . the best man decided we had to go to . . .

J: White Castle.

A: To the White Castle (giggling), like the commercial. So we went through the drive-thru, just ordered a pop. Nobody else did. We just got a pop and then we went into the reception with a White Castle pop.

J: (Laughs)

A: Everyone thought we had stopped and ate. "Oh no," they said, "we've been waiting here to eat and you went and ate!" But we didn't.

Here, the details of the balloons after the wedding and the White Castle trip seemed to serve as the unique symbols of their wedding. We would hazard a guess that many couples cherish similar distinctive details of this sort in their wedding story to differentiate their own special day from the rituals of others. The details serve as markers to set their story apart from the many similar events they have attended or heard about.

In contrast, other couples seemed surprisingly low in details of the ceremony, considering the extensive work many reported going into planning the wedding. Although one got the impression that they had taken great care in selecting the flowers, the gowns, the music, the ceremony details, these were not elaborated on. For these couples, small scenes seemed to stick out in their minds (the pregnant bridesmaid who had to keep leaving the ceremony to use the restroom; the normally stoic father who cried all the way down the aisle; the mysterious guest, invited by the groom's mother, whom no one seemed to know). In general, however, these couples described the wedding as big or small, and perhaps specified the number of attendants. Other than that, however, the occasion was simply described as "beautiful," "real nice," "cool," "great," "so fun," and so forth, with little else in the way of details. Perhaps in retrospect these couples found that no touches in the ceremony clearly set their wedding experience apart from many others. Therefore, rather than repeat the fairly standard details of the ceremony, they chose to insert a few distinguishing anecdotes of memorable events (e.g., the pregnant bridesmaid) and focus on the overall emotional impact of the occasion. In fact, the most common themes or aspects of the wedding story were fairly general, such as "it was a good time, it went well" (18%), and an "opportunity for family to be together/consolidate" (13%). More extreme categories, such as "grand finale" or "fulfilling a lifelong fantasy," were used very rarely (1% and 3%, respectively).

Overall, the most common theme for the wedding was that of it being a social occasion (24%), followed closely by it being a generally positive experience (20%), or it symbolizing a public commitment (18%). Negative reactions of any sort were not common (18%), and very extreme positive reactions (an affective high point of the relationship) were even less common (14%). Despite all their planning and preparation, the couples mostly seemed to keep the wedding in perspective, seeing it as a positive opportunity to affirm their commitment to each other in front of family and friends, but not as a major life-altering experience. Unique details were cherished and elaborated on, and the rest were encompassed into an impression of a generally positive and enjoyable experience. Having withstood the difficulties involved in arranging and performing the public commitment of their marriage vows, most couples seemed to look back at the experience as a good thing that worked out well for them. One cannot help but wonder whether, like an initiation rite, the difficulties attendant in planning the myriad elaborate details served to leave the couple even more strongly bonded than if the transition had been easier.

The Honeymoon. The majority of couples reported some sort of formal honeymoon, but not all. Approximately 30% of couples did not give a honeymoon story, either skipping that part of the narrative altogether (12%) or talking about what life was like right after they were married but making it clear they had no formal honeymoon as such (18%). The remaining 70% described some sort of formal honeymoon experience, ranging from a simple driving tour around Michigan to an elaborate all-expenses-paid package in Jamaica. Some couples still provided stories of key events that stuck out in their minds (e.g., Angie and Chris told an amusing story about almost losing their tickets, as well as the one about getting their sunburns). However, more couples began to move to a more descriptive mode here (e.g., "All the meals and stuff were included. You can eat as much as you want and didn't have to pay for nothing. And those people love rum and everything. . . . They had like two bars out on the beach. . . . You just stayed drunk there if you didn't watch yourself. . . . It was real nice. The weather was nice.").

The honeymoon seemed to be a positive, relaxing experience for most. The most common rating for source of tension was "none—no tension" (33%), and twice as much tension arose from issues between the couple and others (26%) as between the couple members (13%). The few tensions that did arise came mostly around the area of honeymoon mishaps: problems with arrangements or travel (27%) or issues around the couple members' work or job, such as "getting enough time off" (11%). There were some instances of couples experiencing interpersonal tensions as well (19%), mostly minor squabbles. The major themes that arose included "travel, sightseeing, and entertainment" (28%), "a period of seclusion/privacy" (11%), and "general satisfaction" (11%). Overall, positive themes far outweighed negative themes (64% to 22%; 15% coded "other"). As expected, the honeymoon seemed to serve as an enjoyable interlude and pleasant diversion for most couples.

Current Life.   As noted in the style section, once we moved into the present life section, most couples ceased to tell stories and instead gave a general description of their current life situation, often emphasizing that it was largely continuous with their life before they got married. They described the division of household chores (Darla: "I come home and he always cooks dinner, you know. That makes it nice. He has dinner ready for me"), their leisure-time activities (Chris: "We have friends that come over quite often. We play cards and we watch movies on the video recorder. But basically, her and I, we like to stay at home, just be with each other"), their minor conflicts (Mike: "How much I don't clean up the sink after I'm finished shaving. It's about the biggest argument we've ever had, if anything, is when I leave the bathroom a mess"), their daily routines (Alison: ". . . go feed the ducks in Northville, balance the checkbook. . . . Go over the bills and talk about the day and watch TV and go to the grocery store"), or their work schedules (Denise: "Now I'm in the intensive care unit. . . . So I'll be taking classes for the first of the year").

Tensions in the current life were most often between the husband and wife (30%), although this was closely followed by tensions between the couple and outside (24%). Common types of tension included couple relations (22%), money/finances (14%), and work/job (14%). These tensions seldom extended to serious problems at this point, however. The couple relations tensions generally consisted of the small problems in getting adjusted to life together which we've already seen mentioned briefly (e.g., dividing up household chores, squabbling over messes, getting used to sharing space and possessions). Some tensions dealt with differential spending and budgeting habits they had as a couple. Such tensions in some couples seemed trivial but it would not be hard to imagine that they could flower into more extended tensions as the marriage progressed. Work/job tensions were more often in the nature of uncertainties, rather than actual arguments. The mid-1980s was a time of corporate restructuring and downsizing that certainly affected some of our participants. For example, the car plant where John worked was temporarily closed for refitting; meanwhile, he was being transferred around to several other plants. Although he knew he would be called back to his home plant eventually when it reopened, he did not know when that would be nor what his job situation would be in the interim, leading to feelings of uncertainty.

Couples' themes for their present life narrative echoed concerns similar to those revealed in the tensions. Couples were concerned about establishing good relations with each other. Common themes included "getting adjusted to each other or to married life" (10%) and "developing a routine" (8%). They were also concerned about getting themselves on a solid financial footing. Common themes included "financial security or stability" (8%) and "work/job" (19%). Finally, 8% discussed issues related to children. Among these were two groups: those who were already parents and often discussed their childcare responsibilities, particularly arranging for others to help out; and those who did not yet have children, who often discussed differential attitudes each had toward having children soon or putting it off.

Overall, the current life section had a very pragmatic tone, wherein couples described their daily life and current needs and priorities in a very straightforward fashion. The feeling that emerged was less one of blind newlywed bliss and more one of a sensible mutual accommodation to a new set of life circumstances and priorities.

Future. The future section felt very similar to the present life section. Again, it did not consist so much of stories as of general descriptions. Less attention was paid to the relationship between the partners here; most seemed to assume that once they got past the initial minor adjustments, their life together would continue on quite happily. The emphasis was more on their pragmatic goals.

Some emphasized their plans for future housing, either improving their current housing or buying new ("nest building," 14%). For example, Mike and Alison discussed their plans:

A: We wanna skip over the starter home and stay in the apartment while we save up more money and get a house that we can stay in, cause I hate moving. . . .

M: Older house too, that we can possibly work on.

A: With some land and some big trees.

Discussions of future job, education, and career plans also figured prominently, tied in with couples' goals of establishing solid financial security (9% mentioned change/continue in work/job; 13% mentioned change in/enhancement of job/career; 10% mentioned financial security/stability). Troy gives a good feel for this type of discussion, as he outlined their plan to possibly have Denise start up a day-care business in a few years, or else return to school to upgrade her nursing skills:

T: Yeah, I think it's a lot of money in day care, and I don't think it's that
hard of a job. She enjoys nursing now, but I can tell now that after 3 to 5
years, there's a burnout in nursing, like front line nursing. And she'll
like to do something either administrative or she'd have to pursue her
master's. I want to be in a position that if she does decide to pursue her
master's after we have children, then I can financially support the entire
family, so it won't be a problem. She can go back to school if she wants
to, or whatever she wants to do. I don't want us to have to do anything for
financial reasons. I want us to be able to have the flexibility to do what we
wanna do, as opposed to having it dictated to us.

Finally, the issue of wanting children came up most clearly in the future
section, inextricably tied in with the need for a larger house or greater financial stability. Wanting children or wanting more children was a theme
mentioned 19% of the time. Many couples seemed to have some general
idea of when they would like to expand their family, whether in the near
future (Alison: "The objective is to get a house and as soon as we get a
house we have a baby"), the mid-future (Troy: "Considering children.
When to have children. Trying to make sure it's the right time. Estimate
now about ..." Denise: "About 3 years." Troy [chuckling]: "About 2
years"), or the more distant future (Angie: "I don't want kids at least for 5
or more years, 7 years maybe. . . . Right now, you know, I'm too young").
None of the couples announced in their narratives that they did not plan
to have children.

Couples' future stories overwhelmingly fell into a "progressive form"
(94%; anticipating increments in the relationship of a positive kind) rather
than a "regressive form" (2%; anticipating a negative outcome in the relationship) or a "stable form" (2%; no anticipation of changes or increments
in the relationship). See Appendix A for specific categories in each form.
Couples saw their future quietly and steadily improving over time, as they
worked toward their family, career, and financial goals. As Angie summed it
up: "Got lots of plans for the future, you know, just different things that will
happen, but that comes with time. So, we've got a lifetime together."

Summary.   In the courtship, couples focused on several key stories of
their dating years—how they first met, their first date, the proposal, and so
forth. The periods in between these key episodes were often glossed over.
The overall impression was of a quietly positive progression as the couple
steadily grew closer together over time. Many courtships seemed to be egalitarian and to evolve gradually, with both partners agreeing to see each
other or agreeing it was time to get married. When one partner did initiate,
however, it was still overwhelmingly the male.

The wedding planning, in contrast, was still more of a female domain.
Again, in many instances, the couples were quite egalitarian, planning the

ceremony together. When it was left to one partner, however, it was still overwhelmingly the woman. Many couples escaped the wedding planning period without major tensions, and some experienced tensions primarily between themselves and outside individuals. It was not uncommon for the wedding planning to engender some conflict between the couple, though, over the matters of who would be invited or what the details of the ceremony would be like. After all this planning, however, the wedding was generally described in general but positive terms, with emphasis on the unique details that set the couple's ceremony apart from others'. The couple tended to experience the wedding as a fun and positive social occasion, but not as some central grand finale to their dating years.

The honeymoon, when it was taken, was a good opportunity for the couple to relax and enjoy themselves. Couples' experiences tended to be positive. Some couples still focused on some key episodes that stood out in their minds about the honeymoon, but many were beginning to move toward a more descriptive mode.

In the current and future life sections, the tone was definitely descriptive and pragmatic. Couples focused on getting adjusted to each other, on establishing themselves in their careers and achieving financial stability, and on working toward future goals of owning a house and raising children. Although their visions were quite positive, the overall impression was less one of starry-eyed newlyweds, with visions of love in their eyes, and more one of sensible copilots, setting out together on a challenging journey.

Now that we have an overview of the stories in Year 1, we turn in chapter 5 to examining how the stories change over time. Will couples maintain the same quietly positive tone in Years 3 and 7? Will they become more disillusioned as they face the everyday challenges of marriage, resulting in more negative or more conflictful narratives? Or will their stories become more dramatic and intriguing over time as they build up their repertoire of amusing and enlightening stories of their lives together?

TABLE 4.1
Style Variables, Year 1 Narratives, Overall and by Substory

	Overall	Courtship	Wedding	Honeymoon	Present	Future	(Scale)
Integration of Narrative	3.21	3.66	3.31	2.85	2.51	2.26	(5 pt.)
Directiveness of Interviewer	2.12	2.51	2.15	1.85	2.09	1.98	(4 pt.)
Drama of Content	1.48	1.72	1.71	1.38	1.42	1.15	(3 pt.)
Drama of Style—Husband	1.41	1.49	1.55	1.32	1.39	1.32	(3 pt.)
Drama of Style—Wife	1.51	1.62	1.68	1.48	1.45	1.30	(3 pt.)
How Much Conflict?	1.38	1.56	1.39	1.20	1.34	1.38	(4 pt.)
Percent Jointly Told	69	74	68	60	71	70	(%)
Ratio Wife's Involvement to Husband's	1.2	1.20	2.33	1.54	0.98	0.58	(>1 more wife, <1 more husband)
Distribution of Speaking Turns	100	27	44		18	11	(%)
Distribution of Affective Statements	100	28	35		24	12	(%)

Note. For ease of presentation, all numbers have been appropriately reversed so that higher numbers indicate more of the underlying construct (e.g., more integration, more drama, more conflict, etc.). The rightmost column indicates the nature of the scale on which the scores are measured to aid in interpretation of the numbers.

TABLE 4.2
Major Issues of the Overall Narrative

Theme	%
Couple's Relationship	
Positive (general satisfaction with each other, friendship, communication)	24
Positive (showing growth and development, working through problems)	18
Negative (general dissatisfaction)	4
Total	46
Family and Friends Relationship	
Family relations	33
Friend relations	3
Total	36
Children	
Pregnancy	5
Children other than pregnancy	8
Total	13
Other Issues	
Financial concerns (debt/lack of money)	16
Work/Career/Education	29
Home/Home improvement/Buying a home	8
Time (having enough/balancing time)	8
Religious concerns/Church-related	9
Leisure	5
Personal loss/Personal troubles	6

Note. Up to two issues could be coded for each narrative; therefore numbers add up to greater than 100%.

Chapter 5

Beyond the Honeymoon:
Changes in Narratives Over Time

In chapter 4, we examined couples' stories of their relationship in their first year of marriage. In this chapter, we investigate how their stories may have changed when we returned in the couples' third and seventh years of marriage to ask them to tell us their stories again. We treated couples' Year 1 stories in chapter 4 as insights into how average American couples meet, fall in love, and get married—and to a certain extent, they are. To be sure, most people's autobiographical narratives have some basic touch points with the reality of their lived experiences as would be described by an outside observer. But as narrative researchers, we are also well aware that narrative truth is not historical truth (Spence, 1982), and we should not be surprised when stories of even exactly the same events differ from telling to retelling. As we discussed in chapter 2, narratives may well be dynamically affected by the changing contexts of the storytellers' lives, whether those contexts are understood at a cultural, interpersonal, or personal level. Narratives shape and are shaped by changes in the very relationships they both reflect and guide. Thus, we would fully expect that couples' relationship narratives will not remain exactly the same over time, but will change and evolve from Year 1 to Year 3 to Year 7.

PREDICTIONS OF CHANGES

What types of changes might we expect to see in these relationship narratives over time? The literature does not provide a great deal of guidance. Most longitudinal studies using a narrative methodology document changes in children's storytelling abilities as they mature (e.g., Haden, Haine, & Fivush, 1997). A focus on changes in stories across the adult life-span seems less common, though exceptions such as Josselson's (1996) 20-year longitudinal study of women's life narratives certainly do exist. To our knowledge, however, there has been no long-term examination of changes in people's relationship narratives over time and thus our investigation remains primarily exploratory.

However, we did have certain general expectations. Primarily, we expected that over time and with practice couples' relationship narratives would become "better" stories:[1] more finely honed, more dramatic, more integrated stories, clearly emphasizing certain key themes in people's relationships. Such improvement might arise, first, because our couples have gained more practice in telling their stories over time. The relationship narratives do not involve a simple factual recitation of everything that has happened in a couple's relationship. Instead, when telling a good narrative, one selects "from an unlimited array, those moments that the narrator deems significant and arranges them in a coherent order. This fashioning of order is much more than a chronology . . . [It] establishes what counts as the main line of the plot and, thereby, which incidents should be construed as making progress or as retreats or digressions" (Ochberg, 1994, pp. 113–114). As we saw in chapter 4, most couples were readily able to do just that, tell coherent stories from which we were able to extract and code meaningful information.

It seems reasonable to assume that over time and with practice, our couples might become more entertaining storytellers, as they learn which parts of their personal story resonate with their audiences and which parts seem to slow down the narrative flow. They might also have received feedback from their audiences as to how to fill in the gaps or any missing pieces of their stories. Research by Kemper (1990) suggested the possibility of such a practice effect when looking at written accounts. Coders evaluated diary entries made by older adults as more integrated, more technically skilled, and more interesting than entries made by those same adults years earlier when they were less practiced. Over the years, the diarists developed the knack of communicating their life stories in an engaging fashion. We suspect our couples may do the same with their relationship stories.

Practice is not the only reason why we might anticipate "improvement" in the narratives' style over time, however. As noted in chapter 2, we believe these relationship stories are not only used to convey the basic facts of a re-

---

[1]When we use the phrases "better story," "good story," or "improvements in the narrative," we do not wish to pass judgment on the adequacy of the story in any sense other than whether it conforms to a standard understanding of having a complete plot or structure or creates dramatic interest for most listeners.

lationship, but also serve the function of meaning-making. The telling and retelling of relationship narratives over time can help couples explore and understand important themes of their relationship. In their jointly constructed stories, the couple can provide for themselves a common vision of who they are as a couple, and indicate to each other where they are in their relationship.

Again, one might expect that increased experience with the process of meaning-making might lead to the evolution of "better" (i.e., clearer, more dramatic, more integrated, more emotional) stories over time. With deepened perspective and with mutual practice, couples should be able to come to a decision as to which aspects of their story best display their vision of the relationship. "Narratives select the elements of the telling to confer meaning on prior events—events that may not have had such meaning at the time" (Josselson, 1995, p. 35). Additional time and reflection, then, should lead to crisper, clearer, more significant presentations of early relationship events. Indeed, Kemper's (1990) diary study showed the advantages such time and reflection can confer. The most well-elaborated and well-integrated diary entries almost always documented events that had occurred some time (weeks, months, or years) before the entry was recorded. Similarly, the benefit of hindsight, as well as the judicious reconstruction of early memories (see, e.g., Holmberg & Holmes, 1994), may help confer meaning and clarity to the earlier days of the relationship. In addition, if couples have had ample time together to determine their mutual priorities and interests, then the stories of the present and the future might also improve over time as they learn how to communicate what matters to them in a smooth and coherent fashion.

Thus, from both a pragmatic, storytelling perspective, and from a more personal, meaning-making perspective, we would expect to see improvements in the style of couples' narratives over time. We expected they might be more highly integrated, more dramatic, with clearer themes and tensions and fewer omissions or ambiguities.

As mentioned in chapter 4, we would not necessarily expect all parts of the story to be uniformly clear and dramatic. The courtship and wedding stories seem to fall more easily into our cultural notions of a story, with clear development over time toward a well-defined goal. Those were the parts of the narratives that were especially storylike in Year 1. Stories of the present and future fall less clearly into a story form, and thus will probably remain less well-integrated, even with additional practice. Nonetheless, it will be interesting to see what sorts of themes are emphasized in the present and future stories. As couples have more time together to learn about their common goals and desires, do particular themes emerge as common across our sample? Or do couples develop more idiosyncratic views as they learn what makes their marriage unique?

To explore these issues, we examined changes over time in the narratives, from Year 1 to Years 3 and 7. Mirroring the analyses presented in chapter 4, we first focused on changes in the style of the narratives, then turned to changes in the content of the narrative. To look at changes over time in the narratives without changing the group of people being examined, we focused on only the subsample of 144 couples for whom complete stories were available in all 3 years. Please see chapter 3 for complete descriptions of this subsample, and of how it compares to the overall sample.

Sensitive to the fact that changes might be different for different parts of the overall relationship story, we also looked at substories. For each narrative characteristic we examined, we completed what is known as a *repeated-measures analysis of variance*. There were two predictor variables in each analysis: year of story (Years 1, 3, and 7 of marriage) and substory (courtship, wedding, honeymoon, present life, and future). We can thus see whether any significant changes in each measure of narrative style occur over time and whether those changes apply equally to all substories or occur only in certain parts. Table 5.1 shows the overall changes by year, whereas Table 5.2 describes how these year changes differ for different substories. The *F* statistic shown in the last column is a statistical measure of the significance of the differences found. The larger the *F* value, and the more asterisks shown, the less likely it is that differences of this size would be found by chance alone. We begin our analyses by exploring changes in the narratives' style over time.

STYLE OF NARRATIVES

Quality of Storytelling. As noted earlier, our primary expectation was that the couples' stories would get "better" over time, becoming more integrated and more dramatic. A glance at the pattern of results (see Table 5.1 at the end of this chapter) shows that this expectation was not supported. There were significant effects for the year of story variable for all four quality measures: length of story, integration of story, drama of story content, and drama of storytellers' styles.

Contrary to our initial expectations, couples' storytelling abilities did not improve over time. Instead, on virtually every measure, there was a marked decline in narrative quality from Year 1 to Year 3 to Year 7, with the change from Year 3 to Year 7 being the most dramatic. The stories became shorter overall over time, even though there was more history to report as time went on. One could easily argue that by Year 3, and certainly by Year 7, the courtship and the wedding events were more distant than they were during the first year of marriage, accounting for why those parts of the couple story were shorter. But what about the other parts? There was more to report about their history as a married couple at Year 3, and especially at Year 7. And still the stories became shorter as time went on.

The stories also became less integrated over time. In Year 1 and Year 3, the average rating was around the midpoint of the scale, representing "a story or set of stories told intermittently." By Year 7, the average rating had dropped almost a full point on the integration scale, now appearing closest to "conventionalized continuity in response to questions: descriptions." Furthermore, the stories also became less dramatic over time. Recall from chapter 4 that the stories were not especially dramatic to start with. Over time, however, the drama level dropped even further until average ratings for both the content and the style were quite close to 1.0, representing "not at all dramatic."

These drops in the quality of storytelling were most notable for the courtship and wedding stories (see Table 5.2 at the end of this chapter). Recall from chapter 4 that the courtship and wedding stories in particular, and the honeymoon story to a lesser extent, tended to be relatively integrated and dramatic in Year 1. The stories of couples' present and future lives, in contrast, tended to be less dramatic and more descriptive. Our analyses show us, however, that these substory differences tended to get smaller over time. Over time, all aspects of the story tended to move toward the not very dramatic, a primarily descriptive mode seen for the present and future stories alone in Year 1.

Negotiating a Joint Narrative.   What happens to the negotiation of a collaborative narrative style over time? Recall from chapter 4 that the couples overall seemed to negotiate a joint narrative quite well, collaborating strongly and showing relatively little conflict in their storytelling. These analyses show that at least this subsample of couples who stayed together for the full 7 years continued to display these strengths over time, and even increased them slightly. The amount of conflict, low to begin with, dropped slightly more by Year 3; the percentage of all interactions that were positive or neutral (as opposed to negative) started out high and stayed that way over time. The degree of collaboration did drop off slightly in the Year 3 stories, but was back up again by Year 7.

Examination of these effects within each substory suggests that the few changes that did occur primarily took place in the stories of the present and the future, with the conflict levels in those substories dropping to virtually zero in Year 3, and collaboration in those sections showing a slight drop in Year 3. The stories of the earlier stages of the relationship showed fewer changes over time, though they did become slightly more collaborative.

Although the year effects we have been discussing were generally statistically significant, they were quite small on an absolute level, representing only a few percentage points, or tenths of a point on a rating scale, even in the present and future substories where the most substantial changes took place. The overall impression is one of relative stability: Couples did a good job of negotiating a joint narrative in Year 1, and those who stayed together also maintained those strengths over time.

Affective Tone.   The final section of Table 5.1 displays changes over time in the affective tone of the stories. The stories became slightly less affect-laden over time, and the percentage of positive affects also fell slightly. Examination of these results within each substory shows that these overall changes primarily applied to the courtship, wedding, and honeymoon stories (see Table 5.2). For the current and future stories, we see a slightly different pattern: Both actually became slightly more affect-laden in Year 3, with the future story also containing more positive affects in Year 3 before dropping in Year 7. The findings in the previous section also revealed a similar result: Both the present and future stories became more integrated in Year 3, then fell back again in Year 7. Thus, we see slightly "better" present and future stories in Year 3 as compared with Year 1: They are more integrated, more emotional, more positive in tone.

Compare, for example, these future stories by Richard and Janelle. In Year 1, Richard described their future, but in rather vague terms:

> Well, hopefully for us, it will be more of the same. We like to take each day at a time. . . . But you can project certain things, and we want to have children further in the future and raise a family. Hopefully we will continue to grow. Most of the things that we have now remain the same.

In Year 3, Janelle described a much more concrete vision of what the future would hold:

> One of my plans is to go back to school. I realize with a baby it's going to be hard. . . . Definitely our future is the baby, and just trusting in the Lord that he's going to help us. . . . I really think I'm going back to school, because of the baby. . . . 'Cause it's expensive for us, just for the two of us, the cost of living is high.

In Year 1, this couple, like many of our newlyweds, gave the impression of not having thought about the future too deeply. After all, their focus for quite some time in their relationship had been on forming their commitment to each other, then sealing that commitment with the wedding and honeymoon. In the first few months of marriage, they were undoubtedly occupied with the task of adjusting to their new status. The future probably did not loom large in their consideration. By Year 3, however, couples were well established in their married state and many were lining up their immediate and longer-term goals, primarily in terms of whether and when to have children, but also in terms of establishing long-term housing goals and reaching career and educational objectives. Their future story thus gained more focus. Most of the rest of their story, however, showed the same changes we have seen throughout: It was becoming "worse" over time—less integrated, less dramatic, less emotional, less positive.

The stories also underwent some complex changes in terms of the underlying motivations that were emphasized. Recall that in Year 1, the stories were surprisingly agentic in tone, with many of the affects focusing on the couples' needs for self-expression, although we noted that an underlying feeling of the couple working together in achieving their goals was still present. By Year 3, this combination of self-expression and connectedness became somewhat more explicit. Note the dramatic drop in the percentage of all affective statements that express agency or self-expression themes in Table 5.1; the percentage is cut almost in half. There was a slight increase in the percentage of communal affects; however, the interactions reveal that this increase was really only substantial for the courtship story. The other substories remained fairly stable in communal motivations from Year 1 to Year 3. The percentage of stories expressing both agency and connection motivations together also increased slightly over time.

In Year 1, the couples' feelings and needs were fairly directly tied up with achieving their goals: forming a relationship, planning the type of wedding and honeymoon they desired, setting up their household. By Year 3, their affects became somewhat more complex and nuanced. The pattern was now different for different parts of the narrative. The courtship, for example, seemed more romantic and focused on their relationship, with almost all of the affects being communal. The future remained highly agentic, focusing on achieving their goals. And the couples' current life stories represented a complex attempt to seek the balance any relationship must reach between self-expression and connection. Both agency and connection were well represented, and the percentage of statements expressing both desires simultaneously also increased. John expressed the balance many couples are seeking to reach by Year 3:

> Before, when you're single . . . you only worry about yourself. You can take off whenever you want, you don't have to worry about it. When you got kids and stuff like that, you just can't take those days anymore, 'cause now you've got to worry about how they're going to eat, too. It's a whole different thing now. You gotta worry about school, you gotta worry about how they're going to get to college, and insurance. . . . It's like, more than just being a husband, now you've got to be a husband and a father and stuff like that, and kinda balance between the two. . . . I guess that's where we are now. Still having that problem of dividing your time between your work and your family life.

In Year 3, many couples, like John and Darla, were trying to juggle their individual needs, their relationship, and their new roles as parents. It is little wonder that their motivations became quite complex. By Year 7, however, couples seemed to have worked out these balance issues to some extent. They returned to a pattern more reminiscent of Year 1 when agentic themes were emphasized, although mixed themes retained slightly more importance than they did in Year 1. Interestingly, by the time they had been together for 7 years, the emphasis on connection was much less strong overall; in fact, less than 10% of all affects in the wedding/honeymoon, present, and future stories had an explicit connection theme. The statements relevant to connection and feelings of communion seemed to become isolated in the courtship portion of the story, where almost 30% of the affective statements still had communal themes. The couple remembered there were some important feelings and needs associated with their connection in the past. In the present and future, though, the stories seemed to have more of a "working partnership" tone, where the coupled worked on achieving their important goals, sometimes together and sometimes individually. The stories of couples' relationships became much more pragmatic than romantic over time.

Summary. Couples continued to do a good job of negotiating a joint narrative over time. Their stories overall, however, became "worse" as stories over time. They were shorter, less dramatic, less well-integrated, less affectively charged. There were some temporary exceptions to this rule, with the present life and future stories, for example, becoming "better" stories on some measures in Year 3. However, even these substories fell back to low ratings by Year 7. Overall, and contrary to our expectations, couples' narratives seemed to become less dramatic, integrated, and interesting to outside listeners as time went on. We see similar themes echoed in the content section that follows.

CONTENT OF NARRATIVES

When examining the thematic coding for changes in the content of the narratives over time, two major findings emerged. First, the narratives became more ambiguous and more vague over time. Second, over time, the narratives focused less on the couple and their relationship to each other and more on their role as parents and caregivers. Let us examine each of these findings in turn. (All findings discussed in this section are summarized in Table 5.3 at the end of this chapter.)

More Ambiguous Narratives.   We noted in the style section that couples' narratives, especially the courtship and wedding sections, became "worse" as stories over time—shorter, less dramatic, less integrated, less affective. Similar themes emerged when we examined the content coding.

The stories, especially in the earlier stages, became more unclear, more vague. Basic details were often unable to be coded. For example, in the courtship story, it became less clear who initiated the relationship, or who proposed, with the percentages of narratives falling into the "ambiguous" or "unclear" categories increasing. In the wedding, it became less clear who did the planning.

Dramatic tensions present in the story at Year 1 evaporated over time. In each subsection of the story, the percentage of narratives coded as "no tensions present" increased. In the wedding, the percentage of narratives coded for "no differences in wedding planning arise" increased.

The narratives continued to be quite positive, but in a more generic vein. The broadest and vaguest themes became more prominent over time, especially in the early stages of the relationship: The courtship was increasingly described as "generally positive," the wedding as a "good time," the honeymoon as "generally satisfying." There were too many specific themes to show, but this increase in generic themes seemed to come at the expense of all the specific themes, not just one or two in particular. Almost all of the themes showed a gradual decrease over time. As time went on, the narratives, and especially the early stages, seemed to be less about anything in particular. Instead, they became general descriptions of satisfying experiences.

Why did the narratives become less good as stories over time? In retrospect, we have several explanations. First, the narratives serve as a storytelling experience. We wanted the storytelling experience in each year to be as fresh as possible for the respondents. Thus, we used different interviewers in each year, and assured our respondents that we wanted to hear the full story, from the beginning, each time. Nevertheless, couples might have felt at some level that they had already told the researchers the basic story in Year 1, and so we surely did not need to hear it all again. Concerns about being repetitious may have held them back from providing the detail they had in Year 1.

Second, the narratives, contrary to getting better over time and with practice in the telling as we had anticipated, may have actually gotten worse due to lack of that very practice. After all, in our everyday lives, how often do we actually sit down and tell the story of our relationship? Around the time of our wedding, calls for such stories may be more common, as friends and relatives who see us ready to make a lifelong commitment may ask us to review how we reached that state. In Year 1, then, we may have caught the couples after recent practice in telling their relationship story. Over the next few years, though, how much additional practice would they have gained? Calls to review those early events probably do not occur in the normal course of events until the couple's children are old enough to be curious about "how you and Dad met." Our couples are probably too young for that stage; therefore, we may be catching them during a period when their stories are somewhat rusty from disuse.

Third, and we suspect most importantly, our couples may be feeling less of a need to use their narratives as a source of meaning-making over time. Recall from chapter 2 that narratives generally emerge when individuals struggle to come to terms with difficult or at least complex events. In Year 1, when the couples were working to adjust to their newly married state, they may well have felt impelled to carefully review the steps that led them there. By Year 7, however, our couples are "old pros" at the married state. They no longer have to struggle to understand whether the married state is right for them, or seek to justify their decision to marry, to themselves or to anyone else. They can move to a quieter, more interior perspective on marriage. They know why their marriage is right or wrong for them, and expressing that knowledge need not involve elaborate justifications. It is enough to be aware that their courtship was positive, their wedding was good, their honeymoon was satisfying, and so forth. Going into all the details is not necessary; they know where they stand.

As we discuss in chapter 7, this quiet certainty is lacking in less-happy couples. Ironically, it is the couples (and especially the women) who tell the most romantic, idealized, well-integrated stories of the early stages of their relationship who are the least satisfied with their relationship. Those who are undergoing current difficulties dwell on the glory days of the past, reminiscing about when times were better or seeking to understand what went wrong. The majority of our couples, relatively satisfied with their relationships, quietly get on with living their lives in the present.

Change in Focus From Couple to Family.   For many of our couples, the major change involved in living their lives in the present involves the transition to parenthood. Just over a quarter of this subsample had children in Year 1, but that percentage increased to a little more than 50% in Year 3, and fully 91% by Year 7. The vast majority of our couples made the transition to parenthood during the first 7 years of marriage. And as their lives shifted over time, so too did their narratives, moving away from discussion of the couple's adjustment to each other and to the married state, to a focus on children, parenthood, and family issues.

We see this shift in the overall themes of the narrative as a whole. As can be seen in Table 5.3, a focus on the nature of the couple's relationship was a common theme for the whole narrative in Years 1 and 3, appearing in approximately one third of all themes coded. By Year 7, however, relationship themes appeared only 18% of the time. Similar changes appear when we look at the coding for the last few years (in Year 3 and 7 narratives only) and for the present life substory. Themes focusing on the couple's adjustment to each other dropped sharply over time. The couple moved beyond the challenging initial transition to marriage, and no longer had to spend time examining or discussing the nature of their relationship to each other.

Instead, they focused on their next major life challenge, becoming parents. As can be seen in Table 5.3, the narratives became increasingly focused on the couple's children over time, with coding of "children" as a prominent theme doubling or even tripling in frequency across the 7 years. Many couples were as absorbed as this eager new mother:

> It's changed our lives a lot, you know. . . . It's made us a closer, stronger bond together. It's so fun to look at [the baby] and see things about him that are like him, and things about him that are like me. And that's fun, too, you know. So much fun to watch him grow and learn new things, and that's just such a thrill. I never thought it would be. You know, I didn't know what it would be like.

We noted in chapter 4 that the narratives were not solely about the couple's relationship to each other, but also encompass their relations to others in their social network. That observation became even more apparent as time went on, though the couple's relationship to their children became more central than their relationships to their family or friends. Couples' relationships do not emerge in a social vacuum. Their story includes the story of important others in their lives, and as they go on, the most important others seem to be their children. We see that the story of most couples' relationships is not a self-centered Hollywood romance, but rather the story of the emergence of a family.

SUMMARY

Couples' narratives became less clear over time. They continued to be positive, but in a generic vein, with few particulars mentioned. The focus of the narrative shifted from the couple's relationship to each other to their relationship with their children. The picture of quietly positive, not terribly romantic, fairly pragmatic narratives that emerged in chapter 4 continued over the 7 years of marriage. This description characterizes what the narratives look like, on average, across time. In chapters 6 and 7, we explore how couples who differ in their current marital well-being experience different changes in their narratives.

TABLE 5.1
Changes in Style of Narratives Over Time

Measures	Year 1	Year 3	Year 7	F
Quality of Storytelling				
Length of narrative (minutes)	30.5	26.4	20.1	16.86***
Integration (5-pt. scale)	3.05	3.12	2.05	58.90***
Drama: Content (2-pt. scale)[a]	1.39	1.19	—[b]	43.73***
Drama: Style (2-pt. scale)	1.52	1.34	1.10	15.08***
Negotiating a Joint Narrative				
Amount of conflict (4-pt. scale)	1.40	1.22	1.21	4.67*
% of interactions + or 0	96	96	97	1.17
Degree of collaboration (2-pt. scale)[c]	1.74	1.67	1.76	2.63†
Affective Tone				
Total affects (corrected for length)	.054	.051	.040	15.70***
% positive affects	73	68	68	3.03*
% agentic affects	60	32	48	48.90***
% communal affects	24	28	13	26.52***
% affects both agency/communion	10	11	14	2.90†

[a]The 3-point scale used for Drama ratings in Year 1 was converted to a 2-point scale, to allow comparability across years. "Dramatic" and "somewhat dramatic" were collapsed into one "dramatic" category.

[b]Due to a coding problem, this number is unavailable in the Year 7 narratives.

[c]Degree of collaboration was constructed as follows: 1 = all or mostly all one spouse; 2 = collaborative.

†Trend, $p < .10$. *$p < .05$. **$p < .01$. ***$p < .001$.

TABLE 5.2
Differential Changes in Style of Narratives Across Substories

Measures	Effect	F
Quality of Storytelling		
Integration	Courtship and wedding stories show biggest drops; present and future more integrated Year 3, but then less again by Year 7	8.36***
Drama: Content	Courtship and wedding stories show biggest drops	4.83**
Drama: Style	Courtship and wedding stories show biggest drops	2.67**
Negotiating a Joint Narrative		
Amount of conflict	Present and future stories drop most, in Year 3	2.48*
% of interactions + or 0	No significant differences across substories	0.37
Degree of collaboration	Courtship and wedding stories slightly more collaborative over time; other stories somewhat less	2.91**

(Continued)

TABLE 5.2
(Continued)

Measures	Effect	F
Affective Tone		
Total affects	Courtship and wedding stories show biggest drops; present and future stories up slightly in Year 3, less again by Year 7	3.69**
% positive affects	All substories become less positive over time, except future—more positive Year 3, less again by Year 7	2.03[†]
% agentic affects	All substories large drop Year 3, up again somewhat Year 7; except future: more stable	6.52***
% communal affects	Courtship increases Year 3, then drops somewhat Year 7; all other substories stable Years 1 and 3, then large drop in Year 7	2.70*
% affects both agency/ connection	No significant difference across substories	0.79

[†]Trend, $p < .10$. *$p < .05$. **$p < .01$. ***$p < .001$.

TABLE 5.3
Changes in Content of Narratives Over Time

Measure	Year 1	Year 3	Year 7
More Ambiguous, Generic Narratives			
Who initiated relationship? Ambiguous	6	12	27
Who proposed? Unclear	16	32	30
Who planned wedding? Unclear/No discussion	19	40	40
No tensions: Courtship	13	40	36
Wedding	13	38	34
Honeymoon	33	61	49
Present	20	49	41
Future	33	67	72
No differences in planning wedding	33	53	64
Courtship: "Generally positive"	12	14	25
Wedding: "Good time"	20	26	36
Honeymoon: "General satisfaction"	8	14	43
Change in Focus From Couple to Family			
Overall themes: Couple relations	45	53	28
Last few years: Adjustment to marriage	—	20	10
Present: Adjustment to marriage	24	15	14
Overall themes: Children	15	26	45
Last few years: Children	—	14	28
Present: Children	6	12	22
Overall themes: Friends and family	48	19	23

Note. Numbers represent percentage of all responses given to a question that fall into the category noted. "Adjustment to marriage" includes "Getting adjusted to each other/married life," "Developing a routine/settling down," and "Developing as a spouse."

Chapter 6

Tales of Love and Woe:
The Interconnections
Between Relationship Narratives
and Marital Well-Being

In the next four chapters, we turn to a consideration of how the narratives might vary depending on the interpersonal or personal characteristics of the storytellers involved: their marital well-being, their current marital attitudes, their gender, or their ethnicity. In this first of the four chapters, we examine how participants' current marital well-being, their overall feelings toward their relationship, relates to the stories they tell. Do the narratives of happy couples differ in systematic ways from those told by unhappy couples, either at a single point in time or in how they have changed over the years? Or, as another way of looking at the same question, do those who tell particular types of relationship narratives tend to be unhappy, versus happy, in their relationship, again either at a single point in time or over the years? In this chapter, our examination of the links between marital well-being and narratives is primarily exploratory. We examine a variety of aspects of the narratives, both their style and content, to see, empirically, which ones tend to differentiate between happy and unhappy couples. In chapter 7, we turn to more focused questions and explore how changes in current marital feelings over time predict reconstructions in the narratives. First, however, let us examine how couples' current relationship feelings are related to the relationship stories they choose to tell.

Most psychologically minded social scientists have been trained to assume that the memories we report in speaking about our lives are not necessarily the "whole truth" about what really happened way back when. The Freudian revolution in the first part of the 20th century made it commonplace to assume that in our life stories, our current needs and feelings guide us to consider only certain past events and to think about these events in specific ways, sometimes emphasizing and sometimes ignoring what might have happened. We can repress, elaborate, and distort.

This insight led personality theorists in the middle of the 20th century to gather systematic stories and develop reliable ways to code those stories for what they reveal about an individual's personal meaning. A wealth of research went into diagnosing various needs (achievement, affiliation, intimacy, power, fear of failure, fear of success, fear of sex), all from stories told about pictures (see Smith, 1992, for a compilation of such research). Furthermore, McAdams (1985) developed similar procedures, not from stories told about pictures, but from stories people told about their own lives, as if they were composing a set of chapters for a book. From these autobiographies, McAdams diagnosed not only the needs people might have, but also the images they carry around about the meaning of their life, or the ideals they try to live by.

McAdams' research reminds us that autobiographies are fascinating reading, not simply because people's lives are "stranger than fiction," but also because we enjoy inferring certain feelings people must have had, given that they talked of the events in their lives the way they did. We are aware, as mentioned in chapter 2, that the stories people tell to others often reveal personal meanings, and we relish the opportunity to analyze important people's stories and develop a deeper look at what kind of motivations and feelings they might have had. When we read Eleanor Roosevelt's (1992) autobiography, we cannot help but notice that Eleanor never spoke of Lucy Mercer, who was Franklin Roosevelt's secretary and lover in the early part of their marriage and his loving companion in his later years. Not speaking about Lucy tells us a great deal about the bitterness that Eleanor must have felt in keeping up the pretense of a good marriage for Franklin's public image, let alone the deeper wounds she may have had about being a rejected wife. To the reader of Eleanor Roosevelt's autobiography, noticing her silence about Lucy Mercer adds an additional dimension to Eleanor's analysis of her own political career. We interpret something about Eleanor by observing the way she chose to tell her story.

Likewise, in this chapter we gain deeper insight into our couples' feelings by observing how they told their relationship stories. In the process, we explore two general themes about the couples in our study and about how their dynamic relationships might have a bearing on the stories they told us about their relationship, their tales of love and woe.

The first theme is that couples' feelings about their current marriage influence the way couples tell their relationship story. Their feelings affect how they remember and emphasize certain aspects of their past together, and how they color their ideas and emotions in their story, in keeping with their current psychological take on their marriage. Happy couples emphasize certain things, and unhappy couples might emphasize other things, even if ostensibly both groups are following the interviewers' instructions and reporting on the "story of their relationship." In chapter 2, we spoke of the interpersonal and psychological functions that stories serve in precisely these ways.

Our primary assumption when beginning these analyses was that couples who are happier in their current relationship have thought through and integrated their feelings about their marriage, and are comfortable sharing those feelings with others. Therefore, we expected that happier couples would be more likely to tell integrated, emotionally involved stories, whereas less happy couples would be more reluctant to discuss their feelings and would be more likely to stick to simple descriptions, which would be less likely to touch on sensitive issues. However, as noted in chapter 2, there is also some indication that problems or stressors might encourage individuals to form more complex narratives, in an effort to deal with and understand their feelings. Thus, at times we might expect more complex and affect-laden narratives to arise from less-happy couples. As we have reasons to expect findings in either direction, we keep our analyses in this chapter largely exploratory. In what ways do the stories told by happier couples differ from those told by less-happy couples?

Our second theme in this chapter is that once couples tell their stories with certain contents, once they speak out loud about their lives in certain ways, these images can become guideposts for their future adjustments as a couple. In this theme, we explore the hypothesis, preposterous as it might seem, that stories can link to forces that bear on future adjustments, the kind of hypothesis that Adler (1917) long ago spoke of as people having "guiding fictions" for integrating their lives. The stories couples tell are not only emblematic of the way they currently operate in their relationship; they may also come to exert a subtle influence over how they choose to operate as a couple in the future.

We should bear in mind when we consider this proposal that we do not literally mean that the narrative causes future adjustment. Rather, we suggest that the narrative can be diagnostic of other things already going on in the couple's life, or about to go on in the near future, all of which can, in turn, affect the couple's future adjustment. Furthermore, we are also aware that telling a very personal story about a relationship may be in fact the very first time that a wife or husband has heard his or her spouse speak of certain issues, and that such revelations might affect their relationship in a highly dynamic way. The story might induce them to talk more with each other about what they have said or have not said about their courtship or their wedding. We must also remember that the couple is telling their story to a stranger, and what is revealed under such circumstances could be unsettling for some people, and could give them cause to ponder their lives together. Thus, the narrative is not a direct causal agent of future adjustment, but is reflective of dynamic aspects of the couple's ongoing adjustments to one another, which in some complex way might set into motion future adjustments.

We searched our data for evidence of both of these general themes. We used two types of statistical analyses in our search. The first simply asked whether either a husband's or a wife's reported marital well-being in a given year was correlated with the appearance of specific kinds of story features. The measure of marital well-being we used was one employed in many analyses in the Early Years of Marriage project. It is *Marital Happiness,* or the degree to which spouses positively answer six questions concerning their feelings about their marriage in an individually given interview. These questions are as follows:

1. Taking things altogether, how would you describe your marriage? Would you say your marriage is very happy, a little happier than average, just about average, or not too happy?

2. When you think about your marriage and what each of you puts into it, how happy do you feel? Would you say very happy, fairly happy, or not too happy?

3. All and all, how satisfied are you with your marriage? Would you say you are very satisfied, somewhat satisfied, or not very satisfied?

4. How certain would you say you are that the two of you will be married five years from now? Would you say very certain, fairly certain, not too certain, or not at all certain?

5. How stable do you feel your marriage is? Would you say very stable, fairly stable, not too stable, or not stable at all?

6. In the last few months, how often have you considered leaving your wife/husband? Often, sometimes, rarely, or never?

We created a single index by assigning values to each of the responses to a given question, with the lowest values for the least positive responses and the highest values for the most positive responses and corresponding values for the responses in between. The index was the sum of the values from each item. Because husbands and wives answered these questions separately, we could generate a husband's happiness index and a wife's happiness index for each couple. All our analyses were done on each spouse's index separately. Although it would have been simpler to add the two indices together and have a combined measure for the couple's happiness, we resisted doing that, as much of the thinking and research on marriage speaks to different meanings of marriage for men and women (see Bernard, 1972). Indeed, chapter 8 focuses on gender differences we revealed in our analyses of the couples' narratives over the course of this study. We speak of some of those differences here, as we discover ways in which the narrative responses seem to reflect men's perceptions of happiness differently from the way they reflect women's perceptions of happiness.

The second set of analyses goes one step further. We used Growth Curve Analyses (Singer, 1998) to see whether having certain narrative features in a story is associated with marital happiness, not just within the same year that the narrative was told, but also with changes in marital happiness over time. Thus, these analyses ask: When we find changes in certain narrative features over the 7 years of the study, does that also predict corresponding changes over time in a respondent's marital well-being? If it does, we have reasonable evidence that the narrative feature may represent something important about how the couples' marriages evolved over the first 7 years. We use the more complicated Growth Curve Analyses and the simpler correlations intermittently in presenting the results that follow.

MARITAL HAPPINESS MAY INFLUENCE STORYTELLING

In this section of the chapter, we explore findings relevant to our first theme: A couple's marital well-being (or lack thereof) may direct them to tell certain kinds of stories. In compiling these instances, we cannot legitimately say that the person's feelings about the marriage "directed" him or her to help construct a certain kind of story. We are not dealing explicitly with cause–effect findings. After all, one could say that when a couple tells a certain kind of story, this reflects back on the couple's feelings about their marriage, or one could say that having a certain narrative feature in a story *and* being happily or unhappily married are both reflections of some unknown third factor. Nevertheless, our results do allow us to consider the possibility that a couple's well-being can direct them to think of their story in certain ways. In fact, it seems easier to think about these findings in that way, and we tend to do that in the interpretations we present later in this section. It makes a better story about what is going on. Scientific interpretations, after all, are largely researchers' stories or constructions about events, and are probably not the whole truth either. Thus, our storyline in this section is based on the inference that people's feelings influence the story characteristics. Our scientific training requires us to admit that other interpretations of these data are possible, but as narrative researchers, we argue that our version helps construct a clearer understanding about the findings.

In the sections that follow, we cover four ways that marital happiness seemed to direct individuals to construct a certain kind of story: (a) Feelings reported in stories reflected how gratified partners felt about their marriages; (b) feelings reported in stories reflected the problems people experienced in their marriages; (c) telling a "good" story about experiences at times represented an attempt to cope with difficulties, but at other times reflected respondents' pleasure in having mastered something important in their lives; and (d) telling specific types of stories about courtship reflected feelings about the marriage. We discuss each of these findings in turn and present the specific results on which we base our discussion in the tables at the end of the chapter, for those who are interested. Those who prefer text to numbers should be able to follow our presentation without consulting the tables.

Feelings Reported in Stories Reflected How Gratified Partners Felt About Being Married. Couples' stories about their weddings and their honeymoons were diagnostic of how happily married they were as their marriages progressed over the 7 years of the study. The happier they felt about their marriage over time, the more likely they were to tell stories about these early events as times when they harbored many feelings, both hopes and needs, both pleasures and anxieties (see Result 1 in Tables 6.1 and 6.2).[1] Evidently, as married couples retained the glow of well-being typically thought to be true of couples at the time of their wedding and honeymoon, they increasingly remembered those early occasions as moments of great sentiment.

Recall Chris and Angie's example from chapter 4, when they described with amusement the story of getting bad sunburns on their first day in Florida. They also recalled the panic they felt when, on the way to the airport, they discovered that their plane tickets to Florida were missing. Their story of the honeymoon was crammed with such sentimental tidbits in Year 1, and remained so over time. Happy in their marriage, they happily dwelled on the emotions aroused in those early days.

The reverse can be said about couples who became increasingly unhappy by Year 3, for they seemed to steadily purge their early relationship memories of much sentiment as time passed. For them, the wedding and honeymoon were increasingly described as emotionless events. Their stories focused more and more on simple descriptions of outside events as they happened, avoiding descriptions of interior states. For example, one couple told a story in Year 1 that was dominated by a honeymoon car trip in the northeastern part of the United States. In Year 1, when they were happy, the honeymoon was a major focus of their story. By Year 3, when

---

[1]We should also point out that this finding does not simply reflect happier people telling longer stories, and hence having more of any given characteristic. In all of our analyses of feelings in this chapter, we divided the number of feelings by the length of the story, thereby adjusting for any differences in overall story length.

their marital happiness had dropped sharply, this once-treasured trip was hardly mentioned at all, and then, only in passing.

Feelings Reported in Stories Reflected People Working on Problems They Experienced in Marriage.   The findings in the previous section seemed so sensible, we were expecting them to be repeated in many ways. We were in for a big surprise. We had forgotten that a focus on a couple's feelings could reflect not only a sense of gratification but also, under certain circumstances, their frustrations. In chapter 2, when describing the functions of narratives, we said that people often use stories as a way to cope with traumatic or problematic experiences. Although we do not want to suggest that the transition to marriage and the ongoing challenges of married life are traumatic experiences, we are aware that these experiences can be difficult at times. Those who are encountering some difficulties making the adjustment to marriage might use the narratives as a vehicle to work through these issues. An emphasis on feelings and emotions may, at times, reflect such an attempt to grapple with challenging issues.

For example, both husbands and wives who were unhappy in their first year of marriage imbued their current life story with more statements of feelings and needs, and with more psychological tension, than did husbands and wives who were happy in their marriage (see Results 2 and 3 in both Tables 6.1 and 6.2). It is especially interesting to note that the feelings or tensions mentioned were not necessarily negative. Many of the feelings were positive, or simple statements of what the couple wants or likes. The tensions mentioned were not generally major conflicts; instead, they often had to do with an unusual event like buying a house, or coping with a minor ongoing challenge, such as working out a schedule for getting household chores done. Also interesting is that these patterns of results did not emerge in the Year 3 or Year 7 stories.

It seems that couples who were unhappy with marriage during the first year used their storytelling as a way to examine and explore the everyday feelings and tensions that arose in their relationship. They were not simply venting negative feelings. They included statements about the good things that were happening as well as the bad things. It is as if their lack of adjustment alerted them to their current feelings and the tensions of daily life when they told their story. The storytelling became an expression of their wish for adjustment to the new married role, one with which they may not have felt they were coping well.

For example, here is part of the story one couple who was relatively unhappy during the first year told us about their present life:

Husband: Well, we're still here. It's working. I'm not working, but I just got called back. I go back in two weeks . . . so my vacation is over. Things are pretty good, I guess, no problems.

Wife:	No, nothing really.
H:	We generally got things that we want, not everything. We don't have a house yet, but we're not. . . . We got, you know if we need something, we got it, so. Financially, we're pretty . . .
W:	I think it's pretty stable right now.
H:	Yeah, we can make it. We can make it on one of us working too, so. It's better when both of us are working, but we can make it when only one of us works and stuff, so we're doing all right.
Interviewer:	Tell me the kind of things you do during the week.
W:	Daily routine? Get up and go to work (chuckling). Usually we really don't do very much. I mean we really don't have a lot of outside activities. We're home quite a bit, at least I think we do, you know, once in awhile we go out . . . and he has things he likes to do and things he doesn't like to do with me like shopping.

This excerpt did not focus on major difficulties in the relationship; in fact, the couple insisted that things were going well and they were experiencing no major problems. Under the surface, however, it is clear that there were many feelings being discussed about being unemployed and not having things they wanted. Even when they were asked to tell the interviewer what they did on a daily basis, the wife talked about things he liked to do and didn't like to do with her. In this short excerpt many feelings emerged, explicitly and implicitly. Such a focus on feelings in the current life was a sign of problematic issues in the relationship.

More interesting is that for wives, but not husbands, this same phenomenon was true of the couples' stories about the courtship (see Result 4 in Table 6.1). Current difficulties in marriage not only translated into a focus on current feelings; at least for women, they also translated into a focus on past feelings, centered on the earlier stages of the courtship. This result may appear to contradict the finding we reported in the last section that happy wives and husbands were more likely to speak of their feelings in their stories of wedding and honeymoon. There is, however, an interesting difference. Happy women in Year 1 seemed to be savoring the stage of their relationship when they sealed their commitments publicly, whereas unhappy women focused on looking backward to the time *before* that commitment, perhaps asking themselves how did it all happen. Women faced with difficulties adjusting to marriage in their first year were motivated to look back and explore the feelings encountered when they first met their husband— what they liked about and wanted from each other, what was distressing. Such stories about the past may represent an effort to cope with difficulties in the present. That men do not show the same result perhaps suggests that men do not as easily channel their current feelings into feelings encountered in the past. In fact, there is evidence to support the idea that women tend to ruminate more than men (Nolen-Hoeksema & Jackson, 2001; Nolen-Hoeksema, Larson, & Grayson, 1999).

It is instructive to note that these same patterns of results did not exist in Year 3 and Year 7. Marital unhappiness of men and women after the first year did not translate directly into an emphasis on feelings or tensions in the couples' current life stories or into wives' reports of affects during their courtships. Perhaps unhappiness experienced in the first year of marriage reflects a general uneasiness about adjusting to a new role and coping with its demands. Society also teaches us that this transition should be a time of great happiness rather than uncertainty. The narrative approach thus may give couples the opportunity to vent such uneasiness. Such vague uneasiness translates into a pervasive, but unfocused, emphasis on affects and tensions.

After the first year of marriage, unhappiness seemed to be rooted in more specific complaints: not having enough time for each other, the interferences of raising children, or financial concerns. These more focused issues did come up in the narrative, but the feelings they aroused tended to have less pervasive affective consequences for the story. Instead, in Year 3 and Year 7, particular issues that arose in the narratives seemed to serve as signals for ongoing marital difficulties.

For example, we found that the unhappier women were in their third year of marriage, the more likely the issue of lack of commitment was to come up in couples' stories (see Result 5 in Table 6.1). This complaint of a lack of commitment seemed to be a central disappointment of unhappy wives in Year 3. As another example, for both men and women in Year 7, the unhappier they were, the more religion as an issue between them came up in their stories (see Result 6 in Tables 6.1 and 6.2). By Year 7, almost all of the couples had children, and that is often a stimulus for intense discussion of religious differences between spouses, which in turn can be a source of considerable unhappiness in the marriage. Thus, specific issues in the narrative seemed to reflect the unhappiness of spouses in the later years, rather than the general affective tone that was predictive in Year 1.

The specific issue of pregnancy was another theme that arose in stories told by couples who were getting increasingly unhappy across the 7 years of marriage (see Result 7 in Tables 6.1 and 6.2). One unhappily married couple in their seventh year directly stated that the wife got pregnant on their honeymoon, then proceeded to talk about the burdens of raising children. Possibly couples who dwell on the role of a pregnancy in their lives find it difficult to adjust to the ups and downs of married lives, especially with respect to the responsibilities of children; perhaps instead, those who are finding marriage generally difficult tend to focus on the problems of pregnancy as an easy scapegoat for their problems. In either case, a pregnancy-dominated story is a poor prognosticator or reflection of a happy marriage in all of the years of early marriage we observed.

Certain key issues seemed to serve as warning signs of dissatisfaction for the men in our study. Unhappy husbands in their third year of marriage contributed to stories that focused on the period of the couple's life when they were merely living together and not married (see Result 8 in Table 6.2). It is as if unhappy men in Year 3 were longing for their unmarried state, and the couples' stories reflected that. A related finding (see Result 9 in Table 6.2) showed that increases in making cohabitation an issue in the courtship were found in men whose marriages became relatively more unhappy over the years.

Telling a "Good" Story: Good News or Bad News? In chapter 5, we discussed what we mean by a "good" story. We mean what most narrative researchers interested in the structure of a story mean, that the story has a clear beginning, middle, and endpoint, and that the plot is clearly connected. We found that not many parts of the couples' stories in this study fit these stringent criteria for a good story. Nevertheless, they did vary in how integrated the connections were in the flow of events. We call this the *integration* of the story, and we discuss in this section the connection between story integration and spouses' marital happiness.

The most integrated stories were generally about the courtship, sometimes about the wedding and honeymoon, but rarely about the present or future. In fact, by Year 7 the couples' lives were so complicated that virtually all the stories about the present and future had only descriptive comments, with little integration at all between these descriptions. Aside from the fact that some people may have special competences for telling "good stories," is there anything else that a clear, integrated story can reveal? Next we discuss how story integration is indeed important in predicting spouses' well-being.

First, evidence shows that telling clear, integrated stories can at times bode well for the relationship. For example, in Year 3, telling an integrated story about the honeymoon reflected greater happiness for both husbands and wives (see Result 10 in Tables 6.1 and 6.2). Just as more emotional stories about the wedding and honeymoon were predictive of greater happiness, so too were more clear and integrated stories. One might easily argue that the couple who has not yet lost the strong passionate feelings about their marriage enjoys looking back at the time of the honeymoon as an adventure that started it all off. They are still savoring the time of their intimate withdrawal from the world right after they said their vows.

Given that interpretation of what appears to be a straightforward result, it was startling to find that this phenomenon did not last until Year 7. At that time, in fact, we found a reversal for women. The unhappier women were in Year 7, the more likely the couple told an integrated story, not only about the honeymoon, but also about the wedding (see Results 11 and 12 in Table 6.1); furthermore, the more integrated the wedding story became in Year 7, the less happy the wives became over time (see Result 13 in Table 6.1). What changed?

One possibility is that as the passion began to drain for women with the onset of parenting responsibilities in particular, and they began to feel distressed about their marriage, those who looked back at the wedding and honeymoon in integrated plot lines might have been those who were particularly distressed and sought a remembrance of when things were different. Those who were happier in Year 7 evidently could be more matter of fact and descriptive in their talk about their wedding. Those who were not as happy in Year 7 might be "living in the past," a time which served as a sweet contrast to a relationship that has soured. This is similar to findings by Franks, Herzog, Holmberg, and Markus (2002) that show that individuals who have more complex and elaborated past selves are lower in current well-being than are those who put more emphasis on their present and future selves. When present life is not particularly satisfying, one option is to spend more time and energy focusing on the better days of the past. Similarly, Karney and Frye (2002) found that relatively contented spouses tended to downplay the positivity of their relationship in the more distant past, although they saw the more recent past as increasingly positive. A focus on the present or recent past seems to be healthy, but dwelling on the more distant past is not.

What about a focus on the future? There was one instance in the results where telling an integrated or more elaborated story about the future rather than one about the past was a sign of a happily married couple. This occurred for males in Year 3 (see Result 14 in Table 6.2). This finding is also parallel to what Franks et al. (2002) found. In that study, those with more highly elaborated future selves experienced higher personal well-being. Likewise, in our study, emphasizing the future of the relationship bodes well for marital well-being, but focusing on the distant past does not.

Husbands did not seem to go back into the distant past to cope with current difficulties as often as wives did. They did show similar effects in their stories of the more recent past, however. In the first year of marriage, more integrated stories about the wedding, a relatively recent event, occurred when husbands were relatively unhappy (see Result 15 in Table 6.2). A ready interpretation of this result is that from their distress evolved a good story about the wedding, what went into the planning, and what happened before, during, and after the ceremony, including the hoopla that goes with it. It is almost like a reminder to the couple that despite the husband's misgivings, they did indeed embark on a life together.

Telling Specific Kinds of Stories About Courtship Reflected Feelings About the Marriage. There are a number of favorite scripts or myths about how courtships in urban settings in the United States take place. Men and women are undoubtedly susceptible to them. When couples react to these common scripts, rather than focusing on their own unique experience, what does it tell us about their feelings toward each other? We found two patterns of findings that are revealing in this respect.

The first is that husbands were especially unhappy in their marriage in Year 7 when the couple's story indicated that the wife and not the husband was the initiator of the courtship (see Result 16 in Table 6.2). As we saw in chapter 4, despite the progress of the women's movement, it was still far more common for the man to initiate the dating relationship. Cases of mutual initiation, where both partners agreed to begin dating, were not unusual, but a complete role reversal, in which the woman was the primary initiator, was still quite rare. Our findings suggest that such a role reversal is not a comfortable story for men to maintain.

By Year 7, once the facts of how the woman may have played an active role in the courtship have had a chance to fade, couples had the option of moving to a different scenario, one in which they simply glossed over who initiated the relationship and the initiator became ambiguous. Such scenarios did in fact increase sharply in usage over the years (see results in chapter 5). Some couples, however, did not take this route, and continued to focus on the female as initiator. Men in these couples became increasingly unhappy, continuing to be saddled with a storyline that challenges their sense of independence, free choice, or even their masculinity.

For women, there was also a Year 7 courtship plot that reflected distress with their marriages. Surprisingly, that danger signal was painting any kind of romantic or passionate picture of their courtship (see Result 17 in Table 6.1). These findings were indeed surprising to us; we might have assumed that a lively, passionate view of their courtship would reflect good feelings about their marriages, but the opposite seemed to be true.

Again, it seems that those women who spend time harkening back to the distant past may be showing signs of yearning for past happiness, rather than focusing on the present. When wives speak of their courtship after the earliest years of marriage in other than an offhand, pragmatic way, they may be trying to recoup a lost time, a time when their lives were exciting. The same trend was there for the husbands, but it was clearest for the wives. Thus, especially for women, stories about the past can be compensatory for what is absent in the present. They are engaging in a kind of reminiscence of when things were good, almost as if they are asking themselves what went wrong.

Following are excerpts from the Year 7 courtship stories of two women. One was happily married in Year 7 and the other was not. Consider the differences. The happily married woman in Year 7 said this of her courtship:

> So I met him, just the typical teenage years in school. We met through a mutual friend, and then . . . it developed. Yeah, just developed over the years, you know, as we got older, it just developed into a full fledged relationship. . . . It wasn't anything really elaborate. I mean, we got married in the park.

In contrast, the unhappily married woman's story is much more engaging and romantic:

> We had pizza and beer, and he fell madly in love with me and said "Let's go for a walk." Right? We went for a walk that night, and then he asked me out for the next night, and then after that, and the day after that. And then he left for two weeks to go to Texas to visit his family. When he came back, he called me and we started dating.

Instead of the quiet compatibility of the happily married woman, this woman emphasizes the strong feelings and passionate pursuit of her husband in the early stages. He was "madly in love," and couldn't seem to see enough of her. The tone of the happily married wife about the courtship is clearly matter-of-fact, whereas the tone of the unhappily married woman is more romantically engaged. We would argue that the unhappily married woman was harkening back to the sweeter time because she now felt that they were struggling, particularly over financial matters, which she later talked about as "seeping into every other area."

STORYTELLING MAY INFLUENCE MARITAL HAPPINESS

So far, we have focused on our first theme, that marital happiness might elicit certain types of stories. We now turn to our second theme, that telling stories of a certain kind can represent the meanings couples make of their lives, meanings that can then go on to guide their future adjustment. There are three findings we have not yet presented that more directly point to the power of the narrative in a given year as a potential basis for future marital adjustment in a later year. These findings suggest to us that couples may be living out a story they have created, or at least that a story told early on is indicative of ongoing problems in the marriage, and can serve as an early warning signal of future maladjustment.

Lack of Commitment. The first finding indicates that when lack of commitment was a major issue of the story in Year 3, women not only tended to be unhappy about their marriage in that year, but also tended to be unhappier 4 years down the road, in Year 7 (see Result 18 in Table 6.1). We can imagine that saying out loud in a story to a stranger, as well as to one's spouse and to oneself, that there is a problem of commitment in the marriage is a stark statement about what is happening in a couple's relationship. Unfortunately, such statements can easily become self-fulfilling prophecies that the couple lives out over the subsequent years, to the particular distress of women.

That the issue affected the happiness of women more than men fits the gender stereotype that issues of commitment in relationships are a major concern for women and less of a worry for men. It is important to note that during Year 3, most of the couples were starting to have a family, if they did not already have one. This transition makes a woman especially vulnerable to the problem of lack of commitment on the husband's part. The transition to the parent role can exacerbate worrying about commitment once the issue has been raised. And certainly once the question arises, there are many ways in which a spouse can gather more information to confirm a spouse's lack of commitment.

We looked at the Year 3 story of a couple who had become progressively unhappier from Year 3 to Year 7, and caught early evidence of a concern for lack of commitment on both the husband's and wife's part. The wife put it in terms of each of them wanting their freedom, when she explained their style of living during their first 2 years of marriage:

> He has his [bills] and I have mine, and sometimes he helps me a lot. I'm no help, but we basically try and split up everything. Although we basically have our own thing. We've always been that way. Like his Mom says, he drives his car, and I drive my car. It's not that often you will see us together. His mother, she worries a lot. I guess it's his freedom, and I like my freedom, even though we're still one. I think that's why we lasted so long. He let me have my freedom and I let him have his freedom, but when it's time for us to come together, we're one, you know. His mother can't seem to understand that.

Note that the woman does not explicitly state that this rather loose marital arrangement is a problem; in fact, she insists it works quite well for them. But perhaps her mother-in-law saw something she did not at the time. The discussion of the issue of commitment noted here proved to be a forerunner to problems in the relationship that led to a sharp drop in this couple's marital well-being by Year 7. Once commitment comes into question, deeper problems of marital well-being seem to emerge.

Wife as Pursuer/Initiator.   The second finding that suggests narratives may shape subsequent well-being is that when couples in Year 3 told stories about wives having been the pursuer in their courtships, husbands in Year 7 expressed considerable unhappiness in their marriage (see Result 19 in Table 6.2). We previously noted the connection between courtship stories that discussed the woman being the active pursuer and the husband's discontent at that same time. With this result, however, we can take our argument one step further and say that in the minds of men, living out such a marriage might actively contribute to later unhappiness. Perhaps men feel "caught" by their wives when the courtship story is expressed as female-dominated and, over time, that feeling extends to their sense of marital well-being. It is almost as if they were accepting a passive position in the marriage, and as this position is viewed as being counter to what "real men" are like, they are increasingly unhappy in their marriages.

The final finding in this section is closely related: When couples in Year 3 told stories about wives having been the initiator in their courtships, husbands in Year 7 expressed considerable unhappiness in their marriage (see Result 20 in Table 6.2). Female domination can also be the connotation of a story where women are the initiator of the courtship at the beginning. Again, when men become aware of this as a characteristic of the story they tell with their wives about their courtship, they can feel threatened and begin to worry about what their marriage means. Thus, we have found that certain themes in the narratives, such as wives being either the initiators or the pursuers in the courtship, serve as warnings that when the course of the marital relationship is experienced by men and women as somehow not fitting the standard cultural script, there can be added stress in the relationship. When such themes appear in the narrative, it likely indicates that the couple voicing them may be having special difficulty coping with that stress.

SUMMARY

We found considerable evidence for the first of the themes with which we started this chapter, asking about the connection between marital happiness and the kinds of narratives that the couples constructed between Years 1 and 7 of their marriage. How happy husbands and wives were was closely connected to the kinds of stories they told, the feelings they attributed to their discussion, the issues and problems that became the foci of their concerns, and even how "good" a story they told. Sometimes the results indicated that the story constructions represented the gratifications they felt from their marriage. Sometimes the story constructions represented attempts to master problems they were facing, or ways of recalling times when life was better. The different parts of the relationship story—the courtship, the wedding and honeymoon, the present and future lives—evoked different functions for storytelling. During the first year, for example, happy couples were speaking with more feelings about their weddings and honeymoons than were unhappy couples, but unhappy couples were speaking with more feelings about their present life.

And it gets more complicated than that. For example, a given part of the story evoked different functions at different points of the marriage. Thoughts about the honeymoon seemed to engage savoring feelings in Year 3, but by Year 7 engaged what seemed to be sad reminiscences. Thus, in working out how marital well-being affects couples' stories, we must be aware of both what part of the story is being told and how long the couple has been married.

We also have to bear in mind that in the web of findings the results were rarely parallel for men and women. It would not be hard to conclude that men and women are happy and unhappy in their marriages about different matters and have different ways of evaluating their marriage. We discuss these issues further in chapter 8.

We also found evidence that the connection of marital happiness to story construction was sometimes different for African-American couples as compared to White couples. We did not deal with these differences in this chapter, but have reserved the results for chapter 9, in which we discuss ethnic differences in the narratives.

We were less impressed with the results substantiating our second theme, that stories can be guiding fictions for couples that might affect the future well-being of husbands and wives. There were some results in that direction but they were not powerful. However, we should remind ourselves and the reader that, although we interpreted most of our findings as instances where marital happiness influenced story construction, it could very well be that stories guided and influenced feelings about marriage as well. It could very well be that during the storytelling procedure, one spouse might hear what his or her partner felt about their courtship for the very first time. It could very well be that feelings about the marriage crystallize when the couple tells their story to a nonjudgmental, kindly stranger. And once heard, the subsequent interactions of the couple can change. After all, human interactions of any sort, including storytelling, are a continuous dynamic process. Stories never end, but are told, retold, and changed, as chapter 5 demonstrated. The feelings that a couple has for each other must be a powerful factor in affecting and being affected by those complicated processes.

Some of the thematic results presented here might also represent failures of a marriage to conform to individuals' internalized preconceptions. People do have relatively consensual ideas of the key events in a marriage, as well as the order in which these events should occur, although their notions of marriage are not as clear as those for dating relationships (Holmberg & Cameron, 1997). A typical view of a marriage in our culture might well include a relationship initiated by the man, blessed by family and friends in a religious setting, and featuring heartfelt commitment on the part of both the husband and the wife. Living together before marriage, or having a child together before marriage, do not form part of the cultural script for most people.

Thus, the effects we have seen for pregnancy, cohabitation, lack of commitment, and religious-differences issues, like the problems with wife-initiated courtships, might well reflect marriages that are not comfortably conforming to participants' preconceived notions of what marriages should be. Such violations of expectations can potentially add stress and strain to a relationship. Other research indicates that individuals who see their relationship as progressing in line with their expectations for typical relationship progression are happier than those whose relationships violate their expectations (Holmberg & Mackenzie, 2002). These discomforts and strains are being echoed and reflected in couples' narratives, and we find that the more they become a central issue, the unhappier the couples are, and the unhappier still they tend to become over time.

In chapter 7, we take a closer look at how dynamic changes in the couple's relationship feelings over time are associated with changes in the narratives they choose to tell.

TABLE 6.1

Summary of Significant Findings Linking Wives'
Marital Happiness to Narrative Features

		Wives' Marital Happiness	
Measure	*Result No.*	*Effect*	*Statistic*
Affective Style	1	Increases in using affects about the wedding or honeymoon associated with increases in marital happiness over the years	$\beta = 2.11**$
	2	More affects regarding current life in Year 1 associated with lower marital happiness in Year 1	$r = -.26*$
	4	More affects regarding courtship in Year 1 associated with lower marital happiness in Year 1	$r = -.43***$
Thematic Content	3	No tension in story about current life in Year 1 associated with higher marital happiness in Year 1	$r = .20*$
	5	Thematic issue regarding lack of commitment in Year 3 associated with lower marital happiness in Year 3	$r = -.23*$
	6	Thematic issue regarding religion in Year 7 associated with lower marital happiness in Year 7	$r = -.26^{\dagger}$
	7	Decreases in pregnancy as an issue in the story associated with increases in marital happiness over the years	$\beta = -.23**$
	17	Nonromantic, pragmatic positive story of courtship in Year 7 associated with higher marital happiness in Year 7	$r = .25*$
	18	Not attending to lack of commitment in Year 3 associated with increases in marital happiness over the years	$F = 3.36**$ (Year int.)
Narrative Style	10	Telling a more integrated story about honeymoon in Year 3 associated with higher marital happiness in Year 3	$r = .23*$
	11	Telling a more integrated story about honeymoon in Year 7 associated with lower marital happiness in Year 7	$r = -.31*$
	12	Telling a more integrated story about the wedding in Year 7 associated with lower marital happiness in Year 7	$r = -.50**$
	13	Increases in integration regarding the wedding associated with decreases in marital happiness over the years	$F = 4.68**$ (Year int.)

Note. Result number indicates the order the findings are discussed in the text.
†Trend, $p < .10$. $*p < .05$. $**p < .01$. $***p < .001$.

TABLE 6.2
Summary of Significant Findings Linking Husbands'
Marital Happiness to Narrative Features

		Husbands' Marital Happiness	
Measure	*Result No.*	*Effect*	*Statistic*
Affective Style	1	Increases in using affects about the wedding or honeymoon associated with increases in marital happiness over the years	$\beta = 1.85$**
	2	More affects regarding current life in Year 1 associated with lower marital happiness in Year 1	$r = -.23$*
Thematic Content	3	No tension in story about the current life in Year 1 associated with higher marital happiness in Year 1	$r = .18^{\dagger}$
	6	Mentioning thematic issue regarding religion in Year 7 related to lower marital happiness in Year 7	$r = -.29$*
	7	Decreases in pregnancy as an issue in the story associated with increases in marital happiness over the years	$\beta = -.22$*
	8	Mention of thematic issue regarding cohabitation in Year 3 associated with lower marital happiness in Year 3	$r = -.31$**
	9	Decreases in cohabitation as an issue in the courtship associated with increases in marital happiness over the years	$\beta = -.13$*
	16	Telling a female-initiated courtship story in Year 7 is associated with lower marital happiness in Year 7	$r = -.32$**
	19	Telling a story with wife as pursuer in Year 3 is associated with lower marital happiness in Year 7	$r = -.28$**
	20	Telling a female-initiated courtship story in Year 3 is associated with lower marital happiness in Year 7	$r = -.35$***
Narrative Style	10	Telling a more integrated story about the honeymoon in Year 3 is associated with higher marital happiness in Year 3	$r = .22$*
	14	Telling a more integrated story about the future in Year 3 is associated with higher marital happiness in Year 3	$r = .22$*
	15	Telling a more integrated story about the wedding in Year 1 is associated with lower marital happiness in Year 1	$r = -.28$*

Note. Result number indicates the order the findings are discussed in the text. Results with beta and F statistics come from Growth Curve Analyses. Results with Pearson's r are from correlational analyses.

†Trend, $p < .10$. *$p < .05$. **$p < .01$. ***$p < .001$.

Chapter 7

Changing Our Yesterdays: Reconstruction of Early Relationship Memories

As we saw in chapter 6, spouses' evaluations of their own marital happiness had much to do with how couples constructed their relationship story. In some instances, it seemed as though the couples were changing their memories, or at least their descriptions, of past events in their relationship history to coincide with or to offset their present feelings about their marriage. In this chapter, we take a closer look at these types of findings, with the guidance of recent theories and research about the way people reconstruct their memories. We test a few critical hypotheses relevant to the processes of memory reconstruction as they apply to telling stories about the past.

As we suggested in chapter 6, there is good reason to expect that such a coloring of stories based on current needs and concerns would occur. As we are all aware, memories do not always provide a complete and accurate record of past experiences. Memories show a general pattern of fading over time, such that most adults find retrieving even a dozen distinct memories of their childhood to be a relatively difficult task (Winkielman & Schwarz, 2001). People do not simply let go of faded past memories, however. Over longer time periods, as details recede, people seldom say "I just don't remember" when prompted to recall past events. Instead, they seem to unconsciously fill in any gaps they may experience with their beliefs regarding what might have happened. This tendency results in memories that appear clear and detailed to an outside observer and are held with a high degree of confidence by the person doing the remembering. And yet these memories can be shown to contain major inaccuracies, when compared with respondents' initial reports of the events (Schmolck, Buffalo, & Squire, 2000). In the most extreme cases, the false-memory literature suggests that individuals, in a subtle negotiation with their interviewers, can at times be led to construct clear and confident memories of past events that never occurred (Porter, Birt, Yuille, & Lehman, 2000).

Listening to our couples' narratives, we get little sense of such large-scale memory reconstruction. Their stories show very clear and recognizable similarities from Years 1 through 7. Frequently, the same cherished events and key anecdotes are relayed each year. Each couple has their favored stories and their individual style. We have no doubt that even if we removed all identifying information, coders fresh to the narratives could come in, read the transcripts, and immediately match up couples' Year 1 stories with their Year 3 and 7 stories, with a high degree of accuracy.

What we do see in our narratives, however, are shifts in tone and emphasis. The same anecdotes may be told, but they may be detailed at one time and brief at another. One year, a particular incident may appear charged with affect and emotion; another time, it may be reported in an offhand manner. At one time, it's issue A that gets more emphasis and "airtime"; at another point, it's issue B.

Are such shifts in tone and emphasis dependent only upon the whims of the couple at the time of retelling? Is the relative emphasis on particular issues merely a random reflection of whatever happens to pop into the couples' heads as they develop their story? As narrative researchers, and recalling the results from the previous chapter, we would naturally argue no. Individuals construct their stories to give appropriate meaning to a set of events, given the particular storytelling context, and their needs and desires at the time of the telling. Thus, individuals' current issues and concerns will shape and mold their stories of the past. This process is largely unconscious. From the storytellers' point of view, the tales are constructed from whatever may happen to pop into their heads at the time; it is just that what "happens" to pop into their heads are incidents that reflect their current feelings and concerns. Thus, we would expect couples' current feelings and attitudes toward their relationship at the time of telling their story to color their reported memories of early relationship events.

There is a small but growing literature on reconstruction of relationship memories that supports this point of view. McFarland and Ross (1987), for example, asked dating couples to report their feelings toward their partners at one point in time. Two months later, participants returned to complete the same measures a second time and to recall the ratings they had given initially. Respondents' feelings toward their partners at Time 2 seemed to color their memories of Time 1. Those who felt more negative toward their partner at Time 2 also recalled their Time 1 ratings as having been relatively negative, more negative than they in fact had been. Those who felt more positive toward their partner at Time 2 showed reciprocal effects, exaggerating how positive their past feelings were. Couples remembered their past relationship feelings as having been relatively similar to the present time, even when these past feelings had actually been quite different from what they were now.

More recent research, also focusing on global evaluations of the relationship, suggests that over longer periods of time individuals do not always emphasize the similarity of current and past feelings. At least in the earlier stages of a relationship, people seem to be motivated to construct a sense of improvement over time. For example, Karney and Coombs (2000) found that wives in the first 10 years of marriage recalled their feelings toward their husbands when they were newlyweds as having been more negative than they in fact had been. This reconstruction allowed them to sense that their relationship had improved over time when in fact it had declined. It is as if the wives in the study were unconsciously aware of some recent research showing that reconstructing improvements over time in a relationship, especially in the recent past, predicts confidence in the future of the relationship (Grote & Frieze, 1998; Karney & Frye, 2002).

These studies suggest that people's memories of the overall state of the relationship in the past can be reconstructed in ways that are related to their current relationship feelings. Can memories of more concrete events in the relationship's past, such as we have in the narratives, also be shaped by current feelings? Again, previous research suggests they can. Overall ratings of specific interactions, for example, do seem to be shaped by current relationship feelings. Duck, Pond, and Leatham (1991) had pairs of friends engage in an interaction, then complete a number of rating scales of that interaction. Six weeks later, the friends returned and recalled their earlier ratings, and also provided current assessments of the quality of the friendship. Current satisfaction and intimacy predicted memory changes, with those having particularly satisfying friendships recalling the interaction as having been even more satisfying than when it had initially been rated. Similarly, Holmberg and Holmes (1994) found that levels of trust in a relationship predicted memory reconstruction for reactions toward a particular event. Particularly trusting individuals recalled their attributions and feelings toward specific events in increasingly charitable ways over time (see also Sorrentino, Holmes, Hanna, & Sharp, 1995).

Studies that look for changes in memory for the content of specific events, rather than summative ratings of those events, are rarer. Deciding what constitutes accurate as opposed to inaccurate recall is relatively simple when one is dealing with numbers on a rating scale, but difficult when one is dealing with open-ended recall. Sillars, Weisberg, Burggraf, and Zietlow (1990) found that satisfaction levels predicted which aspects of a particular conversation were focused on in memory. Less satisfied couples were more accurate at recalling confronting statements and other negatively toned statements than were more satisfied couples.

Some of our own earlier work using Year 1 and Year 3 data from the current study also speaks to the issue of how memories for earlier events are shaped by current relationship feelings. For example, we compared a set of 13 couples who were high in marital happiness in both Years 1 and 3 to another group of 13 couples who were equally happy in Year 1 but much less happy by Year 3. The two groups' narratives looked similar in Year 1. However, by Year 3 the group who was less happy had imbued their memories for earlier stages of the relationship with more negative affect and more statements expressing ambivalence toward the relationship (see Holmberg & Holmes, 1994).

In another study, Holmberg and Veroff (1996) looked at how changes in more specific relationship attitudes affected more specific relationship memories. We found, for example, that husbands who put less emphasis on egalitarianism in Year 3 than in Year 1 were also less likely to speak of the wedding as jointly planned in Year 3 than they were in Year 1. For African-American respondents, those who put less emphasis over time on minimizing conflict with their spouse were also more likely to speak of tensions in the wedding narrative over time. Thus, changes in couples' feelings about the relationship (whether these feelings are their overall feelings or their attitudes toward more specific relationship aspects) seem to be related to changes in their memories for early relationship events.

It should be noted that our narrative coding is not sufficiently detailed to disentangle exactly how these early memories are changing. As Karney and Frye (2002) noted, there are at least three possibilities. First, couples could be engaging in wholesale memory reconstruction, dramatically changing the nature of early relationship events, or even manufacturing events that never actually happened. "Flashbulb" memory research suggests such dramatic memory changes can at times occur (e.g., Schmolck et al., 2000). In this paradigm, respondents believe they have a vivid mental picture of exactly where and when they were when they received news of a dramatic world event. However, tracking their memories over time reveals that their recall sometimes undergoes major distortions.

Our readings of the narratives, however, suggest that the changes are not quite so overt. Instead, one or both of the remaining possibilities seem more likely. First, couples could be remembering specific events relatively accurately but through a process of selective attention discuss only those particular events that fit well with their current relationship perspectives. As noted earlier, some events were described in detail at one point but were mentioned only in passing at another. The events that are more likely to be dwelt on in recall might be those events that best fit with current relationship feelings.

Finally, couples could in fact be recalling exactly the same set of events, in the same amount of detail, at two different times. Their stories would still sound quite different, however, if their evaluations and perspectives on those events had changed. Wedding disagreements might be acknowledged, but described as "no big deal" at one point in time. At a later point in time, those same disagreements might be presented as problematic. Through shifts in tone and emphasis, the meaning presented by the narrative could change, even if the underlying events had remained relatively stable.

In this chapter, then, we explore how our couples' current attitudes toward their relationship might affect their stories of the early stages of their relationship. In chapter 6, we examined all available aspects of the narratives to see how they might predict well-being, either concurrently or over time. Here, our focus is more specific. We look at how individuals' relationship feelings change across all 7 years, and see whether those changes in feelings predict particular changes in how their relationship story is remembered and told.

Given the available codes, we were not looking for changes in specific event details but for changes in the general tone of the stories. We divided our analyses into two parts: The first set of analyses investigated how changes in participants' global feelings toward their relationship were related to changes in the overall affective tone of the stories they told about the past across time, an extension of some of the analyses we described in chapter 6. We looked at three aspects of the affective tone of the stories: How emotional couples' stories were overall; how positive or negative couples were about the feelings they brought up in the stories; and how self-involved or communal they were in the feelings they brought up. The second set of analyses investigated how changes in more specific relationship attitudes in the couple affected the content of the stories they reconstructed about the past. In this second set, we looked at two different aspects of the content of stories: How changes in egalitarian attitudes about the roles wives and husbands play in marriage predicted memories of who initiated the courtship, who proposed, who planned the wedding, and so on; and how feelings regarding the acceptability of conflict in marriage predicted changes in memories for tensions and conflicts in the early stages of the relationship.

GLOBAL EFFECTS: CHANGES IN MARITAL HAPPINESS AS PREDICTORS OF CHANGES IN AFFECTIVE TONE

Our first set of analyses answered research questions similar to those tackled in Holmberg and Holmes (1994): How did changes in overall relationship well-being over time predict changes in the overall affective tone of early relationship memories? As noted earlier, in our previous study we compared a small set of couples who remained high in marital well-being across the first 3 years with a set of couples whose marital well-being dropped. Here, we use the same overall measure of marital well-being as our predictor variable (discussed in detail in chap. 6). Recall that this measure consisted of six items that tapped into couples' overall satisfaction with their marriage.

Given the larger sample size and an additional year of data, however, we can now use a different approach to investigating the predictive effects of changes in marital well-being on past memories over time, namely *growth curve analyses*, as discussed in chapter 6. Growth curve analyses ask whether changes in one variable over time can predict changes in a second variable over the same time period. Here, we examined how changes in marital happiness over the first 7 years of marriage were connected with changes in the overall affective tone for the past in the narratives over that same time period. For the variables we predicted, we first looked at the overall level of affectivity in the narratives. How emotional are couples' stories overall? Next, we examined the direction, or valence, of affective statements in the narratives: What percentage of all affective statements are positive? What percentage are negative? Finally, we looked at the underlying motivation expressed in these affects: Were couples focusing on *agency*, on fulfilling their individual goals and desires, as they related their story of their past together? Were they focusing on *connection* goals, or their desire to be close and establish their relationship? Or, were they focusing on both *agency* and *connection* goals simultaneously, actively attempting to balance their own needs and desires with those of the relationship? (See chap. 3 or Appendix B for a review of the codes for agency or connection goals as aspects of affects mentioned in the stories.)

It would not be at all surprising if couples who became less happy in their marriage over time also came to describe the present and future stages of their relationship in less positive terms, as we found in some results in chapter 6. If they were in fact less happy, then we certainly might expect them to, for example, display more negative affect when recounting the story of their relationship today. In this chapter, however, we are more interested in how their current feelings colored their descriptions of the early stages of the relationship. Thus, in all the analyses in this chapter, we only looked at the earliest substories, those of the courtship, wedding, and honeymoon. Those events are in the past at all three time periods. If couples were simply reporting the "objective truth" of these past events, their stories should appear quite similar at each time period, regardless of their current feelings. We suspect, however, that as their marital well-being changed, so too would the tone of their descriptions of those early stages. Let's examine what we found.

Overall Emotionality of Stories.   We began by echoing some of the analyses conducted in chapter 6, in which we looked at the overall level of emotions expressed in the early relationship stages. As couples changed in their levels of well-being over time, did their stories of their courtship, wedding, and honeymoon tend to become more, or less, emotional overall? We in fact found no such changes over time. There was a general tendency for happier couples to tell more affect-laden stories, but this average tendency showed no sign of shifting over time. We thus see no evidence here of memory reconstruction.

Given chapter 6's findings, these null results are not surprising. We saw there that the connection between generally emotion-laden stories and well-being is not a simple one. Sometimes emotional stories signal good feelings about the relationship and sometimes they indicate areas of concern. Emotional memories seem to be positively associated with well-being in the short term, but in the longer term a more pragmatic tone seems to be the better approach. These conflicting tendencies would tend to obscure any trends toward systematic memory reconstruction. Given these complications, we quickly decided a more productive approach would be to break down the overall affect scores into their component parts. First, we looked at whether the affects mentioned in the early relationship stories tended to be primarily positive or negative.

Positivity/Negativity of Affective Statements.   To our surprise, we found no significant effects in the most obvious place to look, namely, the valence of the affective statements made, or how positive or negative the affective statements were. We expected, similar to what we had found previously (Holmberg & Holmes, 1994), that as couples became increasingly unhappy, they would tell stories that were increasingly laden with negative feelings. This did not happen. Among the couples who provided stories in all three years, changes in overall marital well-being did not predict changes in the percentage of either negative or positive affects contained in the early relationship stories.

Why did we find different results than we had found previously? One possible explanation lies in the analysis strategy. In our previous work, we singled out a small group of couples who experienced a very dramatic drop in their well-being over a 2-year period and found corresponding changes in their narratives. The current analyses looked at all the participants; perhaps the many couples who experienced relatively small changes in their well-being obscured the effects that might be seen in the few couples who experienced a large drop.

In a second and related explanation, our sample may have worked against us. Many couples in the study had divorced or separated over the 7-year period. Those who experienced the largest and most dramatic drops in well-being, and perhaps correspondingly dramatic changes in their memories, may have already selected themselves out of our sample by splitting up. The current analyses, by looking only at those couples who stayed together for 7 years, may be less likely to show dramatic memory changes.

Third, previous research shows that the stage of the relationship and the length of time involved can affect the nature of memory reconstruction. Over short periods of time (e.g., S. Duck et al., 1991; Holmberg & Holmes, 1994; McFarland & Ross, 1987), memory reconstruction seems to serve to confirm current feelings. Those who become more positive in their relationship feelings over time also recall the past in a more positive fashion; those who become more negative recall the past more negatively. Over longer periods of time, however, opposite effects can occur. Relatively happy couples may now begin to derogate the earlier stages of their relationship to make the present seem better by comparison and to foster a sense of current well-being (see, e.g., Karney & Coombs, 2000; Karney & Frye, 2002; Sprecher, 1999). Over the first 7 years of marriage, we may see a mix of these effects. Some happy couples remembered the good times of the past, some downplayed the good times in the past and focused on the good times in the present. The net result shows no strong effect on the overall positivity of couples' stories of early relationship events.

We saw results consistent with this argument in chapter 6. In the shorter term, more emotional memories of some early relationship stages (e.g., wedding and honeymoon) were positively related to happiness; in the longer term, more emotional memories of the past (e.g., particularly romantic courtship stories) were negatively related to happiness. Thus, current marital well-being may increase affective statements about the past in either a positive or negative direction. Such a phenomenon makes it unlikely to find marital well-being effects on only positive or only negative affective statements.

Motivation of Affective Statements. Where we did see effects was in more subtle measures that tapped into the motivations underlying affective statements in the early narratives. Here, we did find changes in marital well-being over time that predicted changes in the affective tone of the stories, at least for husbands. For the more statistically minded, descriptions of the exact effects are found in Table 7.1.

Recall from chapter 5 that narratives of the earlier stages of the relationship tended to start out surprisingly high in agentic statements in Year 1. In Year 3, the percentage of agentic statements fell off sharply, only to rebound slightly in Year 7. All of our couples tended to display this same U-shaped pattern, and all looked quite similar in Year 1. In Year 3, however, husbands' well-being began to have an effect. Although all groups dropped off in their percentage of agentic statements, happier husbands showed less of a drop than did unhappy husbands. The effects of happiness were stronger still in Year 7; by this point, happy husbands were participating in narratives that displayed considerably more agentic themes than less-happy husbands. Thus, over time, the happiest husbands were those who were in couples where agentic themes, themes of maintaining individual goals and desires over time, continued to be emphasized (see Result 1 in Table 7.1). Furthermore, there was also an effect of ethnicity. The effects just described were particularly strong for African-American husbands (see Result 2 in Table 7.1).

When we analyzed the percentage of affective statements reflecting themes of connection or communion, we found the mirror image of the aforementioned effects. These communal statements showed an overall pattern of increasing in Year 3, before falling back again in Year 7. This inverted-U pattern held for all groups, and all groups looked fairly similar in Years 1 and 3. By Year 7, however, we again see effects of husbands' well-being. Here, happier husbands participated in narratives that showed less communal affect (see Result 3 in Table 7.1). And again, the effect was particularly strong for the African-American husbands (see Result 4 in Table 7.1). Men, and especially African-American men, seemed happiest over time when they participated in narratives that did not place undue emphasis on themes of connection.

When we combine these two findings, we see a picture of those husbands who maintain higher well-being over time participating in narratives that place relatively more emphasis on meeting individual needs and goals and relatively less emphasis on merging, or submerging, in the couple. Cross and Madson (1997) reviewed the literature and suggested that men's self-concepts place more emphasis on agentic needs such as achievement or separation, whereas women's self-concepts place more emphasis on communal needs such as forming and maintaining affectional bonds. As a whole, the relationship narrative is likely to resonate better with women's more communal self-concepts. In the glow of the newlywed state, men may well be willing to accommodate such stories, but over time, the happiest husbands were those in couples who spun relationship tales that resonated to their needs, that continued to acknowledge the importance of individual goals and desires, and that downplayed somewhat the joys and agonies of forming a bond together.

Consider Troy and Denise's Year 7 story, for example. Their courtship, by this point, is portrayed as logical and goal-oriented. As Troy put it:

When we got together the second time, we knew that either we were going to be real serious, or not do it. And we decided to do it, so it was at that point that we knew we were a couple for life. I graduated. Denise had another year of school left, so I came home for a year, got an apartment, and lived in the apartment for about 3 months. Then I moved home with my parents, decid-

ing to save some money, because at that time I think we had actually determined we were going to get married. . . . So at that point, we knew what we
wanted to do. Denise graduated the following April. She came home, moved
in with her parents, saved quite a bit of money toward the wedding, and then
we had . . . the wedding.

Troy's story may not be excessively romantic, but it illustrates what may be
a comfortable tale for many males, one where the couple got together and
decided what they wanted to do, carefully completed their individual needs
and goals first, then proceeded forward to marriage when the time was right.
Both husband and wife were then emotionally and financially prepared to
make the commitment. The tone might be very businesslike, but note that
both partners were still very satisfied after 7 years of marriage.

Compare their story to that told by another couple, Jake and Alisha.
Alisha described the circumstances and feelings that first drew them together:

Getting interested in each other? We were interested. We were two hurt people thrown together that needed somebody's help. Well, really he needed
somebody to talk to, and I was willing to listen at that time, to his problems. . . . He says he was in between women, so he was using me to get rid of
these other women. But that I didn't mind too much. Like I said, I had just
been dumped. I had my own life in order. I was getting it in order, and I
needed a male who was my friend.

Jake also emphasized their feelings toward each other in describing how
they first became interested:

I got interested in her because of the women that I . . . had at the time, she
was the more consistent. That was one of the best traits about her. I mean,
aside from the fact that she could talk and had personality. I mean, most of
the women I met . . . most of them have personalities, but most of the time,
hers [Alisha's] was more even keel. It wasn't so much like a serious roller
coaster ride. Like "I hate you today. I love you tomorrow. I hate you today. I
love you to death." It was kinda like, you know, nice. And I needed a little
calmness, cause I was seriously between these people who had me real insecure. If I walked out of the room, it was frazzle city. So finally came time to
deal with that part, and I didn't have to call her [Alisha] every day, saying
"Baby, I love you; baby, I love you."

Jake and Alisha's emphasis on their feelings and emotions toward each
other might sound more like a conventionally romantic narrative. Such an
emphasis on connections and the state of the relationship, however, may
not be the most comfortable stance toward the relationship for some males.
Note that by Year 7, this couple was relatively dissatisfied with their relationship. One gets the sense that Jake might have found that marriage in fact re-

quired a little more "Baby, I love you" than he was prepared for. For men, negotiating a relationship where there is a good balance between agentic and communal needs seems to be important.

Note also that this sense of negotiation and balance between agency and communion cannot become too overt. Recall that we also coded statements that simultaneously reflected both agentic and communal needs. These statements mostly had to do with wanting a relationship to be a particular way. Particularly in Year 3, happier males were lower in these statements than unhappy males (see Result 5 in Table 7.1). Happier males did not seem to have to consciously wrestle with the issue of how they wanted their relationships to be in their narratives. Instead, over time they were able to subtly negotiate a stance that did not deny communal needs, but downplayed those needs slightly in favor of a somewhat more individualistic stance.

These findings are all accentuated in the African-American respondents' narratives. As we describe in chapter 9, maintaining a sense of individuality within the context of the couple relationship is particularly important to African-American respondents. Especially for African-American males, who may at times feel blocked from pursuing their individual needs and goals by ongoing racism, being able to maintain a sense of individuality within the context of their relationship over the years can be especially important. These results are a good example of the types of subtle, less-than-conscious effects that emerge from a narrative analysis, and which may not emerge as clearly using standardized items.

We do not see parallel findings for the wives' well-being. As was mentioned briefly in chapters 4 and 6, and is explored in more detail in chapter 8, women seem to have slightly clearer memories for early relationship events than do men. With these clearer memories, women may be somewhat less prone to rework the broad sweep of their past in service of current goals. More likely, however, motivations were not their key issue; a relational narrative may already serve their more relational self-concepts rather well. We saw in chapter 6 that different features of the narrative, such as story integration and romance of plot, were more closely tied to women's overall relational well-being. However, women's attitudes toward more specific relationship issues did predict changes in their narratives over time, as we see in the next section.

SPECIFIC EFFECTS: CHANGES IN EGALITARIAN AND CONFLICT ATTITUDES AS PREDICTORS OF CHANGES IN MEMORIES

In this section, we examine how changes in particular relationship attitudes predicted more circumscribed features of the narratives. We conducted similar analyses in a previous study, looking only at data from Years 1 and 3

(Holmberg & Veroff, 1996). There, as here, we looked at changes in respondents' "Rules for Marriage" over time. As part of the couple interview, partners individually rated how important each of 16 different rules was in their own relationship (e.g., "Be sure to have some private time away from each other"; "Know the people your spouse spends leisure time with"). As a means of investigating couples' negotiation strategies, they were then given 10 minutes to work out joint importance ratings. Their discussions were tape-recorded. In the current analyses, however, we looked only at the initial ratings that partners completed individually. They completed ratings of the same set of 16 rules each year; we were thus able to track changes in the importance they assigned to a number of specific marital attitudes.

Egalitarianism. In our previous study (Holmberg & Veroff, 1996), we found that changes in egalitarianism over time predicted changes in memories of how the wedding planning was divided. We looked for similar effects here, to see if those who became more egalitarian were, over time, more likely to recall the wedding as having been jointly planned or the initiation of the relationship or proposal as having been a mutual decision.

We found no effects of egalitarianism in our current analyses. The problem may have been one of small sample sizes in certain groups when we looked across all three time periods. We compared those who rated egalitarian attitudes as highly important in all three interviews to those who initially viewed egalitarianism as important but then came to see it as less important over time. Very few women let go of their egalitarian views over time; most fell into the group rating these attitudes as very important in all 3 years. Conversely, and somewhat sadly, only a few men held on to their egalitarian views over time. Even those who rated such attitudes as very important in Year 1 saw them as less important over time. Perhaps when faced with the challenges of raising children, husbands found a completely egalitarian approach to the relationship more difficult to maintain. In any case, our small sample sizes may have worked against finding significance in these analyses. We did, however, find significant effects of the other set of attitudes we investigated, those that dealt with the acceptance of conflict in the relationship.

Conflict Minimization. Several of the Rules for Marriage dealt with partners' acceptance of conflict within the relationship. A representative item, and the one we focused on in the analyses, was "Control the way that you show you are angry with each other." We formed two groups of respondents: those who said this rule was very important in all 3 years of the study, and those who said this rule was very important in Year 1 but saw it as less important by Year 7. We then compared these two groups' average scores across the years on two different measures.

The first measure assessed how much conflict couples were coded as experiencing during the experience of planning the wedding. This was coded on a 3-point scale, with 1 representing no conflict experienced (or none mentioned), 2 representing some differences settled by compromise or reciprocity, and 3 representing reports of open conflict, either within the couple or between the couple and others. The second measure assessed the average amount of tension coders rated in the early relationship narratives (we averaged across the courtship, wedding, and honeymoon substories, and across the three different sources of tension that could be included for each substory).

We compared the means of these two measures across the years for the two groups described earlier: *conflict minimizers*, who insisted on the importance of controlling their anger at all three time points, and *conflict accepters*, who over time came to see that controlling their anger at all times was not so central. To compare the means, we used what is known as a *repeated-measures analysis of variance*.[1] Analyses were run separately for husbands and wives. Only the results for the wives were significant. For the interested reader, the exact means are shown in Tables 7.2 and 7.3.

Let us first examine changes in memories for the amount of conflict in the wedding planning (see Table 7.2). Over the shorter term, looking only at the changes from Year 1 to Year 3, exactly the sort of effects one might expect occurred. Conflict minimizers had slightly lower scores even in Year 1 than did conflict accepters, although both groups said it was very important to control your anger at this point in time. By Year 3, these small initial differences had been accentuated. Conflict minimizers appeared to have shaded their narratives in the direction of their relationship attitudes. They believed that one should always control one's anger, and they in fact described experiencing considerably less conflict during the wedding planning than they had initially indicated. Uncomfortable with conflict, they purged their narratives of any indication of such conflict over time. Conflict accepters, who became more comfortable with the notion of disagreements over time, did not show these same effects, dropping only slightly in the level of conflict they portrayed.

What is especially interesting is that these sensible effects did not seem to hold up over time. By Year 7, we see a surprising reversal. At this point, conflict accepters were actually describing less conflict in their narratives than were conflict minimizers. What is going on here? One possibility is that conflict minimizers, who have insisted over 7 years that they must control how they show their anger with their spouse, might be feeling the strain. Every

---

[1]Growth curve analyses were not used here because they work better with continuous variables, like the happiness measure. Two-category variables, like the Rules for Marriage ratings, do not work as well in these analyses.

couple is going to have their conflicts, their disagreements, their times when they simply want to yell at each other. Conflict accepters have overtly changed their views, and have said that controlling one's anger at all times is not actually that essential. Conflict minimizers, who continued to maintain their belief in controlling overt displays of tension, might increasingly be letting that tension seep out in more subtle ways, such as in their memories of past events. Such an interpretation is speculative. However, we have seen similar results before: The White respondents in the Holmberg and Veroff (1996) study showed a similar pattern.

Another possibility is that conflict minimizers who were actually successful in living up to their ideals and controlled their anger over 7 years of marriage became more sensitive over time to any indication of conflict. Wedding planning can bring out tensions in the best of couples; those who have succeeded in rarely getting angry at each other in their marriage may come to see wedding conflicts, one of their few disagreements, as relatively bad in retrospect.

Again, it should be noted that we are talking about shadings of tone and emphasis, not wholesale memory reconstruction. As an example of the sort of changes we are describing, following is an excerpt from the narrative of one couple, Ed and Jeannette, in which the wife falls into the conflict minimizer group. As a rule, Jeannette does not like conflict, but she and Ed experienced a severe stressor during the wedding planning, when Ed's friend, who was to perform the ceremony, at the last minute turned out not to be registered as a minister in the state of Michigan. As one can imagine, this caused consternation. Perhaps sensitive to his wife's dislike for disorder and conflict, Ed described the negative reactions they experienced in Year 3, but somewhat downplayed the seriousness of the situation:

> I had a friend that I grew up with, right. He's an ordained preacher, but he had left the state of Michigan before he got ordained. He was supposed to marry us, but when it come down to it, he didn't have the . . . we were out of his jurisdiction. We found that out at the last minute. . . . My wife and me are more and more hysterical. Well, my future wife. My biggest problem was to keep her calm, you know, cause like I say, why worry. We'll work something out, you know. As long as you keep your head level, you know, you think about it, there's a solution to every problem.

Here, problems and tensions clearly were occurring in the wedding planning, but they were not dwelled on. In contrast, look at the same couple's story in Year 7:

> E: One thing about the wedding . . . I had a friend that's one of them preachers, and he was supposed to marry us. He was supposed to marry us, and we find out that he wasn't licensed in Michigan, and we found

> that out at the last minute. . . . She [Jeannette] panicked, you know. She had a fit. That's one thing that I can't get out of. She panicked. It's like I tried to tell her, you know, there'll always be problems, and we can always find a solution. We can always find a solution to the problem, you know, but still, she panicked . . .
>
> J: *Frantic.* Not panicked, but frantic.
>
> E: Eventually we worked it out, you know. I talked to another friend, and I forgot that his father was a preacher.
>
> J: His mother made him go ask him. . . . She said, "Ed, you better marry this girl. If not, she's gonna have a fit."

The tensions Ed and Jeannette experienced were much more obvious in this Year 7 story. Perhaps if they seldom showed their negative emotions to each other, this one time when Jeannette was understandably stressed seemed more like a "fit," more like "panic," as time went on.

Compare these changes to changes seen next, in Angie and Chris's wedding planning narratives. They showed the opposite pattern, with their emphasis on problems in the wedding planning decreasing, not increasing, over time. In Year 3, they described the disagreements between their families over the nature of the wedding celebration in detail:

> C: What the toughest thing about all of it is, myself included and my parents, our religious beliefs. I had never been to a big wedding, and her being Polish Catholic, they have a dance, they have halls, they have all this big extravaganza, and for me, a wedding was two people, and the congregation from the church, you go in, you get married, you all meet out in the overflow room of the church building and our lobby. You have coffee or punch and a piece of cake, and everyone goes home, and you're married . . . and that's it. And so we had to come up with a compromise somewhere between getting her family happy and making my family happy. So I talked to my parents, and she talked to her parents, and we decided that we'd get married in our church, but we would rent a hall and we would have . . . dancing and all that for her family. I felt that was right, because that's what they were used to. And so, that was hard for my parents to swallow. Both sets of parents had to go through something.
>
> A: . . . Him going to a wedding where there's liquor and dancing and everything was like "Um, okay. . . ." (chuckles). So, we both gave up a little bit, just trying to please everybody.

Angie is a conflict accepter. She became more comfortable with the notion of conflict in her relationship over time, and participated freely and easily in a narrative that spoke of conflicts and tensions. By Year 7, in contrast to Ed and Jeannette, Angie and Chris seem to have moved on. They described the same disagreement, but in a much more brief, offhand fashion:

C: So we had to decide how we were gonna do this. I wasn't really following any set religion at the time, but yet, to appease my parents, I didn't want to do anything that would hurt them. So we decided that, you know, my parents wanted to help, but they wouldn't pay for alcohol and things like that. So that's how we worked it out. We got married at my parents' church, and then we held the reception at a hall, and we had dancing and drinking. . . . Both of our parents were real adult and mature about the whole situation. They handled it really well, and they got along. That was nice, that both sets of parents could be sociable. And it was, in the years to come it's helped too.

Angie and Chris didn't dwell on the wedding planning difficulties in Year 7, as Ed and Jeannette did. They acknowledged them, but didn't seem to feel, now that sufficient time had passed, that the conflict was any big deal. Conflict minimizers, like Jeannette, though, seemed to dwell on the difficulties more as time passed. As can be seen in Table 7.3, we see similar effects when we look at the average level of tension in the early portion of the narrative. Conflict minimizers participated in narratives wherein the tensions became stronger over time, while conflict accepters showed a drop in tensions in their Year 7 stories. Again, this effect could represent a rather psychodynamic spilling over of repressed tension from conflict minimizers, or a simple contrast effect: If they indeed displayed little tension in their day-to-day relationships, any tensions they did experience in the past might come to seem more and more unusual and worthy of exploration over time.

SUMMARY

In this chapter, we have seen that at both the interpersonal and the personal levels described in chapter 2, current feelings can shape the narratives of early relationship. For men, their overall well-being was related to the motivations expressed in their narratives about their past together. Happier men reconstructed narratives where there was relatively more emphasis on agency, and less on communion or connection, as compared to less happy men. An emphasis on meeting individual needs and goals seemed to serve as a more comfortable relationship narrative mode for men, particularly African-American men, when they reconstructed their memories.

Women did not show the same effects on their motivations. Where we did see narrative shaping for women was in the area of interpersonal conflict, a topic that is often highly charged for women. Women who came to accept a certain level of conflict in their relationship, who came to believe that it was not always necessary to control their anger, seemed freer to move on and let early conflicts and tensions fade away. Ironically, women who insisted that all anger must be controlled had narratives that became more charged with tension over time, and were less able to let go of wedding planning conflicts in Year 7. If controlling emotions was a central issue to them, they continued to explore issues of tension and conflict in their narratives, perhaps seeking to understand and learn lessons from times when they were unable to live up to their own high standards.

Both sets of findings support our belief that individuals' current perspectives on their relationship can reach back and color their relationship narratives in predictable ways. Current individual feelings and attitudes play a role in reconstructing the memories that make up the narratives. In chapters 8 and 9, we turn to examining how personal characteristics such as gender and ethnicity may play similar roles in shaping couples' narratives over time.

TABLE 7.1

Summary of Significant Findings Linking Husbands' Current Marital Happiness to Changes in the Narrative's Affective Tone Over Time

Measure	Result No.	Effect	Statistic
% Agentic Statements	1	Happy husbands have relatively more agentic statements in Year 3, and especially in Year 7, than unhappy husbands	$F = 3.57$* (Yr. × Happ. Int.)
	2	African-American husbands higher in agency than White husbands, but only in Year 3, and especially Year 7	$F = 4.30$* (Race × Yr. Int.)
% Communal Statements	3	Happy husbands have relatively fewer communal statements than unhappy husbands, in Year 7	$F = 4.14$* (Yr. × Happ. Int.)
	4	African-American husbands lower in communal statements than White husbands, but only in Year 7	$F = 4.38$* (Race × Yr. Int.)
% Statements Both Agentic and Communal	5	Happy husbands have relatively fewer statements reflecting agency and communion simultaneously, in Year 3	$F = 3.76$* (Yr. × Happ. Int.)

Note. Result number indicates the order the findings are discussed in the text.
*$p < .05$.

TABLE 7.2
Changes Over Time in Ratings of Degree of Conflict
in Wedding Planning, for Wives Who Are Conflict
Minimizers Versus Conflict Accepters

Group	Year 1	Year 3	Year 7
Conflict Minimizers	1.91	1.30	1.35
Conflict Accepters	2.20	2.00	1.13

Note. Degree of conflict is rated on a 3-point scale, with higher numbers indicating more conflict. Conflict minimizers are those who say it is very important for spouses to control the way they show they are angry with each other, in all 3 years. Conflict accepters rate this rule as very important in Year 1, but rate it as less important by Year 7. Year × Group interaction, $F = 3.63$, $p = .03$.

TABLE 7.3
Changes Over Time in Ratings of Average Degree
of Tension in Early Relationship Story, for Wives
Who Are Conflict Minimizers Versus Conflict Accepters

Group	Year 1	Year 3	Year 7
Conflict Minimizers	1.22	1.43	1.50
Conflict Accepters	1.31	1.35	1.18

Note. Degree of tension is rated on a 2-point scale, with higher numbers indicating more tension. Tension is averaged across all mentions in the courtship, wedding, and honeymoon substories. See Table 7.2 for description of groups. Year × Group interaction, $F = 3.16$, $p = .05$.

Gender as a Factor
Affecting Narratives

Every time we open our mouths to say something, we reveal many qualities about ourselves: certainly our nationality, often our station in life, and perhaps even our gender. In this chapter, we investigate the role that gender had in affecting the narratives the couples in our study told. What did men or women reveal of their gender, either in the way they told their stories (narrative style), or in the particular issues they chose to focus on (narrative content)? Although we briefly examined similar questions in chapter 4, we were only considering newlyweds' stories in Year 1. Here, we extend our analyses to include thrice-told tales in Years 1, 3, and 7. We are again interested in differences husbands and wives displayed when they told the story of their relationship, but we also include whether these differences have implications for their well-being in their marriages.

To highlight the types of differences we were looking for, consider the following brief passages from two couples' narratives. Can we detect ways that the husband's and wife's responses in each instance differ in style or content, ways that may be typical of male and female modes of telling these stories?

Couple 1:

Interviewer: How did the two of you become interested in each other?

Fred: Ah, well, I suppose as we went out more, we found out what I like and what she likes. She was always pretty athletic herself. So, I suppose we shared a lot in common.

Sue: It was real easy, because we could talk a lot. We just hit it off. I think we went out and one night we just sat and we talked the whole time. We went to a show and it was really easy to communicate with each other. At first, it was kind of weird, because I thought, I bet we're just going to end up being friends, because you know, usually friends can talk really well together.

Couple 2:

Interviewer:	How have things changed since your wedding? How are things now?
Claire:	Things now are pretty good. I think we're starting to get used to each other. We still have some disagreements, but not too many. Oh, we haven't really fought or argued or anything in a long time. I think we did that more at the beginning, just trying to get little things out and that, and plus getting used to each other's schedules. We weren't really that used to it, you know, maybe him not being around when I wanted him or vice versa.
Stuart:	Busy. I would say things are very busy now. Because she is finishing school. To me, that was a very important thing.

In the first excerpt, Fred suggested he and Sue "hit it off" because of shared interests. They each found out what the other liked and then became attracted to each other. Sue, on the other hand, emphasized the long discussions and ease with which they could talk to one another. In the second excerpt, we see that Claire described her present marriage as pretty good because they had been able to work out the difficulties in getting to know each other that existed at the beginning of the marriage. She also believed that currently they were experiencing less conflict and fewer disagreements. Claire focused on the amount and kind of affect in the relationship to describe the present state of affairs in her marriage. In contrast, when asked about the present, Stuart described his current life with Claire as busy, because she was finishing school. He did not emphasize the level of affect in the marriage. Are these two couples typical? Do they reflect distinct patterns in the ways that wives versus husbands told their relationship stories? Our challenge in this chapter is to identify and interpret such gender differences.

In the general social science literature, many scholars have been intrigued with the concept of gender and its implications for what people say and do in their interactions with others. In fact, there is research to support the notion that there are notable gender differences between the speech of women and men (e.g., Tannen, 1990). Men and women tend to differ in the way they speak, as well as in the types of things they prefer to speak about. Tannen summarized these gender differences by describing men's preference for "report talk," in which the primary goal is to communicate information, and women's preference for "rapport talk," in which the primary goal is to establish a sense of connection between conversational partners.

Why might such gender differences exist? Some scholars argue that gender is innate and essentially unchanging. Thus, when we speak of gender, it is associated with the biological qualities (being male or female) of individual persons. This viewpoint assumes that differences in language or storytelling are due to innate differences between males and females, perhaps in the way their brains are "wired." Many propose that such differences might stem from evolution, given the somewhat different reproductive challenges faced by the two sexes.

Alternatively, others have proposed the viewpoint we take in this chapter, that *gendered language* is learned through our culture, or created through social interaction in specific situations or contexts. In this view, gender differences in storytelling are linked to long-term sociostructural and cultural differences between males and females, and also to most men's and women's differential experiences in their own development. These socialization histories are recreated in the context of telling a story.

As we take the latter approach to the examination of gender and narratives, we want to make it clear that we do not believe that every male or every female speaks in a particular way. There are trends that, on average, distinguish men's and women's narratives; however, there are always going to be exceptions to these overall trends. According to West and Zimmerman (1987), men and women do not possess gender, but rather men and women "do" gender. Most often, when individuals "do" gender, they conform to the stereotypical gendered systems of our society and thus gender differences tend to emerge, on average.

Thus, as with many other scholars who have become intrigued by the implications of gender for research on interpersonal relationships, we asked ourselves what gender might mean for the stories that couples tell about their lives together. Are men and women similar in how they participate in these jointly told narratives about their relationship? Do the narratives they produce as a couple reflect the way they feel about their marriage, as individuals? In this chapter, we consider whether men and women differ in the way they tell the relationship narratives, and whether the resulting narratives are connected to their marital happiness in similar or different ways.

Because we used a narrative in which married couples were asked to tell their relationship story together, we have no direct way to compare relationship stories that might have been told by either partner alone. Nevertheless, we coded their joint stories in sufficient detail to know who spoke of certain kinds of feelings in the narrative, how dramatic each of them was in telling the joint story, and how they interacted with each other when they told their joint story. These codings can be informative about some important gender comparisons. Furthermore, we can reexamine the chapter on narratives in relation to marital well-being (chap. 7), to analyze ways that narrative assessments had different meanings for wives' and husbands' well-being.

GENDER DIFFERENCES IN NARRATIVE STYLE

Is there any reason to believe that men and women would participate in telling the story of their relationship differently? Although research on general speech differences between men and women does exist, research directly relevant to gender differences in relationship narratives is limited. Nevertheless, we had a few preconceptions about how gender differences might be relevant to this situation.

Our primary preconception was that women would engage in the narrative task more fully than would men. We expected women to talk more, and to express more feelings about the way events happened. We see such differences emerging even in the brief passages at the beginning of the chapter: In both couples, the wives gave lengthier responses to the interviewers' questions, responses that focused more on the feelings and emotions that existed between the partners. Husbands' responses were shorter and more matter-of-fact.

There are several reasons to expect to see such differences in the narratives. First, as mentioned in chapter 4, even from as young as age 3, females display more detailed autobiographical memories than males (Reese, Haden, & Fivush, 1996). Women seem to encode many events in their daily lives in more detail than do men (Seidlitz & Diener, 1998). Events in women's close relationships seem to accentuate this pattern, with women displaying much clearer and more vivid relationship memories than men (Ross & Holmberg, 1992). Whether these differences exist because relationships are more important to women has been speculated (Acitelli & Young, 1996), but not clearly demonstrated.

The proposed gender differences might arise not so much because of the content of the narratives, with their focus on close relationships, but rather because of the nature of the narrative task itself. Women may take particularly well to the storytelling format. Ong (1982) suggested that women may be more likely to use the oral tradition to tell their lives to others because they were deprived in becoming literate early on. Storytelling may also fit well with a feminine "way of knowing" (Belenky, Clinchy, Goldberger, & Tarule, 1986). It affords women an opportunity to be more contextual, to set the stage for events, to give rich nuances rather than bare facts. In contrast, a more analytical or rational "way of knowing" is assumed to be more typical of men's thinking. We saw such differences in our first couple's excerpt: Fred was very logical about how he and his wife became interested in each other. He said that they had common interests that naturally brought them together. Sue was more detailed and contextual in how she described their attraction. She discussed the process by which their communication drove the attraction, and in fact, she thought at first that given the communication ease, she and her husband might be just friends.

Women may also be more at ease in our particular task because the interviewers for our study, and thus the major outside audience for the narratives, were all women. Under such conditions, husbands may be more taciturn about their points of view about the relationship experiences. Because the husbands were outnumbered, so to speak, they might have tended to be less forthcoming.

For any or all of these reasons, then, we expected that women would engage more fully in our narrative task than would the men. Some of the findings were quite clear-cut and in line with our preconceptions. It is important to point out that all of the results we present later took into account the total length of the stories. Each measure of affect we mention was divided by the overall length of the story. Furthermore, we should mention that we did all of the analyses with two samples. First, we examined the narrative qualities in Year 1 with everyone who completed a narrative in that year. Then, we looked at the narrative qualities in Years 1, 3, and 7 for only those couples who were still married in Year 7 of the study. This later assessment allowed us to look at change over time with the same couples. In most instances, the results were consistent across all 3 study years; in the few cases where the results were different across time, we note these differences.

Affective Statements.   First, we examined the affective statements made by husbands versus wives, to see whether wives were significantly more likely to be emotionally oriented in their storytelling, as our excerpts might lead us to expect. Indeed, we found that women used many more statements about feelings in the joint stories than men did (see Result 1 in Table 8.1 at the end of this chapter). More fine-grained analyses (not shown in Table 8.1) revealed that this result was highly robust. Women exceeded men in mentioning both positive feelings (e.g., "happy about the wedding" or "I hoped things would keep going as well") and negative feelings (e.g., "felt bad that we didn't have enough money" or "I didn't want to still be going to school when we were married"). The overall pattern of results about the positive feelings was weaker, however, when attributing positive feelings to one's spouse (see Result 2 in Table 8.1). That is, when we looked at who was the speaker in the affects coded and the source of the affects coded, there were still more women who spoke of the feelings their husbands had then there were men who spoke of the feelings their wives had. However, this result was not as strong as the other results mentioned. Even in this instance, however, the general pattern of wives having more affects than their husbands reemerged strongly in Year 7, when husbands were especially silent about positive feelings their spouse had.

Wives also revealed more affects than did husbands in every substory. We had considered the possibility that men might speak more of their affective concerns in the present substory. We thought that if the men viewed themselves as traditional breadwinners, they might have shared their emotions about the touchy issue of finances while talking about their current lives. We were wrong. Women's feelings still predominated in the stories about the present (see Result 3 in Table 8.1). Furthermore, the trends were there for each of the 3 study years.

When we broke down the affective statements according to who experienced the emotions, we saw the only reversal in the overall trend of women making more affective statements: Husbands did speak more of their own feelings than their wives did (see Result 4 in Table 8.1). However, women also spoke more of their own feelings and of feelings attributed to both members of the couple, including negative feelings of this type (see Results 5, 6, and 7 in Table 8.1). Husbands did speak of their own feelings, but wives spoke of their own feelings and the couples' feelings, and spoke more of feelings overall than did the husbands. Given these results, we can tentatively conclude that the joint narratives reflected the wives' feelings about the relationship more than they did the husbands'.

Furthermore, the wives seemed to feel more and more comfortable over time "owning" the feelings for both members of the couple. Wives were more likely than husbands to speak of the couple's feelings: for example, "We just hit it off" (Sue), or "We haven't fought or argued in a long time" (Claire; see Result 6 in Table 8.1). This trend was minimal in Year 1, as noted in chapter 4, but it built across the years, becoming especially strong in Year 7 (see over-time pattern in Table 8.2). This use of the first person plural may be the epitome of a nonconscious relationship orientation to telling a story, and it evolves into an even clearer style in women's language as the marriages progress. This is an important result. It seems that throughout the marriage, women are more likely than men to develop a relationship stance about their emotional life. In contrast, men in Year 7 lost much of the small relationship stance they'd had in the earlier years.

Thus, as we had suspected, women engaged with the task of telling their relationship story more than their husbands did and displayed more comfort when revealing the emotional underpinnings of their marriage.

Dramatic Style. Corroborating this general conclusion was the fact that women were judged by our coders to have a more dramatic style of story presentation than the men in telling all sections of the story except those about the future (see Result 8 in Table 8.1). One might say that women had more flair for telling the story as an unfolding plot. They generally seemed to get into the swing of telling a story that expressed feelings, perhaps even using it as a vehicle for finding meaning in the way their marriage developed. For instance, take Sue in the example at the beginning of this chapter. She told the story of their budding relationship as an unfolding plot. She comfortably elaborated on the process of getting to know Fred, speaking of their ability to communicate and giving several examples to back up her point. She mused on what such an ability to communicate might mean for a relationship and suggested that she thought the two of them might end up being just friends, given that friends are able to talk so well with one another. In contrast, Fred gave a relatively brief, factual response to the question of how they became interested in each other, describing it as a meeting of common minds. Likewise, throughout most of the narratives, both men and women contributed to the unfolding stories but women's responses tended to be slightly more detailed, elaborate, and emotion-packed, whereas the men's were more to the point.

It was interesting to realize, however, that when we controlled for substory we did find a reversal of direction, showing that men tended to have a more dramatic style than women in telling the story of the future (see Result 8 in Table 8.1 again). Perhaps men chime in when they feel they are supposed to be in charge of the direction their marriage is going. For example, in the future section of Fred's Year 1 relationship narrative, he became quite passionate and dramatic about buying a house:

> I just know that we will look to buy a house. A house is so important and I want to find one, so that we buy it and move in. *That* is what we need to do right away!

It is interesting to note, however, that this result dissipated somewhat after Year 1, suggesting that men who did enthusiastically chime in about the future in the early years of marriage may have been negatively sanctioned and changed their style in later years. This is pure speculation, of course, but interesting to consider. Women seem to "own" the narratives somewhat more than their husbands do. Might the wives feel uncomfortable when their husbands chime in?

Interaction. From coding the interactions between husband and wife in telling the joint story, we also examined different styles of husbands' and wives' storytelling. Nothing very different emerged regarding how much husbands and wives made collaborating or confirming statements. But there were significant differences in how much they corrected or made a conflicting comment regarding what their spouses said. Women tended to make more conflicting interruptions, again controlling for the length of the story. However, this result seemed to be mostly true about the courtship section of the story (see Result 9 in Table 8.1). In the following, John and Darla bantered with each other about how they got together initially, and about the presumed beau in Darla's life at the beginning of the courtship, when they were both seniors in high school:

J: We had a class together and she knew me before I knew who she was. I guess I called her or something like that.

D: Don't you remember when Charlene gave you the phone number? Louise. I gave the phone number to Charlene and Charlene gave it to Louise and told you to call me.

J: Oh, okay.

D: That's how it happened. That's how I remembered how it happened. Then you called me and that was it.

J: That was it.

D: We just began seeing each other.

J: Well, yeah, we were becoming a couple. Well, I don't know who you were seeing. Ah, there was somebody else at first.

D: Who, me?

J: Yeah.

D: Uh uh!

J: But he was friend.

D: It was a family friend.

J: Yeah, it was a family friend, but . . .

D: Well, in the beginning.

J: It wasn't really like that, it . . .

D: Well, not on his part, but it was with me.

J: To this day, they won't tell me the truth.

D: *I'm* telling you now, I'm telling the truth.

Darla interrupted John in several places, trying to set him right about how the courtship occurred and especially about the other man in her life. These interruptions to correct the story John was trying to get off his chest are the types of conflictive interactions women in the sample engaged in more often than did men. They were not hostile or demeaning statements; the women simply seemed to feel that they had more clear-cut memories of their courtship. When their husbands said something inconsistent with that story, women felt compelled to set the record straight. Perhaps men have similarly clear-cut memories about other aspects of their lives, such as how they chose their work. They might be affected similarly if they were talking about work in a joint story with their wives. Men would feel compelled to set the record straight if their wives were a little off in telling the story of their career development. In other words, women may feel they "own" the courtship story more than their husbands, and in feeling especially proprietary about it, might be prone to correct any deviations their husbands offer.

Summary. Telling a joint story about their relationship brought out ways of responding to the request that were quite different for the wives when compared to the husbands. Wives were freer in spontaneously talking about feelings in each section of their story, both positive and negative ones. Although husbands spoke more of their own feelings, the general pattern of results suggests that the stories are weighted by the wives' affective portrayals of their lives and their relationship. Furthermore, wives' style in telling the relationship story was judged to be more dramatic than was their husbands' style, by and large corroborating the view introduced in chapter 4 that the flow of the relationship story tends to be directed by wives. We found that wives corrected husbands' statements more often than husbands corrected wives' statements.

An interpretation of these results might be that the relationship story, especially the courtship part, may be especially important to women's ways of thinking about themselves and their lives. Other research (Ross & Holmberg, 1992) suggests this finding would hold true even if the spouses were telling their stories separately. The relationship story seems to be one thought of by both partners as a particular domain of women.

It would be exciting to do another comparable study, not of relationship stories but of work stories, or how each member of a married couple selected their type of work. Would women again be more affective and conflict more with their husbands' statements? Or would the fact that work was more clearly in men's domains make men more affective and likely to conflict with their wives, if they thought their wives did not tell the work story quite right? We are not sure what the results would be. Such a study would help resolve whether the results we found reflected a general narrative style difference between men and women, or are differences that emerge only when the focus of the narrative is on relationships, traditionally the domain of women.

GENDER DIFFERENCES IN NARRATIVES' PREDICTION OF MARITAL WELL-BEING

In reviewing the chapter 7 analyses of the way narrative characteristics were intertwined with the well-being men and women expressed about their marriage in general, we noticed that some of the findings were evident only for women, and others were evident only for men. We reasoned that these gender-specific findings might tell us something either about the meanings men and women make about their marriage, or about the differential significance that a particular narrative characteristic might have for husbands and wives. Some of the results showed positive correlations between marital happiness and a narrative characteristic either for women or men, but not for both. Other results showed negative correlations, again either for women or men, but not for both (see Table 8.3 for a complete listing). Again, the causal direction is not certain. We don't know whether marital well-being is affecting narrative construction, or narrative construction is affecting marital well-being. In either case, it is clear that gender makes a difference. What gender differences do we see?

The Role of Women as Relationship Watcher. There is some evidence (Acitelli & Young, 1996) to suggest that women are more relationship oriented, both in thinking and talking, than are men. Thus, an important expectation of women, both in and out of relationships, may be to become the person who tends to relationship concerns, particularly between her husband and herself. One critical concern for the wife, therefore, is that her husband develop a commitment to their marriage as something important to him, a commitment not because, for example, she may have gotten pregnant before or early in marriage, but because he feels good about their relationship and how they get along. Two of the findings in Table 8.3 illustrate that assertion. Courtship stories of women unhappy in Year 1 brought up the issue of pregnancy, and in Year 3 brought up concerns about their husbands' lack of commitment. These results do not apply to the men.

In general, unlike men, women who were unhappy in marriage in Year 1 peppered their courtship stories with utterances about feelings, something, as we learned in the previous section, that is generally more common in women. This affective focus seemed particularly strong when women were concerned about their relationship. You might say unhappy women, in reliving the courtship in their stories, asked themselves: What went wrong? What feelings did I ignore? Unhappy men did not seem to do that, perhaps because reliving the past is not seen as something integral to the male role.

By Year 7, unhappily married women helped tell joint stories that had elaborate presentations of their wedding and honeymoon. We speculated earlier (see chap. 7) that unhappily married women in Year 7 may be longing for the times when there was hope and pleasure associated with the idea of being married. They held on to detailed, integrated pictures of their wedding and honeymoon, whereas happily married women seemed content to make light mention of these events and move on to aspects of their present relationship with husbands and children. We bring up this interpretation again in our discussion of the role of women as the relationship watcher. When women believe they have failed in a relationship, they may turn to the times when they thought their role performance was more adequate.

The Role of Men as Independent Beings in Control of Their Own Lives. A long-standing myth ingrained in most men's psyches is that they can move about in their lives independently and be in control of the outcomes of whatever they pursue. Marriage can play havoc with this myth. The dependence of women and children on husbands can exert a kind of power over their ways of being that counter mythic role expectations for independence. To find that they are deeply involved and dependent on women is enough to raise considerable anxiety, at least for men who have taken on the male stereotype of what they should be.

To the extent that these male role expectations influence many men, we can speculate about the connection of narratives to marital happiness that are specific to men. First of all, we found the courtship stories of couples in which men were particularly unhappy in Year 3 were more likely to raise the issue of the couple's living together before they were married, certainly a mark of someone who was tied down even before the marriage. Second, courtship stories where the woman initiated the courtship were found more frequently among unhappily married men in Year 7 than among happily married men. Being pursued by a woman is considered less than ideal for men who subscribe to macho role expectations. Third, wedding stories with more integrated plots were apparent in the couple stories of unhappily married men in Year 1 and less apparent in the stories of happily married men. In Year 1, men who were unsure of marriage and thought of it as something they, as independent men, should have resisted, may have considered the wedding as the day that sealed their fate. Thus, when the couple recounted their wedding in a coherent, integrated story of how preparations were made and carried out, it only accented the men's concerns about being married in the first place.

Thus far, we have discussed findings suggesting that men who think that marriage brings far too many demands and constraints may resist no longer being the person in charge or in control of their lives. In this same vein, we can approach the one distinctive finding about men who were happy in marriage. In Year 3, happily married men were members of couples who gave a clear-cut, integrated story about their future. These men evidently participated in the control of their married lives, something they value for fulfilling their perceived gender role.

SUMMARY

Our joint relationship narratives were indeed gendered. The two couples portrayed at the beginning of the chapter were not atypical, but illuminated distinct patterns of how women and men speak about their relationships. Women's ways of constructing the relationship story with their husbands seemed to dominate the outcome. Women expressed more affective concerns of all types in all sections of the story than did men. They took the couple point of view in the story more than the men did, and corrected men's accounts more than men corrected their accounts. We feel that the narrative style of understanding such a vital relationship as marriage permits women to fulfill general cultural role expectations of being the relationship watcher. We believe men tag along, so to speak. Indeed, there are general cultural expectations for men to be uncomfortable with affective outpourings about their marriages. We suspect men would be that way even if they were telling their story individually, and even if they were telling their story to a male rather than to a female interviewer.

This is not to say that men did not contribute to the jointly told story. Their presence undoubtedly helped construct the stories in particular ways. They implicitly went along with what was said. Furthermore, the fact that their own evaluation of the marriage correlated with some of the narrative characteristics suggests that men were not merely passive observers in the storytelling context. Men's concerns about male roles colored the couple stories. For example, unhappily married men were more likely to have participated in a story that stated the courtship was initiated by their wives.

What might our findings suggest for the prevention of or intervention in unhappy marriages? First, there is the fact that there are cultural expectations for women to be the controllers of interactions and communication in the marital relationship. We might suggest that couples become aware of these expectations as factors that can influence them as much as their own personal styles. It is important for women to realize that men might find it difficult to express affective benefits and concerns about the relationship. In turn, it may be important for husbands to understand that when their wives bring up affective concerns, it may not always be because they have problems in the marriage. Instead, husbands should understand that their wives are fulfilling cultural expectations of how women should speak (or tell stories) about their relationship. Finally, in terms of content, our findings suggest that couples might want to emphasize the present and future parts of their marriage rather than the past (especially the wedding and honeymoon). For both men and women, integrated wedding and/or honeymoon stories were associated with unhappiness.

In any case, we have ample evidence that one's gender has an effect in the construction of the narrative. Gender must continually be considered in making sense of many of our findings. The expectations we have for men and women implicitly govern the differential styles they have in approaching a narrative. The emphasis, or de-emphasis, of certain contents by one gender or the other may permit men and women to feel appropriate or adequate in their roles as married men and women.

TABLE 8.1
Significant Mean Differences Between Husbands
and Wives in Narrative Styles, Observed in Couples
in Their First Year of Marriage ($N = 302$)

Result No.	Measure	Husbands		Wives		Paired t Tests
		Mean	SD	Mean	SD	(H–W)
1	Number of affective statements	.1057	.0063	.1165	.0063	−2.00*
2	Positive affects mentioned about spouse's feelings	.0034	.0048	.0039	.0032	−1.24
3	Affects mentioned about current life	.0247	.0229	.0321	.0227	−4.47**
4	Affects attributed to husband	.0633	.0415	.0125	.0130	20.59***
5	Affects attributed to wife	.0107	.012	.067	.0396	−23.21***
6	Affects attributed to husband and wife as a couple	.0215	.0190	.0240	.0213	−1.66†
7	Negative affects attributed to husband and wife as a couple	.0035	.0051	.0044	.0060	−2.13*
8	Dramatic style of storytelling					
	Re: Courtship	1.49	.036	1.62	.038	−3.37**
	Re: Wedding	1.50	.038	1.67	.040	−4.12***
	Re: Present	1.35	.034	1.42	.035	−1.72†
	Re: Future	1.30	.030	1.24	.034	1.98*
9	Number of conflicting interruptions of spouse					
	Re: Courtship	.0030	.0011	.0034	.0013	−2.08*

Note. All means are divided by story length.
†Trend, $p < .10$. *$p < .05$. **$p < .01$. ***$p < .001$.

TABLE 8.2
Mean Gender Differences in Affects Attributed to Both Husband
and Wife as a Couple, by Year, for Couples
Who Told Stories in All 3 Years

Sample	N	Husbands		Wives		Paired t Tests
		Mean	SD	Mean	SD	(H–W)
Year 1	131	.0227	.0210	.0254	.0204	−1.09
Year 3	91	.0220	.0197	.0316	.0305	−2.70**
Year 7	136	.0181	.0198	.0303	.0254	−4.52***

Note. Mean is divided by story length.
**$p < .01$. ***$p < .001$.

TABLE 8.3
Summary of Results Showing Gender-Specific Connections
of Marital Well-Being to Narrative Characteristics

Year	Negative Effects on Women Only
1	Large number of affects about the courtship
1	Presence of themes of pregnancy
3	Presence of themes of lack of commitment in courtship
7	Telling an integrated story about the honeymoon or wedding

Year	Negative Effects on Men Only
1	Telling an integrated story about the wedding
3	Bringing up the cohabitation issue in courtship
7	Indicating that it was a female-initiated courtship

Year	Positive Effects on Women Only
7	The overall plot of the courtship was unromantic and pragmatic

Year	Positive Effects on Men Only
3	Telling an integrated story of the future

Chapter 9

Ethnicity as a Factor
Affecting Narratives

Most studies of marriage investigate the universal principles that operate at different stages of a relationship for most couples. As much as we would like to emerge from our study with universal principles about the meanings couples impose about their marriages and the way narratives are told and retold, we know we must leave the door open for finding results that are specific to an African-American context as opposed to a White context, and vice versa. White couples generally face structural circumstances that are strikingly different from African-American couples. Whites generally face fewer obstacles and encounter fewer injustices in their worlds. Thus, as we indicated in the earlier chapters, individuals can have different meanings of what marriages are or should be, based on whether they are embedded in one or the other of these two subcultural contexts. We have already discussed in chapter 8 how the experiences of being male or female in a marriage can have unique meanings that are revealed in the narratives. In this chapter, we examine the extent to which unique meanings emerge, depending on whether the couple is African-American or White.

A number of published studies from our project (Chadiha, Veroff, & Leber, 1998; Orbuch, Veroff, & Holmberg, 1993; Veroff, Chadiha, Leber, & Sutherland, 1993) have illustrated the ways these differential meanings might have operated in Year 1 of our marriage study for African-American couples as compared to White couples. The results suggested either that the same narrative imagery may have different underlying meanings among Blacks and Whites, or that the normative experiences of African-American as compared to White culture elicits different narrative styles, themes, or interactions. In this chapter, we develop these same ideas even further, by including the couple narratives in Years 3 and 7 and seeing how the storytelling may have changed or remained stable over all study years, both within and between the two ethnic groups.

Before we highlight the new analyses, which focus on the narratives over time, it is important to highlight some of the previous findings from Year 1. These findings give us clues about what to examine or expect from our analyses in this chapter. First, Chadiha et al. (1998) found that in Year 1 stories, African-Americans more than Whites had themes that centered around the couple's relationship and how it changed as the couple got to know each other and entered into marriage. For example, consider what Denise and Troy, an African-American couple, said about their courtship in Year 1:

D: We just kept seeing each other after that. And then, I guess our relationship got stronger and everything, you know.

T: We just enjoyed going out together.

D: And then, we stayed together so long, everybody kept saying, we are not going to get married. We are not going to get married. Eventually, we started talking about marriage.

T: Yes, we began talking about getting married. We were finally there.

By contrast, Whites, more than African-Americans, told stories that contained themes about the couple's work and accomplishments, as well as the topic of having enough time to do the things they needed to do. Let us look at Joy and Steve, a White couple who, in Year 1, talked about wanting more time to achieve their individual goals before they got married:

J: I just wasn't ready to get married. There were things I wanted to do and I wanted all that stuff. At the beginning we didn't really see each other a whole lot, you know, maybe once a week. Sometimes not for a couple of weeks. With working and school, we had busy schedules.

S: I've always been a hard worker, save my money. I was, you know, content with staying busy. I had my own car, paid for my first car, by myself and all that. I also had enough brothers and sisters that were married and things. I didn't really need that, you know.

J: Yeah, I don't know. I didn't like the guys my age. They were immature. I liked guys who were more settled, less wild. When I met Steve, although I wasn't ready to get married right away, he was stable and a hard worker. He kept saying, well, not until I get out of school and things like that. Luckily, some things came up and then he gave me a ring. I was surprised at that time, because I didn't think he wanted to right then, that early, and then I had said to him, I want to finish school. I was afraid that if I got married, I wouldn't finish school.

In simple terms, we might say that African-American couples, at least in their initial stories, were trying to make sense of their relationship, whereas the White couples were taking the existence of their relationship more for granted, and were instead focused on building up the accoutrements of a good marriage through their pursuit of success in their jobs. These themes can alert us to the possibility that early on, perhaps even before they are married, African-American newlyweds may be more directly wary about whether marriage will work for them. The divorce or separation rate among African-Americans is higher than it is among Whites, and this fact may cast many courting and newlywed African-American couples into doubtful concerns about their relationship.

Second, Veroff, Chadiha, et al. (1993) studied the affects and interactions couples displayed in their storytelling and found different approaches to marriage in the two ethnic groups. There was, again, a hint of greater marital wariness among African-American stories compared to the White stories, from affects divulged in the narratives and from the way the couples collaborated on the narrative task. Among Blacks, affective statements were more likely to be statements about what they wanted, rather than about what they felt. It was almost as if the African-American couples were more intent on telling what they needed from the relationship than on telling how they were reacting to it. Many more of the African-American stories dealt with the husbands' needs and feelings, as if that were something that had to be more strongly considered among the Black couples. By contrast, White couples were more likely to talk about how they were feeling about something as a couple. Furthermore, when White couples collaborated well in the way they interacted, it reflected happy marriages. This was not the case for the Black couples, for whom collaboration in telling the stories of their relationship did not necessarily imply that they were doing fine.

We come away from these findings with the notion that there might be a stronger mindset among Whites to think in couple terms about their marriage and to collaborate with their spouse. In contrast, there seems to be more of a mindset among the African-American couples to think about the individuals involved in a marital relationship and to protect the needs and wants of those individuals. Now, we must remember from the Chadiha et al. (1998) study mentioned previously that African-American couples were more focused on relationship issues. Thus, it is not that Black couples avoided interpersonal issues altogether. It is just that these couples seemed more guarded about protecting individual concerns when thinking about their relationship. We might interpret this tendency as the same wariness we noted previously, perhaps a wariness enlisted to counter their concerns that they might easily separate or divorce, like so many other African-American couples who married in the last part of the 20th century.

Third, Veroff, Chadiha, et al. (1993) also found that when there was conflict about the storyline, it was more likely to come from the African-American couples. Although the interactions between most husbands and wives as they told their stories were predominantly collaborative, with spouses helping each other cooperatively in telling the story, conflicts between husband and wife in the telling of the story were more likely to appear in the stories of Black, rather than White, couples. From this finding, we are reminded of other research showing that conflict, in the form of friendly jostling, is a highly acceptable form of communication in everyday African-American interactions (Kochman, 1981). In fact, Orbuch et al. (1993) wondered whether this conflictful style of interaction is good or problematic for the well-being of the marriage. They found that Black couples whose narratives reported some tension between husband and wife during the courtship story were in fact higher in marital well-being 2 years later. Such was not the case for the White couples. This result suggests that hindsight attention to the tensions that existed in a couple as they got acquainted and decided to marry bodes well for African-American marriages.

It is important to note that Orbuch et al. (1993) also found that, for both Black and White couples, having a generally positive but not highly romanticized view of the courtship in their stories foretold happy marriages 2 years later. This result suggests that the tensions between the couple shown in the Black courtship stories were minor, perhaps simply reflecting the lively interactions that may underlie a generally positive view of a relationship in African-American couples. This interpretation may tie into the African-American conflict style discussed earlier (Kochman, 1981).

Finally, it is important to note that there were also other narrative indicators of African-American marital well-being that were not found for Whites in Veroff, Chadiha, et al.'s (1993) study. For example, only for Black women did narratives that dealt with religious issues coincide with positive feelings of marital well-being. And only for Black men did narratives that dealt either with children or with finances coincide with negative feelings of marital well-being. For Black men, these results come as close as any to showing that men who question their ability to provide for a family might have trouble with marriage. With the history of racism in the United States, it is not a long stretch to think that Black men's wariness about marriage might originate in the ways the economic system has for so long been unequal for African-American males. In many ways, these findings from the narratives were clearer than any that were uncovered in direct questions about problems in couples' marriages. It might be that for most African-Americans, the narrative method is more consonant with long-standing oral traditions in Black culture (see Heath, 1994). Many African-Americans may feel freer to expand on their lives in a story form than in a set of answers to a highly standardized interview schedule.

Based on this evidence from the Year 1 narratives, we began the present analyses with two major hypotheses for ways that African-Americans and Whites might differ in their relationship narratives over the first 7 years of marriage. First, we expected African-Americans to display more wariness about their relationships than White couples. Second, we expected Black couples to be more individualistic in the marriage stories than White couples.

RESULTS FROM OUR CURRENT ANALYSES

Before we begin to highlight how African-American couples and White couples differed in their narratives about their relationships, and what these differences seemed to reveal about marriage for these two groups, we should emphasize that in many ways the two groups were similar. We looked at many comparisons between African-American and White couples for which no significant differences emerged. Indeed, the compelling overall conclusion should be that the cultural context plays a minor role in fashioning the relationship stories these couples tell. The stories that African-American and White couples told over all 3 study years were quite similar in style and content. This fact may get lost in our presentation because we emphasize ways in which they differed in the next sections. Nevertheless, we should bear their overall similarities in mind when we differentiate the groups.

The two hypotheses we started with were based on analyses of the Year 1 relationship narratives. It turns out that when Years 3 and 7 were included in the present analyses, we found little direct evidence for these hypotheses. In fact, there was some evidence that White couples, more than African-American couples, conflicted with each other when telling their courtship story, a result totally opposite to our assumption that African-Americans would be more conflictful and less collaborative. What do we make of these results that fail to support our initial hypotheses, based on Year 1 evidence? We have two interpretations.

First, we must keep in mind that both in our study and in the country generally, African-Americans divorce at a higher rate than Whites. This differential divorce rate could have been a basis of our null results, finding nothing from the analyses of narratives over 7 years to support the "wariness hypothesis" or the "individual versus couple focus hypothesis." Because couples who divorced sometime during the first 7 years of their marriage were largely excluded from the present chapter's 7-year look at the narratives, and because more of these couples were African-American than White, we may no longer be dealing with African-American couples who were particularly wary about marriage, or who maintained a strong individual focus. Those who were particularly wary or individually oriented had no doubt either changed their focus to remain married or decided to divorce.

Another interpretation of why we had little support for hypotheses generated from looking at only the Year 1 data is that we were now dealing with couples over time, over 7 years. As their marriages progressed, perhaps African-American couples began to drop their initial cautions and took more collaborative stances to their marriages in subsequent years. As the African-American couples started marriage, they may have been wary of the idea of marriage, not necessarily because of their partners or their particular relationships, but because they were engaging in relatively non-normative behavior within the African-American community. With time, their stance toward marriage may have mellowed, becoming more like the everyday acceptance of the married state common in the dominant cultural perspective.

Despite not finding the hypothesized differences between White and African-American attitudes toward marriage, we did observe other ways in which African-Americans and Whites differed in their relationship stories. First, we turn to the courtship section of the stories.

Courtship.   In their courtship narratives, African-Americans were more likely to speak about living together before marriage, and about being pregnant before marriage (see Results 1 and 2 in Table 9.1 at the end of the chapter). Because we analyzed the quantitative data from the study and found that somewhat more African-Americans lived together as a couple before marriage and for longer periods of time, and many more of them had children before marriage (Veroff, Douvan, & Hatchett, 1995), these results ipso facto are not especially revealing. Yet they do set the stage for thinking about another result, one that showed more African-American than White couples focused on religious issues when speaking of their courtship in their narratives (see Result 3 in Table 9.1). A few social scientists have noted the importance of the Black church in organizing the African-American community, and the church's influence may come dramatically into play in bringing Black couples to the altar to take their marriage vows, possibly to legitimate children conceived or born before marriage. This certainly may be true for White couples as well, but this finding suggests that religious commitments are more prominent for African-Americans in forging marriages in the first place. We return to this idea when we discuss the wedding, in the next section.

There were other ways that African-Americans and Whites differed in relating the stories of their courtship. It was clear that African-American couples were remembering their courtship in a more romantic way. They, more than Whites, discussed the courtship as a pursuit either by the wife (see Result 4 in Table 9.1) or the husband (see Result 5 in Table 9.1). Whites were much more pragmatic, simply speaking of how the relationship slowly evolved, without much dramatic flair in describing how that took place (see Result 6 in Table 9.1). Supporting this pragmatic emphasis among the White couples was the fact that compared to African-Americans, White couples were more likely to introduce concerns about education (see Result 7 in Table 9.1) and careers (see Result 8 in Table 9.1) into the picture of their courtships.

The notion that Blacks had a more romantic, dramatic flair in speaking of their courtship was also in keeping with an additional finding: The stories told by Black couples in general were longer than the stories told by White couples, both in the courtship and in the overall narrative (see Result 9 in Table 9.1). We imagine that the Black couples told longer stories because it requires more time and effort to develop and relate a romantic plot than it would to tell a more humdrum story. As an aside, we should point out that African-American couples being more verbose than the White couples in their narratives might suggest that a narrative style of information-gathering tends to be more consonant with Black culture and discourse. As a further aside, we should note that when we controlled for this difference in length of the narrative, we did find that African-American wives, compared to the White wives, brought up more affective statements in general (see Result 10 in Table 9.1).

When we examined the link between length of the narrative and marital well-being, it appeared that telling a long story had special meaning for White wives. For them, when they produced longer stories with their husbands, they also felt that their marriages were happier (see Result 11 in Table 9.1). Although there may well be a direct causal link between story length and happiness for White women, we also see possible indirect linkages. It may be that White women think that when they, as couples, become more elaborate in storytelling, it implies or reflects a smoothly working relationship. Alternatively, a highly elaborated story might mean that they are working through problems they are experiencing in their marriage. In fact, previous research (J. M. Gottman, 1994) suggested that when White husbands were "expansive" in talking about their relationship, couples were less likely to divorce 2 years later. Comfortable, open relationship talk may be especially valued by White women. Black couples may be more comfortable with the oral tradition; they therefore talk more extensively but do not necessarily see the sheer amount of talk as particularly diagnostic of a strong relationship.

For Black couples, it was the presence of particular issues in the narrative, rather than the sheer length of the narrative, that was important. For example, among African-American couples, but not among White couples, if the courtship plot described the woman as having taken the initiative, the men experienced lower marital happiness, especially as the marriage progressed in Years 3 and 7 (see Result 12 in Table 9.1). Evidently, this counternormative gender stereotype with regard to courtship makes Black husbands feel particularly defensive. Although Black men can be nontraditional in many facets of marriage, such as helping around the house and child care (Orbuch & Eyster, 1997), having their wives perceived as the dominant initiators of the marriage does not seem to sit well with their sense of masculinity. It may be okay to be nontraditional inside the family, but the public image must still be one of a strong, dominant Black male, what Majors and Billson (1992) termed the "cool pose" when applied to single African-American men.

Such explanations are sensible, but we have no clear understanding of why these findings should hold only for African-American men and not for White men, for whom desired public images must be similar. We can speculate that White men continue to be reinforced for their masculinity and masculine behaviors in the world of work, as a general rule. Because of this public reinforcement, they may not be as threatened by, or as defensive about, counternormative gender role behaviors in public. In contrast, Black men are not often reinforced for their masculinity and power in the world of work, given the challenges that many face in employment environments. Thus, the public image of their relationship and the perceived control they have in it are particularly important.

One final result is worth noting when we compare the courtship stories of African-American couples with those of White couples. It appears that when financial matters came up as issues in the stories of the courtship, it had a negative association with the marital well-being of the Black couples over time, but a positive association for the marital well-being of the White couples (see Result 13 in Table 9.1). Our guess is that thinking about financial issues for Black couples often reflects festering employment limitations and the presence of systemic financial obstacles. Such thinking can "spill over" into their marriages. By contrast, thinking about financial issues for White couples often reflects their own problem-solving activities, which in turn can have a good effect on their sense of control over their marriages.

Wedding. White couples were much more likely than Black couples to incorporate feelings into their stories about their wedding (see Result 14 in Table 9.1). These ethnic differences were largely attributable to White women mentioning these affects more frequently than Black women (see Result 14 in Table 9.1). White couples were also more likely to convey to the interviewer that the wedding was a grand social occasion (see Result 15 in Table 9.1), a story line that would support the use of many strong emotions. African-American wedding stories had a slightly different tone. Although many of the Black couples also highlighted the good times people had at their wedding, they, more than the White couples, tended to focus on an important psychological meaning of the wedding—that the wedding served as a public demonstration of the couple's commitment to one another (see Result 16 in Table 9.1). This sense of commitment is a meaning of the wedding ceremony emphasized in many religious approaches. Because we learned in the last section that religious ideas figured more frequently in African-American stories of the courtship, we were not surprised to see similar themes emerge in the wedding story, as well.

Honeymoon. White couples told much more integrated stories about their honeymoons than Black couples did (see Result 17 in Table 9.1). This finding made us suspicious. When setting up the code for the narratives, we listened to many tapes and knew we had heard a number of highly integrated stories of the honeymoon by the Black couples, in keeping with their elaborate narrative style. We looked closely at the coding for the honeymoon story and found that African-Americans were in fact much less likely to have a honeymoon story at all (see Result 18 in Table 9.1). African-Americans in our sample simply did not take standard honeymoons as often as the White couples did. Thus, White couples can more easily make use of these stored memories as they evaluate their married lives. In chapter 6, we found that voicing integrated memories about a honeymoon had both positive and negative connections with couples' well-being: positive connections in Year 3 (joyful reminiscence) and negative connections in Year 7 (looking back to happier times). At this point, we need to realize that the functions that the memories of honeymoons served were much more relevant for the White couples in our sample than for their African-American counterparts.

Present. The African-American and White couples were quite similar in what they told us about their present lives in their stories. By and large, few couples told us about any tensions in their present lives, at least tensions that would warrant a story structure. Those who did tended to be unhappy, as we discovered in chapter 6. In the analyses for this chapter, we saw that particular finding was stronger for the African-American couples than it was for the White couples (see Results 19 and 20 in Table 9.1). Thus, reporting no tension about the present in a spontaneous story had a more positive meaning in African-American couples than in White couples. Given the high divorce or separation rate, African-American couples may feel especially vulnerable when they enter marriage. Experiencing very smooth relationships with few tensions may aid them in dropping any residual wariness they may feel toward the married state.

Future. In the same way, stories without tension about the future had more positive meanings for the Black husbands than they did for the Whites (see Result 21 in Table 9.1). African-American couples who did forge stories with tension about either the present or the future may have been reflecting their own unhappiness with their marriages. We may have another instance when there is more direct expression of feelings in the narrative method for African-Americans than there is for the White couples.

SUMMARY

We found little evidence for our initial expectations based on previous analyses of the Year 1 narratives. We hypothesized that African-American couples, in comparison with White couples, would have relationship stories that reflected greater wariness and greater individual as opposed to couple focus. However, what seemed to be true in Year 1 marriage stories did not hold up in their retelling in Years 3 and 7. We reasoned that one way to think about this pattern of results is that couples who were particularly wary or individually focused might have divorced early on in the marriage. Many more African-American couples did divorce during the early years. Another way to think of the pattern of results is to suggest that many couples who started off being wary learned over time to solve problems, and those who started off being individually focused learned to be more cohesive with their spouses. Both interpretations are plausible.

There were a number of ways in which the circumstances of life that generally differentiate our two ethnic groups helped contribute to different themes in their stories. African-American couples, compared to White couples, lived together before marriage for longer periods, more often came into their first marriages with children, and were less well-off financially, especially the husbands. These circumstances gave rise to issues of cohabitation, pregnancy, and finances emerging in the African-American courtship stories more than in the White stories. Financial matters seemed to appear in the stories of the Black couples more than the White couples in a number of ways. Among other things, African-Americans did not tell as many honeymoon stories, simply because fewer of them took an elaborate honeymoon. It seems almost paradoxical then to realize that African-Americans tended to bring up more romantic images about their courtship than did the White couples, who, in turn, were more likely to tell us a highly pragmatic version of their courtship.

It does seem clear that religion played a stronger role in the way African-Americans talked about their marriages. We know from their responses to standard survey questions that the African-American couples were more likely to say they attended church and more likely to say their religion was important in their lives. These findings were reflected in the narrative themes as well. Not only did the theme of religion emerge more frequently in the African-American courtship stories, but also it seemed to be important in the wedding stories. In keeping with a religious interpretation, African-Americans were more likely to focus on the public commitment of marriage vows as what their wedding meant to them. By contrast, White couples, more than Black couples, emphasized the fact that the wedding was a grand social occasion.

We conclude this ethnic group analysis by reminding ourselves and the reader once again that we have been highlighting only the significant differences found in the stories of the two groups, which eclipses the overall pattern of results we found. By and large, there were very few differences between the groups. Most of the comments we made in chapter 4 about how a relationship story is told in our sample applied as much to the African-American group as to the White group. Nevertheless, the differentiations we have been making are also important reminders that these two groups emerge from slightly different social contexts, settings that occasionally engender different characteristics in their relationship stories.

TABLE 9.1

Summary of Significant Results Comparing African-American
and White Couples' Narrative Responses Across Years 1, 3, and 7

Subsection of Narrative	Result No.	Finding as Reported in Text	Direction of Difference	F Test[a]
Courtship	1	Cohabitation is issue raised in narrative	AA > W	8.68**
	2	Pregnancy is issue raised in narrative	AA > W	3.84*
	3	Religion is issue raised in narrative	AA > W	8.94**
	4	Plot of narrative focuses on husband's pursuit of his wife	AA > W	6.99**
	5	Plot of narrative focuses on wife's pursuit of her husband	AA > W	8.80**
	6	Plot of narrative focuses on the pragmatics of an evolving relationship	W > AA	12.24***
	7	Work/career is issue raised in narrative	W > AA	6.44*
	8	Education is issue raised in narrative	W > AA	5.82*
	12	Correlation between a theme of a wife being the prime instigator of courtship and men being unhappy in marriage	AA > W	3.63* (Interaction: Ethnicity × Narrative)
	13	Correlation between having financial issues come up in the story and women being happy in their marriage	W > AA	5.42* (Interaction: Ethnicity × Narrative)
Wedding	14	Number of affects expressed by wives about the wedding/length of story	W > AA	18.84***
	15	Wedding is depicted as a grand social occasion in the narrative	W > AA	6.46**
	16	Wedding is depicted as a public commitment by couple	AA > W	3.61*

(Continued)

TABLE 9.1

(Continued)

Subsection of Narrative	Result No.	Finding as Reported in Text	Direction of Difference	F Test[a]
Honeymoon	17	Narrative about honeymoon is an integrated story	W > AA	5.94*
	18	Told a story about a honeymoon	W > AA	38.51***
Present	19	Correlation between having no tension in the story about the present and wives being happy in their marriage	AA > W	4.01* (Interaction: Ethnicity × Narrative)
	20	Correlation between having no tension in the story about the present and husbands being happy in their marriage	AA > W	4.77* (Interaction: Ethnicity × Narrative)
Future	21	Correlation between having no tension in the story about the future and husbands being happy in their marriage	AA > W	5.95* (Interaction: Ethnicity × Narrative)
Overall	9	Time taken in telling the narrative	AA > W	9.06**
	10	Number of affects brought up by wives in narrative/length of story	AA > W	13.84***
	11	Correlation between time taken in telling the narrative and women being happy in their marriage	W > AA	6.76** (Interaction: Ethnicity × Narrative)

[a]F test used is a test for fixed effects in Growth Curve Analyses. It is equivalent to the square of the unstandardized beta/standard error.

†Trend, $p < .10$. *$p < .05$. **$p < .01$. ***$p < .001$.

Chapter 10

What Have We Learned About Marriage?

Having explored the stories couples told us about their relationship, not just once but three different times over the course of their early years of marriage, we now summarize what we have learned about marriage that was uniquely revealed through our couples' stories. Much has been written about marriage in the social sciences, largely in terms of what accounts for marital adjustment and stability, but also in terms of how marriage buffers individual vulnerabilities. Although the research analyses in this volume have some bearing on these important issues, their overall implications for understanding modern urban marriages are quite different. Our findings have more to do with revealing the way couples experience their married lives. We asked them to talk about their stories in their own words. They told us about how they met, became a couple, and got married; they told us about what life has been like for them as a couple, and the way they picture their future. Thus, through their narratives, the couples in our study told us about the meanings they had made and continued to make of their marital experiences. Given the joint telling of the stories, we also received insights into how they interacted and communicated while relating their experiences. In this summary, we review the main features of how couples characterized these experiences and dealt with this shared narrative task.

OVERVIEW OF STORIES

We begin by giving a brief overview of the major issues and themes that emerged in each of the narrative's substories. We highlight just a few of these common issues here. Chapter 4 has extensive coverage of them.

When we look at the overall issues that dominate the entire narrative, we see issues surrounding a couple's relationship being most central in just under half the couples, with half of these being largely positive presentations of their love for and good communication with each other. Other important but less dominant themes were about family or friends, and employment or careers. As we discussed in chapter 5, issues of childrearing became more central as the marriage progressed.

With regard to couples' recall of their courtships, we also saw that slightly more than half of the couples saw the dominant tension of the courtship sequence as originating within the relationship itself. Few spoke of the awkwardness of extricating themselves from other relationships. Still fewer, to our surprise, talked of children as a source of tension in the courtship. Given that so many of the couples entered their first marriage with children, we were surprised that children played so small a role in the Year 1 narratives. Children do not seem to fit comfortably into the standard newlywed script; couples perhaps did not want to frame their Year 1 narrative as one where they had to get married solely for the sake of their children.

This finding is a specific instance of a more general pattern: Most couples described their courtships as having developed in a smooth, sedate, positive fashion. Only one third of all couples in the study had courtship plots that highlighted any obstacles to a smoothly occurring courtship. Perhaps we are cynical, but it strikes us as unlikely that so many couples would have such completely problem-free courtships. We suspect that at least some of our couples are engaging in a little convenient forgetting or judicious editing, and that they are suppressing, if not repressing, the minor problems they may have once faced in becoming a couple. Positive illusions regarding the courtship may occur in our couples' narratives.

With regard to the wedding, it seemed that most couples managed to negotiate the perils of putting a wedding together relatively well, as least in their retrospective accounts. Some hassles did occur but they weathered them together. The general account of an American urban wedding in the last part of the 20th century details certain common features regarding clothes, attendants, blessings from an officiator, and a party afterward featuring food, drink, and dancing. The most common theme of the wedding sequence was that it was a positive social occasion, true of one third of the wedding stories. This emphasis on fun and sociability overshadowed the more earnest theme of the wedding being a time of public commitment of vows, only apparent in a small number of couples' stories.

The most common types of tension in the couples' present life narratives had to do with their relationships with each other, with money and finances, and with their work or jobs. The tensions perceived in the couples' future life had to do with even more pragmatic matters, often centered around their housing concerns. The present and future stories were thus quite pragmatic, even humdrum. Nevertheless, the overall tone was positive, with the majority of respondents optimistically seeing their lives as progressively improving.

Overall, our couples' stories were certainly not the romantic and dramatic fare of Hollywood romance. Their tales might not make it on the big screen or in the latest Harlequin romance; nevertheless, our couples' stories offered fascinating glimpses into the quiet ups and downs and mutual accommodations of real-life relationships.

After delving into these narratives, four overarching qualities struck us as particularly important. We summarize these general characterizations next.

CHARACTERIZING THE NARRATIVES

Positivity of Couples' Stories.   First, we could not help but be impressed by the quietly positive tone that couples wove in telling their stories. Their tales may not have been filled with hearts and flowers and wild romance, but they definitely were suffused with a quiet sense of caring, of a genuine satisfaction in the relationship and in each other. We might have expected something different, with the divorce rate as high as it is. Our sample was certainly no exception, with more than 30% getting divorced over the 7 years of the study. For most couples, however, we did not seem to be capturing much in the way of building resentments or festering disappointments. Of course, there may have been a selection bias, with those couples who were feeling worst about the relationship at a particular point in time declining to put themselves in a position in which they would have to discuss it. Nonetheless, we collected many relationship narratives over a relatively long period of time, and on the whole, our hearts were gladdened with the positive images they provided of marriage today.

Positive plots predominated in the stories the couples told about the courtship, the wedding, and the way their life was progressing since they were married. There was little report of conflicts between them, and not many openly disagreed while telling the story of their relationship. The wedding was seen as fun. The future was seen as positive. It is true that most of our couples were relatively happy in their relationships, yet even those couples who reported in their survey questions that they were unhappily married spoke relatively little about sad, frustrating, or unhappy events. Listening to almost any of our narratives would leave one with a warm glow about the married state; very few were "downers."

In no way do we think that our couples have only good feelings about their marriage or that they never argue. Rather, we conclude that when they summarized their experiences of marriage for outsiders like the interviewers in our study, these couples overwhelmingly took a positive stance to their marriage. Some might argue that this positive stance is merely social desirability at work. However, one must keep in mind that constructing a coherent narrative is not nearly as simple as electing to circle a high number on a rating scale. Those who legitimately had few positive feelings toward each other would no doubt have found it difficult to negotiate a convincing positive narrative on the fly. Thus, we do not believe that our respondents were simply making up good stories. We believe that as a whole, marriage is a quietly positive and fulfilling experience for most of our respondents, and it was on these positive elements that they elected to focus.

It is interesting to think about how the stories our couples told us would compare to the stories couples seeking counseling would tell a marital therapist. A marital therapist might prod couples into talking about the negative memories and problematic issues they face in their life together. The positive tone we picked up would be dampened or absent, and conflicts and problems would be emphasized. Perhaps the negative press that modern American marriages sometimes get depends in large part on stories couples tell in the therapeutic context. Many authors penning popular self-help books on relationships come from a background of marital counseling. Those who write about marriage may have only heard negative stories from couples seeking change. In contrast, the stories of our more representative sample were reassuringly upbeat.

The Everydayness of Marriage. We want to re-emphasize that our couples' stories, although generally positive, certainly did not depict a state of marital bliss. Instead, the stories our couples told conveyed a sense of the "everydayness" of marriage. The stories were not gripping dramas, but instead focused on couples' small accommodations to each other and to the world around them. We think that these accommodations are exactly what most couples actually experience in marriage, along with only occasional moments of marital bliss and protestations of love. Even newly married couples spend most of their time and energy coping with the day-by-day tasks and adjustments that are needed to forge a life together. If thoughts about charged romantic feelings did come up in their stories, they appeared in their descriptions of their courtships. Yet, not even the majority of courtship stories were romantically plotted, but instead spoke of a generally evolving commitment to one another.

Again, this is not a stereotypical Hollywood romance. In fact, many Hollywood romances end before the couple reaches the altar, perhaps finding, as our couples did, that the courtship stage makes for a better story than does the ongoing reality of married life. Mostly, marriage is not about romantically gazing into each other's eyes, or about nobly sacrificing everything for a partner. Instead, marriage is mostly about balancing the checkbook, picking out the best available home that fits the budget, and deciding who will drive the kids to school next Tuesday. Our couples seem to understand that, even if Hollywood does not. Meeting romantic myths is one thing, living a smooth-running life is another.

In fact, as we saw in chapter 6, it is the unhappy wives who appeared the least likely to have learned this lesson. They painted an increasingly emotional story of the courtship over time, whereas happier wives took a more pragmatic stance. Just as Karney and Coombs (2000) found in their research, happier wives seemed to downplay how good the past was, to some extent. This approach allowed them to see the present as a relative improvement, which seemed to be important for allowing continued optimism toward the future (Karney & Frye, 2002). The happiest couples were not those who tried to live a never-ending romance or dwell on wonderful romantic times in their past. The happiest ones were those who focused on the quiet rewards that come from the everyday give-and-take of a relationship.

The Importance of the Social Network. A ripple effect of the generally pragmatic approach our couples took to marriage is that their relationship stories seldom focused only on themselves and the way they thought and felt about each other. Instead, couples' stories most often included a wealth of supporting characters, a whole network of people who must be consulted or in some way considered during their married life. Marriage is not a duet, but rather a complex orchestral arrangement, one in which many different people's needs and preferences must be considered and negotiated. The courtship stories dealt considerably with family and friends and the nature of the couples' work lives. The wedding stories dealt with the interactions needed to pull off the event in the way the couple wanted it while taking into account the preferences of both partners' families. Even the honeymoon, a period when there is supposed to be a dyadic withdrawal from the world, often touched on the business-world pragmatics of financing a vacation, getting to one's destination, and negotiating side trips and excursions.

Needless to say, the birth and presence of children became new topics of consideration in most couples' marriages, especially after the first year. With the addition of children, their stories became even less couple oriented, and more family oriented. It is fair to say that the stories of our couples' relationships have as much, if not more, to do with their surrounding networks than with a simple focus on themselves. The experience of marriage is a kaleidoscope of social encounters with the world, encounters that are essential if couples are to deal with the reality of being married and becoming parents. Perhaps if the fabric of a marriage begins to shred, the couple might then begin to experience their quarrels and distrust of each other more exclusively, and lose the strands of their network that bind their day-to-day married life.

Privatization of the Marital Experience. That each couple's story depends not only on the unique circumstances of their own relationship, but also on their interactions with a unique set of people in their social network, led us to realize that our search for universal meanings in stories of marriage would be difficult. We tried to group specific story themes under frequently appearing topics. The first part of this chapter summarized some of those common themes for each substory. Nevertheless, in reviewing that summary, we are aware that it gives no profound insight into the nature of the couples' stories. The problem is, to get topics that appear reasonably frequently, one must collapse across coding categories to such an extent that individual voices are lost. Couples' stories are highly diverse. In no case did we easily emerge with general themes apparent among most couples. Rather, we are now led to conclude that each couple finds its own private meanings through their stories. Certainly, there may be some similarities across some groups of couples, but it would be safer to say that what emerges over the early years of marriage is a privatization of each couple's marital experience—definitely affected by cultural norms and scripts, as we have seen, but psychologically grasped by each couple as their own world, their own consolidation of their daily lives within their own set of circumstances. In that sense, marriage is an intimate experience; each couple must think of their life's story as strictly between them, and perhaps not of much interest to others. As researchers of the narrative, we tried to get a glimpse of those worlds when we asked couples to tell the story of their relationship, and we did see some general features, as noted previously. However, we came away from our search impressed with how much the role of marriage elicited unique, private experiences. Thus, the day-to-day living and remembering in a marriage are part of a private, intimate world.

In rendering that private world through the narrative, certain couples told us about key issues in their lives. In fact, we observed in chapter 6 that some of these key issues were interconnected with couples' levels of happiness in their marriage. We will not repeat all of the findings from chapter 6 here, but we do wish to highlight two particular factors predictive of marital well-being, factors that have not gained much attention from marital researchers using more standard self-reports or behavioral observations.

NARRATIVE FACTORS PREDICTING
MARITAL WELL-BEING

Lack of Commitment. Commitment, or rather the lack thereof, certainly emerged as a key issue in the marriage narratives. Some couples made it clear that they were experiencing a lack of commitment by one or both of the partners in the early phases of their marriage. Such a lack of commitment was a key predictor of problems in their well-being, especially for women. Taken alone, that result is perhaps not earth-shaking, but it is a phenomenon that has been hard to measure except through a storytelling method. We can certainly ask a couple to indicate on a scale how likely it is they think the marriage will last or we can ask them about a given factor that may theoretically contribute to commitment. However, standard measures seem to miss out on the felt experience of commitment, that feeling that one's spouse or one's self is wholly pledged to the marriage. Recall our excerpt from the wife whose mother-in-law worried because the couple usually took separate vehicles and were seldom seen together. The wife insisted that this was simply their style, that they still were "one," and that no problems in the relationship should be inferred. She would probably insist they were highly committed to each other. Our coders, however, readily picked up that commitment was in fact an issue in this couple's story, and this lack of commitment predicted a subsequent drop in marital well-being that the couple themselves may not have seen coming.

Thus, in subtle ways, commitment clearly did emerge as an issue for some couples as they talked about changes in feelings as their courtship or marriage progressed. This is not unlike the phenomena that Surra, Hughes, and Jacquet (1999) focused on even more directly, using a storytelling technique that asks a person to look back and review their entire relationship in terms of ups and downs in the strength of their commitment. There is something about the juxtaposition of an unfolding story that can make apparent to both the teller and the audience the dramatization of a commitment. It might well be only when a person appraises his or her marriage over time, considering the entire story sequence, that a sense of waxing and waning commitment emerges. In many instances, the stories we heard from the couples in our study spoke to that concern.

Whether this is a part of the experience of marriage that occurs readily only when couples are in the early stage of family building is an open question. Our guess is that it can be a concern at any stage of a marriage but becomes especially dominant when families are in the process of being formed. Commitment may become less of an issue when the couples have a longer history together and the length of the marriage itself becomes strong evidence for marital commitment. However, when children have grown and the couple is again placed on its own, we speculate that the story of the relationship for the future may once again raise issues about commitment for the couple.

Wife as Initiator.   The second theme relevant to marital well-being that emerged in our study of narratives, a theme that has not been adequately emphasized in other research, is the general intolerance that most couples had for considering the woman to be the central initiator of the relationship. In telling the story of the courtship, some couples indicated that the woman was the primary initiator and/or the pursuer in getting the courtship off the ground. When that happened, our results suggested that men were unhappy in the marriage. Previous research has suggested that men can feel threatened by women who have greater resources outside of the marriage and, thus, greater say and power at home (Orbuch & Eyster, 1997; Steil & Weltman, 1991). What we uncovered in having couples tell their relationship stories was that this concern extended to questions of who had the upper hand in forming the relationship in the first place.

Our couples' stories were certainly not entirely male-dominated. It was not uncommon for descriptions of the relationship initiation to suggest that both partners played a role and mutually agreed to pursue the relationship. Such an understanding did not appear to be particularly problematic for later well-being. It was far less common for women to take the lead outright, however, and when such a gender-role reversal did occur, it did not speak well for the husband's well-being over time. Indeed, over time some couples seemed to learn not to tell or speak of female initiation. Many of these stories were glossed over, and ended up falling into the common code of being unclear who initiated in Years 3 and 7. It is almost as if some couples became aware over time of the difficulty of speaking about women's active role in couple formation, and to put the marriage on a sound footing, they dropped that understanding from their minds. In those couples who did not, who continued to emphasize the woman's role as initiator, the husband was less happy.

Similarly, we saw in chapter 7 that husbands fared better over time if the early relationship narratives emphasized more agentic themes, and deemphasized communal themes. Men were wary of extreme encroachments on their independence; narratives that relayed a sense of men as initiators, capable of pursuing and attaining their personal goals, predicted higher male well-being.

Our two highlighted findings from chapter 6 were just some of the many results concerning how the marital well-being couples reported was associated with characteristics of the narratives they told. From the pattern of other such results, we have many other clues as to the underpinnings of sound marriages. Two examples are worth highlighting. We found that compared to couples in unhappy marriages, couples in happy marriages harbor more feelings about their wedding and honeymoon in narratives. We also found that happy couples told us comparatively more integrative stories about the future. These characteristics are not necessarily correlated with both husbands' and wives' well-being, but at least with one or the other. Nor were they necessarily correlated with well-being in each of the years the narratives were told. Nevertheless, the results in chapter 6 alerted us to aspects of marriage that are related to marital well-being that may have been overlooked by standard research procedures.

In the next two sections, we briefly highlight how the narratives differed for African-American versus White couples, and for men and women. Again, we gain insights that might not have emerged in a more standard survey procedure.

ETHNICITY AND NARRATIVES

In chapter 9, we brought together various results showing that African-American marriages were different from White marriages in a number of ways, but similar in many others. It is instructive to realize that the larger cultural context can have considerable and identical impact on how both groups experience their marriages. But it also is instructive to realize that the Black–White difference, so important in understanding the socioeconomic picture of our society, also translates to some extent into defining the marital experience differently for the two groups. Our study enabled us to highlight these differences. We discuss two next.

Religion in the Narratives. First, we found that religion played more of a part in how the couples met, how they were married, and how their present life was transacted among the African-Americans than among the Whites. Much social science literature has focused on the importance of the church among African-Americans in stabilizing their communities. It was interesting to see how that force extended to the private experience of marriage as well. White couples also spoke of the importance of religion to them, but far less often than did the Black couples. It is one thing to find on a survey that African-American respondents report attending church more frequently than do White respondents; it is another to see how the importance of religion affects the relationship African-Americans have with their spouses.

Honeymoons. The second ethnic difference in the experience of marriage we wish to highlight is the greater role that the honeymoon played in the White marital experience as compared with the Black marital experience. Many African-American couples skipped the honeymoon section of their story altogether, largely because many did not have a honeymoon to speak of. For many African-American couples, it may be a matter of not having the money to cover both a wedding and a honeymoon. Or, because a much larger number of African-American couples entered their marriages with parental responsibilities, it may be that planning a honeymoon with children to attend to created too many logistical problems.

In any case, most White couples had a honeymoon memory as part of their relationship story, whereas many African-American couples did not. The honeymoon is a key period in the standard cultural story, representing a time when romance blooms and couples can escape for secluded time to focus exclusively on each other. Without this standard period to cement their new marital relationship, African-American couples may have to work harder to maintain their own sense of romance.

GENDER AND NARRATIVES

Women as Keepers of Relationship Memories. Finally, what can we say about the role of gender in the marital experience? By far the most important conclusion we drew in this regard was that wives appeared to be the keepers of the memories of the relationship. They were more affectively engaged in telling the stories of the courtship and the wedding. Furthermore, issues about the courtship and wedding that arose in the couples' stories also affected wives' experience of marital happiness and unhappiness to a much greater extent than they did for their husbands. It is not that marriage is less important for men, but rather, it is the keeping of the memories of marriage that seems to be so important for women and less so for men. Jointly produced stories integrating the couple's history with each other seemed to flow more freely from the minds and words of women, and once produced, stayed carefully guarded by the women. Both husbands and wives certainly participated fully in these relationship stories, but the stories seemed to be owned somewhat more by the wives. It would be interesting to see whether women are similarly elaborative regarding other past personal experiences (Seidlitz & Diener, 1998), or whether the effect is more restricted to memories surrounding a relationship, or more specifically a romantic relationship. For these relationship narratives, however, it is clear that gender played an important role.

SUMMARY

Couples' stories of their marriage were quietly positive, not overly romantic tales that largely outlined their everyday accommodations to each other and their experiences with their social networks. Certain issues, such as a lack of commitment and women as initiators, were key predictors of subsequent difficulties in marital well-being. Gender and ethnicity did shape the narratives to some extent, although there were still many similarities between men's and women's stories, and stories told by both Black and White couples. Overall, we were impressed with the diversity of couples' stories.

Marriage remained a unique experience for each couple, making it difficult to draw broad conclusions from couples' stories that would apply to relationships across the board.

Given this diversity in the stories, can we still extract general lessons about the narrative approach to research? In chapter 11, we address that question.

What Have We Learned About Narratives?

Throughout this volume, we have looked at how the narratives married couples told about their lives together were useful in understanding their relationship. We examined how Year 1 narratives spoke to the experiences of newlyweds, how the narratives changed over time, whether the narratives varied by race and gender, what the narratives told us about different levels of well-being, and how well-being shaped the directions the narratives took over time. When all is said and done, what can we now say we have learned about narratives that we did not know before we began?

We would like to get one matter off our chests right from the beginning, because it reflects our own original naiveté about narratives. We asked couples to tell us the story of their relationship, and fully assumed that a storylike quality would emerge as couples got into the swing of talking about their lives. We went so far as to break the overall story down into chapters, or substories: courtship, wedding, honeymoon, present, and future. We coded each of these substories as if for each, couples would have a separate story to tell. Overall, this assumption seemed to be valid for the courtship and the wedding, but was not as useful for the other sections. We learned what we should have realized from the beginning, that telling a story about something can emerge coherently only when there is a clear timed-sequence structure with a defined beginning, middle, and end. Some narrative researchers even insist narratives must contain such a clear unfolding plot before they are willing to call them "stories." The courtship and the wedding sections, and to some extent the honeymoon section, are aspects of a marriage that fit neatly into this conventional story package. They do in fact have beginnings and endings, and relatively clear paths that one can follow to get from one to the other. Much less conveniently packaged in this way are the present life and future sections of the relationship narrative. For these sections, it is not clear how to define a beginning or an end or how to decide which events should be highlighted. Rather than echoing the tightly packaged fare of standard drama, the present and future sections tended to resemble a postmodern, existentialist play, one in which there is no clear plot line but rather an emphasis on the characters' interactions and their attempts to make sense of their unfolding experiences.

It is not that all couples told us coherent and integrated stories about the courtship or the wedding, or that no couples told us such stories when they talked about the present or the future. In fact, we found that when couples told coherent, integrated stories about the future, it was diagnostic of their feelings about the marriage, just as it was when they told us such stories about the courtship or wedding. Even without a conventional story format, there were still thematic contents, affective reactions, and stylistic characteristics that we could observe in the narratives that were useful for understanding a couple's experience. It is not that there was no information of interest in the present and future stories; it is just that calling them "stories" does not really capture their nature.

For at least some aspects of the relationship narrative, then, we must reach the same conclusions as Edwards and Middleton (1986) did, in their study of joint remembering of movie plots:

> Sequential narrative reconstruction . . . is an available, but not a preferred, frame for joint remembering. The group participants spontaneously preferred to exchange memories of what was best, worst, funny, or incredible—memories based on personal reactions and evaluations which were subjected to social comparison and joint validation. (p. 452)

Likewise, at least in the present and future sections, our participants seemed to find it more natural to focus on their general feelings and reactions to their ongoing experiences, rather than attempting to construct a conventional, chronological story.

For us, then, a narrative approach became a convenient way to speak of being systematically open-ended in covering various aspects of the couple's history together. A "story" in the structural or literary sense of the word may emerge from this kind of inquiry or it may not. A researcher could choose to impose an emergent meaning even when there was mere description. We generally chose not to do that. (See Clandidin & Connelly, 2000, for an excellent discussion of these issues.) That we had the couples initially think in terms of a "story" certainly might have had some benefits. We suspect such a frame was beneficial in releasing respondents from thinking that there were specific right and wrong answers they had to come up with. The standard survey research interview, as open-ended as it might be, brings back memories for many respondents of taking tests, or at least answering teachers' questions in school. Furthermore, the plethora of interesting results that emerged from our use of a narrative approach more than compensates for the initial naive methodological assumption we made that our couples would give us a set of conventional stories.

Given our broader approach to the narratives, one that moved beyond an exclusive focus on narratives as stories, what can we say about our findings that may be useful in thinking about narratives in general? Next, we list some generalizations about narratives that came out of a reconsideration of the findings reported in this volume.

NARRATIVES CAN GIVE INSIGHT INTO CURRENT TENSIONS AND CONCERNS

One of our first conclusions was that even when narratives are not richly plotted, they can still provide insights into respondents' current tensions and concerns. As we said, we began our ventures into narratives influenced by the concepts of stories as the basic verbal outputs that we would code. We expected that the temporal sequences described in the stories would be the major basis of meaning-making in the early years of marriage. We busily set up codes for plot lines, sources of tension, dramatic styles, and the like, as if we had been assigned to analyze a collection of short stories in a literature class. When we quickly discovered that most of our couples' stories were pale versions of our expectations, we had to stop and ask ourselves what we had in fact collected.

We found that, even though our couples' narratives were not quite as storylike as we had anticipated, there were still many qualities of storytelling that proved useful in characterizing our narratives and in giving us insights into marital experiences. Although few of the couples truly dramatized their stories, some did have more dramatic flair than others, and so we could still examine the relative degree of drama unfolding in couples' stories. In some instances, we found this quality useful in thinking about the meaning couples were conveying about their marriages. Women, for instance, tended to have a more dramatic style in telling the couple story than did men. We used this finding to understand gender differences in storytelling.

Furthermore, although few of the couples' stories emerged as tightly woven, coherent plots, we still could reliably detect some basic underlying progressions in the way couples spoke of their courtships or their weddings. We had to be less restrictive in what we meant by a plot, and be willing to accept such ideas as "the general flow of the story" when we trained coders. These "plots" led to interesting characterizations of the couples' experiences with the early events in their lives together. For example, we found that the general flow of the story was quite strongly positive in most of our couples' recollections of their courtships, with little attention paid to any obstacles there might have been to their decision to marry. We speculated that some newlywed couples might need to suppress the investigation of the minor courtship difficulties they undoubtedly experienced.

In some instances, we found the analysis of tensions expressed in the couples' stories helpful. Although a literary analysis would be more finely nuanced, we found that simply coding for *any* source of tension mentioned in the different subsections of the story was useful in understanding marriage. For example, we found that if we could characterize African-American couples' stories about their present life as being free of such tensions, then they were particularly happy in their marriages, as measured in our survey data.

We also found that current concerns and issues can spill back over time and affect the tensions presented in the early relationship stories. For example, an increase in the degree of tensions revealed in early relationship narratives was seen for women who were uncomfortable with conflict in their relationship. The narratives may serve as a relatively subtle barometer of feelings respondents are uncomfortable exploring in a more overt fashion.

NARRATIVES CAN BE PROFITABLY ANALYZED FOR THE SATURATION OF AFFECTS

As well as considering the broader thematic analyses of plot, drama, and tension, we also performed a more fine-grained analysis, investigating every single instance of affects (feelings or needs) expressed in couples' stories. This less qualitative approach to narratives paid off, in that the affect coding scheme yielded many *quantitative* results that gave us new insights about couples' *qualitative* experience of their relationship. For example, we found that the number of positive affects far surpassed the number of negative affects, suggesting that couples on the whole experience their marriage quite positively.

We learned that couples did not always signal areas of current concern with an emphasis on negative feelings. Instead, a more subtle elevation of any kind of affect, positive or negative, indicated a focal area for the couple. Occasionally, this focus was on particularly positive events that the couple was savoring; more often, such an affective focus drew attention to problem areas for the couple. Couples were not engaging in extensive use of negative affect, but their overall affective tone was still diagnostic.

In thinking about the narrative task we set for our couples, we realized that it was a story to be told to a stranger by both husband and wife. It makes sense to us now, after the fact, that there would be few overt displays of negative affect. Most couples would want to project a public image of coping, being resilient, having good cheer about what has been happening to them, and being optimistic about the future. In making such assertions, we are perhaps reflecting an American bias for projecting oneself as a stalwart, uncomplaining person, but we suspect it is more widespread. For most couples, this public, relatively formal sphere would not be seen as an appropriate place for unburdening their deepest hurts and fears. They might expose such vulnerabilities to a confidant or to a therapist, but not to a stranger or even to an acquaintance. Instead, these public narratives about a presumably mutual choice to marry would tend to be replete with justifications for why that voluntary decision was a good one. So too, we suspect, would narratives about men and women launched into careers and occupations that they voluntarily pursued. For public display, couples tended to emphasize their role as free agents who made good decisions and were content with their current circumstances. Nevertheless, we still think the couples revealed their lives in meaningful ways. Even if there was an overall positive spin, there was still sufficient variability in style and content to allow meaningful understandings of couples' relative degree of satisfaction with their relationship.

Not all narratives are about freely chosen, relatively positive events, such as our couples' marriage stories. Some narratives center on terrible circumstances like abuse, oppression, accidents, or illness. When narratives center on such negative and unexpected events, we would assert that the situation permits storytellers to let their negative feelings and vulnerabilities all hang out, even to strangers. It is revealing that many past studies using narrative techniques dealt with such matters (e.g., Harvey, Weber, & Orbuch, 1990), with random negative occurrences that cry out for accounts to allow some sense to be made of apparently senseless events. It is no wonder that we and other researchers have often thought of narratives as people's searches for meaning. When the valence is positive and the circumstances are freely chosen, the search for meaning is nowhere near as intense.

NARRATIVES CAN REFLECT THE MEANING OF EVERYDAY LIFE

When we laid out the functions of narratives in chapter 2, we emphasized the role that narratives are thought to play in helping storytellers communicate meaning to themselves and to their audience. We still stand by that way of thinking about narratives, but having seen the results of our research, we now realize that we must expand the notion of meaning. It not only encompasses a highly motivated search to understand exceptional circumstances. It also includes a mature, quiet acceptance of the facets of everyday experience. We found our couples' narratives focused on the more prosaic routines of marriage, not only in how newlyweds adjusted to each other, but also in such matters as the day-by-day experience of courting and being courted, and in the details of planning for a wedding. These pictures of the couples' experiences did not stand out in any dramatic way, and they might not mean much immediately to the audience who hears them. However, one cannot help but notice when listening to the narratives that it is this quiet everyday accommodation that means a lot to the couple. Listen to Jake describe his everyday feelings about his relationship with Alisha:

> She's real good with the kids. When I come home, there's a house here. When there's money to be spent on taking care of the necessities, that doesn't equate into buy all the dresses you can now, and wonder about the electricity later. These necessities, you know, the necessities are taken care of. And you look for that in a mate, because you're trying to deal with something together, not get close with somebody who is steadily wrecking everything.

Jake went on to talk about the pleasures of understanding another person's idiosyncrasies well: "Besides, I know when she's ticked off. [With somebody else], I'd have to figure it out all over again." It is these everyday pleasures, of knowing you can rely on another person, of knowing how to read that other person's mood and feelings, of knowing that other person will help you get through everyday trials and tribulations, that seem to form the heart of the meaning our couples make of their relationship together. We looked for the dramatic in our coding, but we tended to ignore the way mundane details reflected the fabric of many couples' lives together.

We became particularly aware of the importance of these more pragmatic themes after we saw that the more dramatic, and on the surface more romantic, depictions of the courtships were not the way many of the happiest couples presented their courtship. Rather, it was those couples who talked about one thing leading to another, without the romantic illusions, who reported they were the happiest.

Even more revealing was the way that the quality of the narratives changed from Year 1 through Year 7, becoming more and more everyday and less rife with tensions. It was as if the period of adjustment was over. In a well-functioning marriage, couples by Year 7 had more to say about everyday life than about major problems or underlying difficulties. As John put it: "You get married, you have kids, you raise them. I don't plan on being no rock star." That is wise advice. Rock stars are not known for their domestic contentment; our couples' quietly positive lives and stories may not make the cover of *Rolling Stone*, but they do seem to make them happy.

There is a lesson to be learned in all this. Narratives can speak to the everyday lives of people, which could be ignored if we focus only on the dramatic. We would liken it to the phenomenon often experienced in families looking over old photographs. Although the carefully posed and perfectly framed "good pictures" exhibited in albums are pleasant and nostalgic to look at years later, it is often the more careless "rejects" found in a shoe box that speak so vividly of life around the family: the dirty dishes, the casual clothes, the people engaged in conversation. These pictures may not appear to be the best ones at first glance, but they mean a lot to those involved. Furthermore, a sensitive outsider who took the time to consider those images carefully might gain a great deal of insight into that family. Likewise, it takes great skill as a researcher to attend to the mundane, everyday points of experience and magnify them for scrutiny. Some good short story writers do just that. We would assume good narrative researchers can offer similar insights, if they use the proper filters to present the words and ideas that come forth in their audiorecordings.

NARRATIVES CAN BRING YOU CLOSE
TO THE UNDERSTANDING OF PRIVATE WORLDS

It could very well be that what we take to be the everyday pragmatic unfolding of a relationship story has more explicit meaning to the couple than we know how to code. In chapter 2, we spoke of the interpersonal and personal levels of meaning that can influence and shape narratives. Couples can have their own understanding of seemingly trivial events: a cross word that is blown out of proportion, a forgotten item to be purchased at the supermarket, a gesture of understanding at an anxious moment. None of these would emerge as particularly laden with drama or tension in our standard coding schemes, but to the couple or individual, these minor details might communicate much.

Sometimes these subtle personal meanings can be implicitly recognized by the audience. As we noted in comparing the stories across years, clear themes and commonalities emerged for each couple across time. The same basic anecdotes are often relayed each year, but the amount of detail, elaboration, and affective tone may vary. Listening to the narratives, we often caught a glimpse from the overall tone of the affects expressed how the couple might be feeling at an implicit level. The full explicit meaning of these episodes, however, is generally lost on a third party. Narrative researchers must train themselves to listen for these meaningful private sequences.

These private worlds become difficult to translate into quantitative codes of the kind that we created for our study. Perhaps the meanings emerging from this private world can be grouped together with a few others as exemplars of some quality of the narrative proposed by the researcher. More likely, however, they cannot, and then the analysis of the narrative has to be a procedure nothing short of quoting the exact wordings of the relevant portions of the narrative that the researcher suspects convey a private meaning. And even then, a further inquiry by the researcher as to what precisely that quote meant to the storyteller seems called for.

This careful and detailed scrutiny of individual stories is a legitimate procedure used by many narrative researchers. It is probably the best available approach to allow these private meanings to emerge. It is certainly a far cry from the more quantitative analyses we used in our research, in which we relied on grouping characteristics together in abstract codes that could be evaluated by a group of coders with high levels of agreement. Such coding required the assumption that there was a commonality in the meaning of certain narratives, allowing them to be profitably grouped together. We think this approach has merit, and it has allowed us to draw some general conclusions about marriage and narratives. However, having listened to our couples' voices, we must acknowledge that our approach at times misses something crucial. It may well be that, fundamentally, the most private meanings of one couple can never be grouped together with the private meanings of another couple. Hence, there should be room in the investigation of meaning in narratives for both the systematic, quantitative approach we have generally used and the more nuanced, qualitative approach of which we have made only sporadic use.

LIFE COURSE ISSUES IN NARRATIVES

The emergence of private meanings helps to explain one critical pattern of findings in our research. Our study is one of the few to investigate the same individuals' narratives across time. We saw that over the years, as the couples moved from newlyweds to established married couples, their narratives began to follow a less coherent storyline. They became shorter, more descriptive, more lacking in tensions, and less reflective of common themes. We have discussed some pragmatic reasons why we may see this pattern. By Year 7, some couples may have not wanted to be repetitive, and some couples may have been caught up in the fact that there was not much change in their circumstances on which to base a more meaningful story.

More compelling to us, however, was an argument that as a marriage progresses, the tensions of adjustment and working out the married role subside. Rather than being caught up in examining what it means to be a married couple, our participants focused more on living the day-to-day circumstances of married life, even removing any strong emphasis on the future transitions to come. We argued that by Year 7, the couples began to lose a narrative structure of moving toward a goal or of overcoming some basic tension prominent in a more transitional period. Their narratives became attenuated.

We bring this up here to suggest that by Year 7, couples in their narratives might reveal very private worlds as they live them from day to day. But outside of this private everyday understanding, which may or may not be apparent to the researcher, narratives by Year 7 seem less revealing about common dynamic problems faced in daily married life. Perhaps when new transitions occur, such as wives deciding to re-enter the labor force, children going to school full-time, or mature children growing up and leaving home, some new dynamism might engage more common and less private narrative structures again.

Our research certainly supports the idea that narratives may mean different things when told at different points in a person's life. The very same story may serve different functions at different points of the life course. We were struck by this phenomenon when we saw that a well-formed story of the honeymoon told by a couple in the third year of their marriage had very different meanings about the state of their marriage than a very similar story of the honeymoon told in Year 7. In Year 3, coherent honeymoon stories seemed to reflect the radiated glow of women's happy feelings about their marriages, but by Year 7, equally elaborate stories seemed to reflect a nostalgic reminiscence of better times by less-happy wives. Thus, we see how even the same story may have different meanings, depending on the storytellers' current situation or life course stage.

In contrast, we saw that wives who consistently sought to minimize expressions of conflict in their relationship dealt with this issue in different ways at different points in time. Over the shorter term, wives who disliked conflict appeared to purge their narratives of any signs of disagreements. Over longer periods of time, however, this strategy did not seem to work. Over time, conflicts and tensions seemed to creep back in, to the point where those who disliked conflict actually reported having experienced more tensions than those who were more accepting of conflict. The same story may have different meanings at two points in time; the same current needs and concerns might lead to different stories at two points in time. We thus urge narrative researchers to carefully take into account the current life circumstances and life course issues of their storytellers if they wish to obtain nuanced insights into their stories.

NARRATIVES AS BAROMETERS OF STORYTELLERS' EMOTIONAL LIVES

Such nuanced insights can indeed be complex at times. For example, in our web of results we found that sometimes the strong expression of feelings in narratives reflected positive attitudes toward marriage, whereas at other times it appeared to reflect ongoing problems and concerns. In both cases, emotionality in the narratives seemed to reflect the couples' current strong emotions about their relationship, but it was difficult to develop a handle on understanding when the narratives would show positive emotions, and when negative emotions. There seemed to be no one-to-one correspondence between the appearance of positive feelings in a narrative and having positive feelings about the marriage, nor between the appearance of negative feelings in a narrative and having negative feelings about the marriage.

Although we were surprised by these results, we tried to make post hoc sense of the pattern and emerged with a complex insight. We made sense of the findings by considering that being able to own up to negative feelings may be a necessary part of a happy marriage. Likewise, trying to consider the nature and sources of positive feelings can be part of attempting to master a problematic marriage. We see a similar trend in another type of narrative research. Research by McClelland and his students, scoring stories people told in response to pictures for motives of achievement, affiliation, power, and intimacy (see Smith, 1992), showed a parallel phenomenon. High intensity of motivation in that research came from coding both positive and negative affective states mentioned in the stories. It did not appear that the direction of the affect was especially diagnostic of high motivation. What was diagnostic was the dominance of highly charged feelings, whether positive or negative. Affects in narratives seemed to be good guides to the emotional involvements of people in a particular domain but not to their specific history of success or failure within that domain. We conclude the same effect is going on in our couples' narratives: High affectivity is a signal of a focal area of concern, but whether the couple is coping well or poorly in that area is not always indicated. We would speculate that the same effect would occur in any narrative carefully analyzed for affects.

NARRATIVES IN DIFFERENT DOMAINS

The final phenomenon we wish to highlight in our summary of what we have learned about narratives came out of our analysis of gender differences in the narratives. Through our analyses, we came to the conclusion that a relationship story like the one used in our research was largely the domain of women. Other research seems to back up this interpretation. Such a view of narratives as having a domain, which may be more or less central to a given storyteller, should be kept in mind when interpreting any narratives. It is one thing to ask a husband about the story of his marriage, the major execution of which he might defer to his wife, especially if they tell the story together. It would be another thing to ask the same husband about the story of his professional life, even if his wife were involved in help-ing with the story. The work story might more clearly be the husband's do-main, and the gender differences we discovered in the marriage stories might wither.

Recall, for example, that women tended to correct the details of men's relationship memories and the husbands largely deferred to the wives' point of view. Contrast that general finding to this sequence seen in Angie and Chris's Year 7 story:

A: You were assistant manager then. You became . . . you were the assistant manager.

C: No, not yet.

A: Not yet?

C: Not yet.

A: Oh, okay.

Here, we see a clear reversal of the general finding, one where the male is the one who confidently corrects the female's recall and is deferred to. The lesson is that researchers should remain alert to the specific domain of the stories they ask people to create. The relative importance of that do-main to the identity of the storyteller would be important to know. The ability to mold a story that resonates with a storyteller's sense of identity is important, as we saw in the finding that those males who participated in more agentic, less communal stories over time were more satisfied. Even more critical for researchers to attend to, however, would be the relative responsibility a particular person might take for creating meaning in that domain. When a given individual "owns" a particular narrative, aspects of that narrative are likely to provide clearer insights into his or her overall feelings and adjustments, as compared to when he or she is largely follow-ing the other's lead.

SUMMARY

This was an exciting research venture for us. This book is our narrative, or story, of these couples' married lives as told to us through a narrative ap-proach. As survey researchers, we delighted in the chutzpah of inserting a complex narrative procedure into a standard survey setting. True, this de-manded that we make some compromises with our usual interviewing tech-niques in order to guarantee uniformities in interviewing styles. It de-manded that we carefully train our interviewers not to guide the couples' stories in specific directions. It demanded that we work hard at building coding schemes that could do some justice to the rich material emerging from the narratives that couples gave us about their lives. Results were definitely long in coming, especially given the challenges of establishing and maintaining agreement across large numbers of coders.

And yet we would cheerfully say (reconstructing our narratives in retrospect, no doubt) that it was all worth it. The results we found about couples in the throes of the early years of marriage yielded important insights about both marriage and the narrative technique. We look forward to the development of similar narrative approaches to the study of experiences people have during other important transitions in their lives, besides marriage. For example, in Year 7 we collected stories of the birth of the couples' children. We have not touched on those stories here, but they also offer a fascinating glimpse into our couples' lives at a time of high emotion and great change.

We also look forward to a narrative accounting of what happens to marriages as they move out of the early years and into the new demands couples face as they and their children get older. As this book was being written, we were heading into the field to interview these same couples again, now in their 16th year of marriage, which we call the *early middle years of marriage.* They are becoming more established in their careers, their children are growing up, and some are tackling the challenge of parenting teenagers. These couples' lives go on, and there is nothing we enjoy more than continuing to gain glimpses into their private worlds.

References

Acitelli, L. K., & Young, A. M. (1996). Gender and thought in relationships. In G. J. O. Fletcher & J. Fitness (Eds.), *Knowledge structures in close relationships: A social psychological approach* (pp. 147–168). Mahwah, NJ: Lawrence Erlbaum Associates.

Adler, A. (1917). *Neurotic constitution.* New York: Moffat, Ward.

Bartlett, F. C. (1932). *Remembering.* Cambridge, England: Cambridge University Press.

Belenky, M., Clinchy, B., Goldberger, N., & Tarule, J. (1986). *Women's ways of knowing.* New York: Basic Books.

Berger, P. L., & Kellner, H. (1964). Marriage and the construction of social reality. *Diogenes, 46,* 1–23.

Bernard, J. (1972). *The future of marriage.* New York: Bantam.

Blumer, H. (1969). *Symbolic interactionism, perspective and method.* Paramus, NJ: Prentice-Hall.

Bradbury, T. N. (1998). *The developmental course of marital dysfunction.* New York: Cambridge University Press.

Bradbury, T. N., & Fincham, F. D. (1992). Attributions and behavior in marital interaction. *Journal of Personality and Social Psychology, 63*(4), 613–628.

Braithwaite, D. O., Olson, L. N., Golish, T. D., Soukup, C., & Turman, P. (2001). "Becoming a family": Developmental processes represented in blended family discourse. *Journal of Applied Communication Research, 29*(3), 221–247.

Brody, L. R., & Hall, J. A. (1993). Gender and emotion. In M. Lewis & J. M. Haviland (Eds.), *Handbook of emotions* (pp. 447–460). New York: Guilford.

Bruner, J. (1986). *Actual minds, possible worlds.* Cambridge, MA: Harvard University Press.

Bruner, J. (1990). *Acts of meaning.* Cambridge, MA: Harvard University Press.

Cartensen, L. L., Gottman, J. M., & Levenson, R. W. (1995). Emotional behavior in a long-term marriage. *Psychology and Aging, 10,* 140–149.

Chadiha, L., Veroff, J., & Leber, D. (1998). Newlyweds' narrative themes: Meaning in the first year of marriage for African American and White couples. *Journal of Comparative Family Studies, 29*(1), 115–130.

Clandidin, D. J., & Connelly, F. M. (2000). *Narrative inquiry: Experience and story in qualitative research.* San Francisco: Jossey-Bass.

Cooley, C. H. (1902). *Human nature and the social order.* Temecula, CA: Best Books.

Cross, S. E., & Madson, L. (1997). Models of the self: Self-construals and gender. *Psychological Bulletin, 122*(1), 5–37.

Duck, S., Pond, K., & Leatham, G. (1991, July). *Remembering as a context for being in relationships: Different perspectives on the same interaction.* Paper presented at the meeting of the International Network on Personal Relationships, Normal, IL.

Duck, S. W. (1982). A topography of relationship disengagement and dissolution. In S. W. Duck (Ed.), *Personal relationships 4: Dissolving personal relationships* (pp. 1–30). London: Academic Press.

Edwards, D., & Middleton, D. (1986). Joint remembering: Constructing an account of shared experience through conversational discourse. *Discourse Processes, 9,* 423–459.

Frankl, V. E. (1963). *Man's search for meaning: An introduction to logotherapy.* Boston: Beacon Press.

Franks, M. M., Herzog, A. R., Holmberg, D., & Markus, H. R. (2002). *Self-complexity: Linking age and education with self-rated health and depression.* Manuscript submitted for publication.

Gergen, K. J., & Gergen, M. M. (1987). Narratives of relationships. In R. Burnett, P. McGhee, & D. Clarke (Eds.), *Accounting for relationships* (pp. 269–288). New York: Methuen.

Ginsburg, G. P. (1988). Rules, scripts and prototypes in personal relationships. In S. W. Duck (Ed.), *Handbook of personal relationships* (pp. 23–39). New York: Wiley.

Goffman, E. (1959). *The presentation of self in everyday life.* Garden City, NY: Doubleday-Anchor.

Goffman, E. (1971). *Relations in public.* New York: Basic Books.

Gottman, J., Markman, H., & Notarius, C. (1977). The topography of marital conflict: A sequential analysis of verbal and nonverbal behavior. *Journal of Marriage and the Family, 39*(3), 461–477.

Gottman, J. M. (1994). *What predicts divorce? The relationships between marital process and marital outcomes.* Hillsdale, NJ: Lawrence Erlbaum Associates.

Gottman, J. M. (2002). *The relationship cure: A five-step guide to strengthening your marriage, family, and friendships.* New York: Harmony Books.

Gottman, J. M., & Levenson, R. W. (1992). Marital processes predictive of later dissolution: Behavior, physiology, and health. *Journal of Personality & Social Psychology, 63*(2), 221–233.

Grote, N. K., & Frieze, I. H. (1998). "Remembrance of things past": Perceptions of marital love from its beginnings to the present. *Journal of Social and Personal Relationships, 15*(1), 91–109.

Haden, C., Haine, R., & Fivush, R. (1997). Developing narrative structure in parent-child reminiscing across the preschool years. *Developmental Psychology, 33*(2), 295–307.

Hall, J. A., & Halberstadt, A. G. (1994). "Subordination" and sensitivity to nonverbal cues: A study of married working women. *Sex Roles, 31*(3–4), 149–165.

Harvey, J. H., Hendrick, S. S., & Tucker, K. (1988). Self-report methods in studying personal relationships. In S. Duck, D. F. Hay, S. E. Hobfoll, W. Ickes, & B. M. Montgomery (Eds.), *Handbook of personal relationships: Theory, research and interventions* (pp. 99–113). New York: Wiley.

Harvey, J. H., Weber, A. L., & Orbuch, T. L. (1990). *Interpersonal accounts.* Oxford, England: Blackwell.

Heath, S. B. (1994). The project of learning from the inner-city youth perspective. In F. A. Villarruel & R. M. Lerner (Eds.), *Promoting community-based programs for socialization and learning. New directions for child development, No. 63: The Jossey-Bass education series* (pp. 25–34). San Francisco: Jossey-Bass.

Heider, F. (1983). *The psychology of interpersonal relations.* Hillsdale, NJ: Lawrence Erlbaum Associates. (Original work published 1958)

Holmberg, D. (1998, May). *You must remember this: Gender differences in relationship memories and their implications.* Poster presented at the meeting of the American Psychological Society, Washington, DC.

Holmberg, D., & Cameron, T. (1997, July). *What's involved in "happily ever after"? Scripts for married life in married and dating individuals.* Paper presented at the meeting of the International Network on Personal Relationships, Oxford, OH.

Holmberg, D., & Holmes, J. G. (1994). Reconstruction of relationship memories: A mental models approach. In N. Schwarz & S. Sudman (Eds.), *Autobiographical memory and the validity of retrospective reports* (pp. 267–288). New York: Springer-Verlag.

Holmberg, D., & Mackenzie, S. (2002). So far, so good: Scripts for romantic relationship development as predictors of relational well-being. *Journal of Social & Personal Relationships, 19*, 769–788.

Holmberg, D., & Veroff, J. (1996). Rewriting relationship memories: The effects of courtship and wedding scripts. In G. J. O. Fletcher & J. Fitness (Eds.), *Knowledge structures in close relationships: A social psychological approach* (pp. 345–368). Mahwah, NJ: Lawrence Erlbaum Associates.

Huston, T. L., & Chorost, A. F. (1994). Behavioral buffers on the effect of negativity on marital satisfaction: A longitudinal study. *Personal Relationships, 1*(3), 223–239.

Hyde, J. S., & Linn, M. C. (1988). Gender differences in verbal ability: A meta-analysis. *Psychological Bulletin, 104*(1), 53–69.

Josselson, R. (1995). Imagining the real: Empathy, narrative and the dialogic self. In A. Lieblich (Ed.), *The narrative study of lives: Vol. 3. Interpreting experience* (pp. 27–44). Thousand Oaks, CA: Sage.

Josselson, R. (1996). *Revisiting herself: The story of women's identity from college to midlife.* New York: Oxford University Press.

Karney, B. R., & Bradbury, T. N. (1995). The longitudinal course of marital quality and stability: A review of theory, methods and research. *Psychological Bulletin, 118*(1), 3–34.

Karney, B. R., & Coombs, R. H. (2000). Memory bias in long-term close relationships: Consistency or improvement? *Personality and Social Psychology Bulletin, 26*(8), 959–970.

Karney, B. R., & Frye, N. E. (2002). "But we've been getting better lately": Comparing prospective and retrospective views of relationship development. *Journal of Personality & Social Psychology, 82*(2), 222–238.

Kemper, S. (1990). Adults' diaries: Changes made to written narratives across the life span. *Discourse Processes, 13*, 207–223.

Kids & Marriage. (n.d.). Retrieved June 13, 2002, from the World Wide Web: http://www.butlerwebs.com/marriage/kidsandmarriage.htm.

Kochman, T. (1981). *Black and white styles in conflict.* Chicago: University of Chicago Press.

Krech, D., & Crutchfield, R. S. (1948). *Theory and problems of social psychology.* New York: McGraw-Hill.

Lieblich, A., Tuval-Maschiach, R., & Zilber, T. (1998). *Narrative research.* Thousand Oaks, CA: Sage.

Maines, D. (1993). Narrative's moment and sociology's phenomena: Toward a narrative sociology. *Sociological Quarterly, 34*(1), 17–38.

Maines, D. (2001). *The faultline of consciousness: A view of interactionism in sociology.* Hawthorne, NY: Aldine de Gruyter.

Majors, R., & Billson, J. M. (1992). *Cool pose: The dilemmas of Black manhood in America.* New York: Simon & Schuster.

Markman, H. J. (1991). Constructive marital conflict is NOT an oxymoron. *Behavioral Assessment, 13*(1), 83–96.

McAdams, D. P. (1985). *Power, intimacy and the life story: Personological inquiries into identity.* New York: Guilford.

McFarland, C., & Ross, M. (1987). The relation between current impressions and memories of self and dating partners. *Personality and Social Psychology Bulletin, 13*, 228–238.

Mead, G. H. (1934). *Mind, self, and society, from the standpoint of a social behaviorist.* Chicago: University of Chicago Press

Mishler, E. G. (1995). Models of narrative analysis: A typology. *Journal of Narrative & Life History, 5,* 87–123.

Nolen-Hoeksema, S., & Jackson, B. (2001). Mediators of the gender difference in rumination. *Psychology of Women Quarterly, 25,* 37–47.

Nolen-Hoeksema, S., Larson, J., & Grayson, C. (1999). Explaining the gender difference in depressive symptoms. *Journal of Personality & Social Psychology, 77,* 1061–1072.

Norton, A. J., & Miller, L. F. (1992). *Marriage, divorce, and remarriage in the 1990's* (Current Population Reports P23-180). Washington, DC: U.S. Government Printing Office, U.S. Bureau of the Census.

Ochberg, R. L. (1994). Life stories and storied lives. In A. Lieblich & R. Josselson (Eds.), *The narrative study of lives: Vol. 2. Exploring identity and gender* (pp. 113–144). Thousand Oaks, CA: Sage.

Ong, W. (1982). *Orality and literacy.* New York: Norton.

Orbuch, T. L. (1997). People's accounts count: The sociology of accounts. *Annual Review of Sociology, 23,* 455–478.

Orbuch, T. L., & Eyster, S. (1996). *The social context of story-telling: The emergence of meaning for self and couple.* Paper presented at the annual meeting of the International Society for the Study of Personal Relationships, Banff, Alberta, Canada.

Orbuch, T. L., & Eyster, S. (1997). Division of household labor among Black couples and White couples. *Social Forces, 76*(1), 301–322.

Orbuch, T. L., House, J. S., Mero, R. P., & Webster, P. S. (1996). Marital quality over the lifecourse. *Social Psychology Quarterly, 59,* 162–171.

Orbuch, T. L., Veroff, J., Hassan, H., & Horrocks, J. (2002). Who will divorce: A 14-year longitudinal study of Black couples and White couples. *Journal of Social & Personal Relationships, 19,* 171–202.

Orbuch, T. L., Veroff, J., & Holmberg, D. (1993). Becoming a married couple: The emergence of meaning in the first years of marriage. *Journal of Marriage & the Family, 55*(4), 815–826.

Pennebaker, J. W., & Harber, K. D. (1993). A social stage model of collective coping: The Loma Prieta earthquake and the Persian Gulf War. *Journal of Social Issues, 49*(4), 125–145.

Pennebaker, J. W., & Seagal, J. D. (1999). Forming a story: The health benefits of narrative. *Journal of Clinical Psychology, 55*(10), 1243–1254.

Plechaty, M. (1987). Perceptual comparisons of five attitudes among satisfied and unsatisfied couples. *Psychological Reports, 61,* 527–537.

Porter, S., Birt, A. R., Yuille, J. C., & Lehman, D. R. (2000). Negotiating false memories: Interviewer and rememberer characteristics relate to memory distortion. *Psychological Science, 11*(6), 507–510.

Reese, E., Haden, C. A., & Fivush, R. (1996). Mothers, fathers, daughters, sons: Gender differences in autobiographical reminiscing. *Research on Language and Social Interaction, 29*(1), 27–56.

Roosevelt, E. (1992). *The autobiography of Eleanor Roosevelt.* New York: Da Capo Press.

Ross, M., & Holmberg, D. (1992). Are wives' memories for events in relationships more vivid than their husbands' memories? *Journal of Social & Personal Relationships, 9*(4), 585–604.

Schmolck, H., Buffalo, E. A., & Squire, L. R. (2000). Memory distortions develop over time: Recollections of the O.J. Simpson trial verdict after 15 and 32 months. *Psychological Science, 11*(1), 39–45.

Scott, M. B., & Lyman, S. M. (1968). Paranoia, homosexuality and game theory. *Journal of Health & Social Behavior, 9*(3), 179–187.

Seidlitz, L., & Diener, E. (1998). Sex differences in the recall of affective experiences. *Journal of Personality and Social Psychology, 74*(1), 262–271.

Sillars, A. L., Weisberg, J., Burggraf, C. S., & Zietlow, P. H. (1990). Communication and misunderstanding revisited: Married couples' understanding and recall of conversations. *Communication Research, 17*(4), 500–522.

Singer, J. D. (1998). Using SAS PROC MIXED to fit multilevel models, hierarchical models, and individual growth models. *Journal of Educational and Behavioral Statistics, 24*(4), 323–355.

Smith, C. (1992). *Motivation and personality: Handbook of thematic content analysis.* New York: Cambridge University Press.

Sorrentino, R. M., Holmes, J. G., Hanna, S. E., & Sharp, A. (1995). Uncertainty orientation and trust in close relationships: Individual differences in cognitive styles. *Journal of Personality & Social Psychology, 68*(2), 314–327.

Spence, D. (1982). *Narrative truth and historical truth: Meaning and interpretation in psychoanalysis.* New York: Norton.

Sprecher, S. (1999). "I love you more today than yesterday": Romantic partners' perceptions of changes in love and related affect over time. *Journal of Personality & Social Psychology, 76,* 46–53.

Steil, J.M., & Weltman, K. (1991). Marital inequality: The importance of resources, personal attributes, and social norms on career valuing and the allocation of domestic responsibilities. *Sex Roles, 24,* 161–179.

Stryker, S. (1981). Symbolic interactionism: Themes and variations. In M. Rosenberg & R. H. Turner (Eds.), *Sociological perspectives on social psychology* (pp. 3–29). New York: Basic Books.

Stryker, S. (1983). Social psychology from the standpoint of a structural symbolic interactionism. In *Advances in experimental social psychology* (Vol. 16, pp. 181–216). New York: Academic Press.

Surra, C. A., Batchelder, M. L., & Hughes, D. K. (1995). Accounts and the demystification of courtship. In M. A. Fitzpatrick & A. L. Vangelisti (Eds.), *Explaining family interactions* (pp. 112–141). Thousand Oaks, CA: Sage.

Surra, C. A., Hughes, D. K., & Jacquet, S. E. (1999). The development of commitment to marriage: A phenomenological approach. In J. M. Adams & W. H. Jones (Eds.), *Handbook of interpersonal commitment and relationship stability: Perspectives on individual differences* (pp. 125–148). New York: Kluwer/Plenum.

Tallman, I., & Riley, A. (1995). *Gender role expectations and couple interactions in newly married couples.* Unpublished manuscript.

Tannen, D. (1990). *You just don't understand me: Women and men in conversation.* New York: Ballantine.

Taylor, S. E., & Brown, J. D. (1988). Illusion and well-being: A social psychological perspective on mental health. *Psychological Bulletin, 103*(2), 193–210.

Veroff, J., Chadiha, L., Leber, D., & Sutherland, L. (1993). Affects and interactions in newlyweds' narratives: Black and White couples compared. *Journal of Narrative and Life History, 3*(4), 361–390.

Veroff, J., Douvan, E., & Hatchett, S. (1995). *Marital instability: A social and behavioral study of the early years.* Westport, CT: Praeger.

Veroff, J., Sutherland, L., Chadiha, L., & Ortega, R. (1993). Predicting marital quality with narrative assessments of marital experience. *Journal of Marriage and the Family, 55,* 326–337.

Wallerstein, J., & Blakeslee, S. (1996). *The good marriage: How and why love lasts.* London: Warner.

Weiss, R. S. (1975). *Marital separation.* New York: Basic Books.

West, C., & Zimmerman, D. H. (1987). Doing gender. *Gender & Society, 1,* 125–151.

White, M., & Epston, D. (1990). *Narrative means to therapeutic ends.* New York: Norton.

Winkielman, P., & Schwarz, N. (2001). How pleasant was your childhood? Beliefs about memory shape inferences from experienced difficulty of recall. *Psychological Science, 12*(2), 176–179.

Wood, J. (1993). *Gendered lives: Communication, gender, and culture.* Belmont, CA: Wadsworth.

Zilber, T. (1998). Using linguistic features of the narrative to recognize and assess its emotional content. In A. Lieblich, R. Tuval-Maschiach, & T. Zilber (Eds.), *Narrative research.* Thousand Oaks, CA: Sage.

Thematic Coding Manual

CODER: Before you begin the narrative coding, listen to the entire tape. Then indicate what you have observed to be a *major issue* of the entire narrative:

1. Finances (including debt; lack of money)
2. Family relations (including in-laws)
3. Work (including unemployment)
4. Pregnancy
5. Children (excluding pregnancy)
6. Education/career
7. Nest building (buying a home; home improvement; setting up a business)
8. Time—allocation of time; balancing time, measuring time (attention to chronology of events)
9. Religion/church
10. Friends/peer relations
11. Couple's relations—positive (general satisfaction with each other, friendship, communication)
12. Couple's relations—negative (general dissatisfaction, etc.)
13. Couple's relations—growth and development (including lack of and reference to self or marriage)
14. Leisure
15. Couple/family relations

179

16. Personal loss (e.g., death, etc.)
17. Personal troubles/problems
97. [Card]
00. No second issue

CODES THAT ARE REPEATED IN EACH SUBSTORY

General approach to Narrative Task

1. Integrated overall story (with plot elaboration or coherence)
2. A story or set of stories with connections
3. A story or set of stories told intermittently
4. Conventionalized continuity in response to questions; descriptions
5. No continuity; mere answering of questions in question–answer format
9. NA
0. Inap: substory not present/inaudible

How dramatic is the story/content?

(Year 1)

1. Dramatic [Card]
2. Somewhat dramatic [Card]
3. Not at all dramatic
9. NA
0. Inap: substory not present

(Years 3 & 7)

1. Dramatic [Card]
2. Not at all dramatic
9. NA
0. Inap: substory not present

How dramatic is the storyteller(s) style? (How much vivacity, articulateness, elaboration, excitement, and enthusiasm is evident?) (FIRST, CODE HUSBAND'S STYLE; NEXT, CODE WIFE'S.)

(Year 1)

1. Dramatic [Card]

   2. Somewhat dramatic [Card]
   3. Not at all dramatic
   4. Husband didn't contribute to story
   5. Wife didn't contribute to story
   9. NA
   0. Inap: substory not present

(Years 3 & 7)

   1. Dramatic [Card]
   2. Not at all dramatic
   3. Husband didn't contribute to the story
   4. Wife didn't contribute to the story
   9. NA
   0. Inap: substory not present

Source of tension in the substory (Code up to 3 *different* mentions. If greater than 3 mentions, prioritize based on emphasis in the story narrative.)

   1. Tension between the husband and wife
   2. Tension between the husband and outside
   3. Tension between wife and outside
   4. Tension between *couple* and outside
   5. Tension does not involve husband or wife
   6. Personal tensions; internal fear, conflict—husband
   7. Personal tensions; internal fear, conflict—wife
   8. Personal tensions; internal fear, conflict—both husband and wife
   9. NA
   0. Inap: no substory, no second tension

How much tension for each source mentioned? (Code up to number of types above.) NOTE: Code in order of sources mentioned.

(Year 1)

   1. A lot
   2. Some
   3. A little
   4. None

9. NA

0. Inap: no tension/type, no story .

(Years 3 & 7)

1. A lot
2. Some
9. NA
0. Inap: no tension/type, no story

How much is the account of the substory a joint product of husband/wife?

1. Collaborative
2. Mostly wife; some husband
3. Mostly husband; some wife
4. All wife
5. All husband
9. NA
0. Inap: substory not present

How much conflict is there between husband/wife regarding the events in the substory?

1. A lot (more than 3)
2. Some (2–3)
3. A little (1)
4. None
9. NA
0. Inap: substory not present

How directive was the interviewer in developing the account of the substory?

1. Very directive (>3)
2. Moderately directive (2–3)
3. Slightly directive (1)
4. Not directive at all
9. NA
0. Inap: substory not present

Is aspect #1, 2, and 3 of the substory true for husband, true for wife, or true for both? (Code separately for each aspect of each substory.)

1. True for husband
2. True for wife
3. True for both
9. NA
0. Inap: substory not present

Is there an overriding theme in the substory?

(Years 3 & 7)

1. Yes [Card]
2. No

CODES THAT DIFFERED FOR EACH SUBSTORY

Codes Specific to Courtship Story

Type of tension for Courtship Story. Code up to number of sources in the *exact order* as above. NOTE: Code what tension is about for each source; code for type in the order of mention(s) above. CARD any combinations for type(s). Note: Can code a type for more than one source.

(Year 1)

1. Deciding about getting married, including premarital jitters
2. Couple relations (past/present relationship(s) to one another, including fights) [Card]
3. Previous relationship(s) of one partner or the other with another person
4. Family (including in-laws)
5. Own children
6. Friends/peers
7. Work/job
8. Money/finances
9. Education/career
10. Substance abuse
11. Separation (including break-ups)
12. Pregnancy/abortion

13. Infidelity
14. Living arrangements/conditions (having to move, distance from work, congestion)
15. Death
70. Pregnancy (12) and death (15)
97. [Card]
00. Inap: no tension, no story, no further mention

(Years 3 & 7)

Couple Relations

1. Deciding about getting married, including premarital jitters
2. Past/present relationship(s) to one another, including fights
3. Separation and reconciliation (mostly break-ups)
4. Separation (e.g., moving for a job, distance by miles, but does not include break-ups)
5. Infidelity by husband
6. Infidelity by wife
7. Interpersonal conflict and resolution
8. Conflict over finances and resolution
9. Conflict—Other and resolution [Card]
10. General personal differences

Role Conflict—Conflict between the demands of two roles

11. Partner role versus work role conflict
12. Partner role versus parent role conflict
13. Parent role versus work role conflict

Children

14. Husband's own children
15. Wife's own children
16. Pregnancy
17. Abortion
18. Childcare
19. Work schedule and childcare conflict

Education/Career

20. Dissatisfaction with work (including unemployment)

21. Lacking education for job wanted
22. Education versus work—making a choice
23. Education versus partner—making a choice
24. Education versus children—making a choice

Money/Finances

25. Not enough money
26. Conflict on how to spend money
27. Spending styles/habits and conflict

Mental Health

28. Bored
29. Loneliness
30. Depression
31. Misery
32. Scared

Physical Health

33. Sickness/illness
34. Death/miscarriage [Card]

Transportation Problems

35. Lack of a car
36. Conflict in schedules over use of a car

Miscellaneous

37. Family of origin/in-laws [Card]
38. Friends/peers [Card whose friends in the situation]
39. Previous relationships of one or both partners
40. Substance abuse
41. Living arrangements/living conditions
97. [Card]
99. NA
00. Inap: no tension, no story, no second tension, no third tension

Types of Courtship themes in couple narratives

A major judgment is whether or not the overall flow of the narrative regarding the acquaintance–involvement–decision to marry–wedding sequence is:

1. A general augmentation of positive experiences—*Romantic Augmentation*
2. Overcoming negative situation—*Romantic Relief*
3. Neutral non-feeling sequence—*Pragmatic*

Determine what you think are the *three main aspects* of the Courtship story and then code them accordingly. NOTE: More than one subcategory may be coded within a major category. Code up to 3 mentions. Mentions may fall into one or more categories.

Romantic Augmentation (enhancement of a continuously positive sequence)

11. Childhood sweethearts (e.g., dated through h.s., jr. high)
12. Love at first sight (e.g., saw him/her and knew instantly they were meant for each other)
13. Evolving out of friendship (e.g., first friends and then later became a couple)
14. Spiritual destiny (e.g., religious overtones; strong faith/belief)
15. Male in pursuit
16. Female in pursuit
17. Other [Card]
18. General positive progression (no major theme other than the entire sequence being positive)

Romantic Relief (overcoming negative situation)

20. Relief from personal obstacles/loss (e.g., death or other personal loss, sickness, one or the other experiences trouble/loss and relationship helps them to overcome)
21. Male in pursuit
22. Female in pursuit
23. Obstacles from parents (e.g., interference from one or both parents)

24. Physical separation (e.g., break-ups, absence from each other through voluntary or involuntary means, dominant quality is moving apart and getting back together)

25. Shared troubles (e.g., both experience a problem and share in it)

26. Obstacles/rebound from previous relationship(s) of one or both (e.g., one or both had a previous relationship which they overcame in becoming a couple)

27. Boredom relief (e.g., one or both become bored with a previous partner/life)

28. Relationship righting itself (e.g., a stormy, turbulent, cyclical relationship from start to end of courtship; may include 24, but dominant qualities are the adjectives above)

29. Other [Card]

Pragmatic (neutral, non-feeling sequence)

31. Settling down (does not include negative obstacles)

32. Just the next logical step

33. Would make a good parent

34. Pressure from others

35. Pregnancy or children

36. Evolving out of contact (includes work and social contexts)

37. Would make good mate(s) (e.g., compatibility)

39. Other [Card]

99. NA

00. Inap: no courtship story; no second/third aspect

Did any of these issues arise in the courtship story?

NOTE: If more than four mentions, code in order of priority for first four mentions.

1. Parental involvement—High Priority

2. Pregnancy—High Priority

3. Living arrangement—cohabitation

4. Living arrangement—housing

5. Property

6. Finances

7. Work (including unemployment)/job—High Priority

8. Education/career

9. Religion—differences—High Priority
10. Religion—other—High Priority
11. Hassles, frustration—Low Priority
12. Lack of commitment to the relationship—husband—High Priority
13. Lack of commitment to the relationship—wife—High Priority
97. [Card]
00. No courtship story

The Marriage Proposal

1. Both agreed; couple discussed or implicit agreement (e.g., couple lived together and "we talked," "we decided to get married")
2. Husband proposed on own initiative
3. Wife proposed on own initiative
4. Husband proposed on wife's prompting
5. Husband proposed on someone else's prompting
6. Husband proposed; wife rejected but later agreed
8. Other [Card]
9. NA: no discussion of proposal; unclear about proposal
0. No courtship narrative

Primary initiator(s) in starting the courtship (Who pursued the course of establishing the relationship?)

1. Husband was initiator
2. Wife was initiator
3. Both agreed to start (NOTE: Can be implicit agreement, if clearly observed)
4. Husband initiated, wife rejected but later agreed
5. Wife initiated, husband rejected but later agreed
6. Husband's family initiated
7. Wife's family initiated
8. Friends initiated
9. Ambiguous—can't tell [Card]
97. [Card]
00. Inap: no courtship narrative

Social-spatial context in which courtship took place. (Code the major place of courtship interaction—code up to 2 mentions)

1. Workplace
2. School (high school, college, other educational setting)
3. Church or other religious setting
4. Social setting (bar, club, organization, hangouts, movies, vacation, travel, shopping site)
5. Residential (neighborhood, home)
7. Other [Card]
9. NA

Whose workplace?

1. Husband's
2. Wife's
3. Both
9. Can't ascertain
0. Inap: No workplace coded, no courtship story

Codes Specific to Wedding Story

Type of tension for source (Code up to number of sources noted earlier).

(*Year 1*)

1. Wedding arrangements—(involvement of other people)
2. Wedding arrangements—(nature of ritual, size, type of ceremony, etc.)
3. Family of origin/in-laws
4. Children
5. Friends/peers
6. Previous relationships
7. Work/job
8. Money/finances
9. *Anxiety* about getting married and *other worries* just before or during wedding (e.g., wedding jitters)
10. Education/career

70. Wedding arrangements—involvement of others (1) and money/finances (8)

72. Wedding arrangements—nonspecific

97. Other [Card]

00. Inap: No tension; no second tension

(Years 3 & 7)

Couple Relations

1. Interpersonal conflict and resolution
2. Conflict over finances and resolution
3. Conflict—other and resolution
4. General personal differences [Card]

Wedding Arrangements

5. Involvement of others—people
6. Nature of ritual, size, type of ceremony, date, etc.
7. *Anxiety* about getting married and other *worries* just before or during the wedding (e.g., wedding jitters)
8. Involvement of others—money/finances
10. Nonspecific problems with arrangements

Children

11. Childcare
12. Uncooperative (e.g., behavior problems at wedding)
13. Having children/pregnancy/birth/planning children

Money/Finances

14. Not enough money
15. Conflict on how to spend money
16. Spending styles/habits and conflict

Education/Career

17. Lacking education for job wanted
18. Dissatisfaction with work (including unemployment)
19. Education versus work—making a choice

20. Education versus partner—making a choice
21. Education versus children—making a choice

Mental Health

22. Bored
23. Loneliness
24. Depression
25. Misery
26. Scared

Physical Health

27. Sickness/illness
28. Death/miscarriage [Card]

Transportation Problems

29. Lack of use of a car
30. Conflict in schedules over use of a car

Miscellaneous

31. Family of origin/in-laws [Card]
32. Friends/peers [Card whose friend and the situation]
33. Previous relationships of one or both partners
34. Living arrangements/living conditions
97. Other [Card]

Effort in planning the wedding

1. Mostly a joint/communal effort with interaction between the couple
2. Mostly an independent effort carried out solely by female partner
3. Mostly an independent effort carried out by female and other(s)
4. Mostly an independent effort carried out by male partner
5. Mostly an independent effort carried out by male partner and other(s)
6. Planning mostly done by someone else
7. Planning done by couple and others
8. Unclear about effort

9. NA: no discussion of planning the wedding
0. Inap: no wedding narrative

Negotiating the differences in planning and executing the wedding

(Year 1)

1. Conflict in which open disagreement is expressed between the couple
2. Compromise between the couple (one gives in to the desires/wants/whims of the other)
3. Conflict or compromise between the couple or members of the couple and others
4. Support or reciprocity (each does something for the other)
5. No differences in planning/executing
8. Unclear about conflict
9. NA: no discussion of planning or executing the wedding
0. Inap: no wedding narrative

(Years 3 & 7)

1. Conflict in which open disagreement is expressed between the couple
2. Compromise (one gives in to the desires/wants/whims of the other) between the couple
3. Conflict or compromise between the couple or member of the couple and others
4. Support or reciprocity (each spouse does something for the other)
5. No differences expressed in planning/executing
6. Compromise or conflict between the couple and conflict or compromise between the couple or members of the couple and others (A combination of code 1 and code 3)
8. Unclear about conflict
9. NA: no discussion of planning or executing the wedding
0. Inap: no wedding narrative

Possible aspects of the wedding narrative—Determine what you think are the *three main aspects* of the wedding story and then code them accordingly (Code up to three mentions).

Affective High Point

9. Grand finale (e.g., a dazzling affair with lots of activity climaxing their courtship)
10. Emotional experience (e.g., one or both and others show emotions of melancholy, tears, laughter, sweating)
11. Beautiful, serene moment of joy, celebration of love; had a wonderful time (e.g., partners actually described their wedding in terms of "beautiful," "joyful." If they just say "wonderful," code 41)
12. Symbolic and fulfilling lifelong desire, wish, or goal; lifelong fantasy (e.g., hoped to be married in a certain kind of ceremony; the wedding symbolizes a wish/desire or fantasy to be married in a certain way)

Social Occasion

13. Opportunity for family to be together/consolidate (e.g., family involvement is emphasized here; involvement includes their participation in the planning and the wedding)
14. Sociable occasion, no clear indication of family/friends
15. Friends, family all had wonderful time (e.g., use this code when the couple or one of them emphasizes the friends/family having a good time)

Public Commitment

21. Turning point—making the big step (e.g., use this code when doubt has surrounded the outcome of the courtship leading to a wedding, or the couple emphasizes it as a big step)
22. Natural ending of courtship (e.g., together, then the coming to an end of the courtship)
23. Confirmation of commitment to a living arrangement
24. Confirmation of one's religious faith (e.g., strong religious overtones)
25. Rite of passage into a new status (e.g., marriage provides an improvement as seen by one partner or both)
26. Legitimization, but no big deal
27. Show for the family's sake/other's sake (e.g., doing it for the family)
31. Personal commitment—a show of commitment not clearly public (e.g., they were committed and emphasized their personal commitment to each other)

Positive Experience

41. It was a good time; it went well, perfect (e.g., affirming a positive experience)
42. Financially rewarding (e.g., receipt of gifts)

Negative Experience

51. Time of conflict with spouse
52. Time of conflict with family
53. Rude awakening (e.g., the experience of marriage leads to shock or sudden changes)
54. Disappointment/problems with people in logistics of wedding
55. Disappointment over debt assumption and/or disappointment over the lack of gifts
56. General dissatisfaction (hassles, etc.)
57. Lack of support from family
58. Lack of support from friends
59. Lack of support from family/friends
97. Other [Card]
99. NA
00. No story; no second aspect; no third aspect

Codes Specific to Honeymoon Story

General approach to Narrative Task—Honeymoon (1–5 same as all other substories)

Use next four codes if couple describes time right after the wedding, but there was no formal honeymoon:

6. A story or set of stories with connections about right after wedding—no honeymoon
7. A story or set of stories told intermittently about right after the wedding—no honeymoon
8. Conventionalized continuity in response to questions; descriptions—no honeymoon
9. No continuity; mere answering of questions in question–answer format—no honeymoon

Type of tension in honeymoon story/narrative (Code up to number of sources in the *exact order* previously coded)

(Year 1)

1. Couple relationships (e.g., interpersonal) [Card]
2. Honeymoon mishaps (arrangements, travel, other outcomes)
3. Family
4. Children
5. Friends/peers
6. Previous relationships
7. Money/finances
8. Work/job
9. Education/career
10. Scheduling/timing
97. [Card]
00. Inap: no tension, no second tension

(Years 3 & 7)

Couple Relations

1. Interpersonal conflict and resolution
2. Conflict over finances and resolution
3. Conflict—Other and resolution
4. Separation and reconciliation
5. Separation (e.g., physically separated as a result of moving, etc.)
6. General personal differences [Card]
7. Divorce/separation (e.g., dissolving marriage)

Honeymoon Mishaps

8. Arrangements
9. Travel
10. Other outcomes [Card]

Education/Career

11. Education versus work—making a choice
12. Education versus spouse—making a choice
13. Education versus children—making a choice
14. Lacking education for job wanted
15. Dissatisfaction with work (including unemployment)

Children

16. Childcare
17. Having children
18. Not having children
19. Work scheduling and childcare conflict

Money/Finances

20. Not enough money
21. Conflict on how to spend money
22. Spending styles/habits and conflict

Mental Health

23. Bored
24. Loneliness
25. Depression
26. Misery
27. Scared

Physical Health

28. Sickness/illness
29. Death/miscarriage [Card]

Transportation Problems

30. Lack of use of a car
31. Conflict in schedules over use of a car

Role Conflict—conflict between the demands of two roles

32. Spouse role versus work role conflict
33. Spouse role versus parent role conflict
34. Parent role versus work role conflict

Miscellaneous

35. Family of origin/in-laws [Card]
36. Friends/peers [Card whose friends and the situation]
37. Previous relationships of one or both partners
38. Scheduling/timing
39. Living arrangements/living conditions

40. Substance abuse
97. Other [Card]
99. NA
00. Inap: no tension; no second tension; no third tension

Aspects of the Honeymoon Narrative—Determine what you think are the
three main aspects **of the honeymoon story and then code them accordingly**
(Code up to three mentions).

Positive Themes: Couple Took Honeymoon

10. Relief from stress of wedding/life's routine
11. A period of seclusion/privacy (e.g., time to be alone together)
12. Travel, sightseeing, and entertainment
13. General satisfaction (Low Priority)

Negative Themes: Couple Took Honeymoon

20. Disappointment/problems with accommodations, travel
21. Disappointment/problems with people
22. Disappointment/problems with length of honeymoon
23. Disappointment/problems with spouse [Card]
24. General disappointment/problems (Low Priority)
30. Getting adjusted, honeymoon taken

Negative Themes: No Honeymoon Taken

50. Getting adjusted, no honeymoon taken

(Years 3 & 7)

53. Disappointments with people
54. Disappointments with spouse
55. General disappointments/problems [Card]

Positive Themes: No Honeymoon Taken

51. Relief from stress of wedding/life's routine
52. A period of seclusion (e.g., time to be alone)
80. Unconventional honeymoon (honeymoon taken prior to wedding; honeymooned with friends; took two honeymoons)
97. Other [Card]

99. NA

00. Inap: no honeymoon story, no second aspect, no third aspect

Codes Specific to the Story of the Last Couple of Years (Years 3 & 7 Only)

Type of tension in the Last Couple of Years (Code up to number of sources in the *exact order* as above).

Couple Relations

1. Divorce and separation
2. Separation and reconciliation
3. Separation (e.g., physically separated as a result of moving, etc.)
4. Interpersonal conflict and resolution
5. Conflict over finances and resolution
6. Conflict—Other and resolution [Card]
7. General personal differences [Card]

Role Conflict—conflict between the demands of two roles

8. Spouse role versus work role conflict
9. Spouse role versus parent role conflict
10. Parent role versus work role conflict

Children

11. Having children/pregnancy/birth/planning kids
12. Not having children
13. Childcare
14. Work schedule and childcare conflict

Transportation Problems

15. Lack of or no car
16. Conflict in schedules over transportation

Education/Career

17. Lacking education for job wanted
18. Education versus work—making a choice
19. Education versus children—making a choice
20. Education versus spouse—making a choice

21. Dissatisfaction with work (including unemployment)

Money/Finances

22. Not enough money
23. Conflict on how to spend money
24. Spending styles/habits and conflict

Mental Health

25. Bored
26. Loneliness
27. Depression
28. Misery
29. Scared

Physical Health

30. Sickness/illness
31. Death/miscarriage [Card]

Miscellaneous

32. Family of origin/in-laws [Card]
33. Friends/peers [Card whose friends and the situation]
34. Previous relationships of one or both partners
35. Substance abuse
36. Living arrangements/living conditions
97. Other [Card]
99. NA
00. Inap: no tension; no second tension; no third tension

Aspects of the Last Couple of Years—Determine what you think are the *three main aspects* **of the last couple of years story and then code them accordingly.**

Social Domain

10. Work and Job (including unemployment)
11. Establishment/maintenance of ties with friends
12. Religious activity (including spiritual guidance and involvement)
13. Education/career (including job advancement)

14. Leisure (excluding honeymoon) including travel, recreation
15. Involvement in social clubs, civic organizations

Personal Domain—Role Development/Adjustment

20. Getting adjusted to each other/married life (e.g., interdependency as a couple)
21. Developing a routine (e.g., settling down in general; doing household chores)
22. Developing as a spouse/developing marriage
23. Developing as a parent/becoming a better parent (including rearing children)
24. Developing multiple roles (e.g., spouse and parent)
25. Overcoming past personal/family experiences
26. Personal comfort/lack of comfort (general)
27. Counseling (individual or as a couple)
28. Enhancing personal development (exclusive of spouse)
29. Changing priorities (e.g., more responsible, growing up)

Personal Domain

30. Financial security/stability
31. "Nest-building" (e.g., buying furniture, decorating, repairing, setting up a business, buying a house, etc.)
32. Living arrangements (including moving)/living conditions (general quality of life)
33. Major purchases (e.g., car, boat, etc.)

Family Domain

40. Establishment/maintenance of ties with wife's family
41. Establishment/maintenance of ties with husband's family
42. Establishment and achievement of couple's own independence
43. Establishment/maintenance of ties with family (*general* mention) or *both* families
45. Children (including pregnancy, childbirth, and rearing of own children)
46. Adoption
47. Deciding not to have children
70. Staying the same/accepting life as it is—Low Priority
71. Taking it one day at a time—Low Priority

97. Other [Card]

99. NA

00. Inap: no last couple of years story; no second aspect; no third aspect

Codes Specific to Couples' Story of Present Life

**Type of tension in Present Life story (Code up to number of sources in the
exact order coded previously).**

(Year 1)

1. Couple relations [Card]
2. Family of origin/in-laws
3. Children/childcare
4. Friends/peers
5. Previous relationships of one or both partners
6. Money/finances
7. Work/job
8. Education/career
9. Substance abuse
10. Living arrangements/living conditions
11. Time/schedules
97. Other [Card]
99. NA
00. Inap: no tension; no second tension

(Years 3 & 7)

Couple Relations

1. Divorce/separation (e.g., dissolving marriage)
2. Separation, reconciliation
3. Separation (e.g., physically separated as a result of moving, etc.)
4. Interpersonal conflict and resolution
5. Conflict over finances and resolution
6. Conflict—Other and resolution [Card]
7. General personal differences [Card]

Role Conflict—conflict between the demands of two roles

8. Spouse role versus work role conflict

9. Spouse role versus parent role conflict
10. Parent role versus work role conflict

Children

11. Having children
12. Not having children
13. Childcare
14. Work schedule and childcare conflict

Transportation Problems

15. Lack of or no car
16. Conflict in schedules over transportation

Education/Career

17. Lacking education for job wanted
18. Education versus work—making a choice
19. Education versus children—making a choice
20. Education versus spouse—making a choice
21. Dissatisfaction with work (including unemployment)

Money/Finances

22. Not enough money
23. Conflict on how to spend money
24. Spending styles/habits and conflict

Mental Health

25. Bored
26. Loneliness
27. Depression
28. Misery
29. Scared

Physical Health

30. Sickness/illness
31. Death/miscarriage [Card]

Miscellaneous

32. Family of origin/in-laws [Card]
33. Friends/peers [Card whose friends and the situation]
34. Previous relationships of one or both partners
35. Substance abuse
36. Living arrangements/living conditions
97. Other [Card]
99. NA
00. Inap: no tension; no second tension; no third tension

Aspects of Present Life

(Year 1) **CODER: Determine if there is a** *dominant aspect* **(i.e., emphasis on one aspect throughout the section on present life), and code that aspect first; then code second and third mentions in the order that they occur. If no dominant aspect, code in order of mentions. When each partner gives a list of aspects, try to determine if any aspect applies to the** *couple* **as a unit, and give priority to these aspects in coding.**

(Years 3 & 7) **Determine what you think are the** *three main aspects* **of the present life story and then code them accordingly.**

Social Domain

10. Work and job (including unemployment)
11. Establishment/maintenance of ties with friends
12. Religious activity (including spiritual guidance and involvement)
13. Education/career (including job advancement)
14. Leisure (excluding honeymoon) including travel, recreation
15. Involvement in social clubs, civic organizations

Personal Domain—Role Development/Adjustment

20. Getting adjusted to each other/married life (e.g., interdependency as a couple)
21. Developing a routine (e.g., settling down in general; doing household chores)
22. Developing as a spouse/developing marriage
23. Developing as a parent/becoming a better parent (including rearing children)
24. Developing multiple roles (e.g., spouse and parent)

25. Overcoming past personal/family experiences
26. Personal comfort/lack of comfort (general)

Personal Domain

30. Financial security/stability
31. "Nest-building" (e.g., buying furniture, decorating, repairing, setting up a business, buying a house, etc.)
32. Living arrangements (including moving)/living conditions (general quality of life)

Family Domain

40. Establishment/maintenance of ties with wife's family
41. Establishment/maintenance of ties with husband's family
42. Establishment and achievement of couple's own independence
43. Establishment/maintenance of ties with family (*general* mention) or *both* families
45. Children (including pregnancy, childbirth, and rearing of own children)
70. Staying the same/accepting life as it is—Low Priority
71. Taking it one day at a time—Low Priority
97. Other [Card]
99. NA
00. Inap: no present life story; no second aspect; no third aspect

(Years 3 & 7)

Personal Domain—Role Development/Adjustment

27. Counseling (individual or as a couple)
28. Enhancing personal development (exclusive of spouse)
29. Changing priorities (e.g., more responsible, growing up)

Personal Domain

33. Major purchases (e.g., car, boat, etc.)

Family Domain

46. Adoption
47. Deciding not to have children

Codes Specific to Couple's Story of Future

Type of tension in Future Life Story (Code up to number of sources in the *exact order* coded previously).

(Year 1)

1. Couple relations [Card]
2. Family of origin/in-laws
3. Children/childcare
4. Friends/peers
5. Previous relationship(s) of one or both partners
6. Money/finances
7. Work/job
8. Education/career
9. Substance abuse
10. Living arrangements/living conditions
97. Other [Card]
99. NA
00. Inap: No tension; no second tension

(Years 3 & 7)

Couple Relations

1. Divorce/separation (e.g., dissolving marriage)
2. Interpersonal conflict and resolution
3. Conflict over finances and resolution
4. Conflict—Other and resolution [Card]
5. General personal differences [Card]

Role Conflict—conflict between the demands of two roles

6. Spouse role versus work role conflict
7. Spouse role versus parent role conflict
8. Parent role versus work role conflict

Children

9. Having children (pregnancy, birth, planning children)
10. Not having children

11. Childcare
12. Work schedule and childcare conflict

Transportation Problems

13. Lack of or no car
14. Conflict in schedules over transportation

Education/Career

15. Lacking education for job wanted
16. Education versus work—making a choice
17. Education versus children—making a choice
18. Education versus spouse—making a choice
19. Dissatisfaction with work (including unemployment)

Money/Finances

20. Not enough money
21. Conflict on how to spend money
22. Spending styles/habits and conflict

Miscellaneous

23. Family of origin/in-laws [Card]
24. Friends/peers [Card whose friends and the situation]
25. Previous relationships of one or both partners
26. Substance abuse
27. Living arrangements/living conditions
97. Other [Card]
99. NA
00. Inap: no tension; no second tension; no third tension

(Year 1) **CODER: Determine if there is a *dominant aspect* (i.e., emphasis on one aspect throughout the section on future life), and code that aspect first; then code second and third mentions in the order that they occur. If no dominant aspect, code in order of mentions. When each partner gives a list of aspects, try to determine if any aspect applies to the *couple* as a unit, and give priority to these aspects in coding.**

(Years 3 & 7) **Determine what you think are the *three main aspects* of the future life story and then code them accordingly.**

Social Domain—Progressive Form

10. Change/continue in job/work
11. Change in/enhancement of education/career
12. Enhancement of friendship with others
13. Enhancement of family/in-law relations
14. Continue religious activities
15. Leisure (including travel and recreation)

Personal Domain/Role Development/Adjustment—Progressive Form

20. Getting adjusted to marriage (e.g., interdependency as a couple)
21. Developing a routine (e.g., settling down in general; doing household chores)
22. Developing as a spouse/developing marriage
23. Developing as a parent/becoming a better parent (including rearing children)
24. Enhancing personal development without consideration of spouse involvement (e.g., self-actualization, greater self-knowledge, fulfillment of own needs)
25. Wanting children/having (more) children
26. Developing multiple roles (e.g., spouse and parent)

Personal Domain—Progressive Form

30. Financial security/stability
31. "Nest-building" (e.g., buying furniture, decorating, repairing, setting up a business, buying a house, etc.)
35. Having a more comfortable life; a better living arrangement
36. General optimism (e.g., "brighter hopes")—Low Priority

Social Domain—Regressive Form

40. Work/job/career (fear of losing job, not being successful)
41. Loss of connection to family/friends
50. General pessimism (the future looks bleak; can't see that far ahead; no control over the future)—Low Priority

Personal Domain—Regressive Form

(This category includes conditional pessimism, e.g., "if . . .")

60. Becoming financially insecure; facing financial difficulties
61. Family modifications (e.g., having another child; having another child too soon)
65. Facing uncertainty re: living arrangements
66. Facing uncertainty re: role/duties as spouse
67. Pessimism re: living arrangements
68. Pessimism re: role/duties as spouse
97. Other [Card]
99. NA
00. Inap: no future story; no second aspect; no third aspect

(Years 3 & 7)

Personal Domain/Role Development/Adjustment—Progressive Form

27. Counseling (individual or as a couple)

Personal Domain—Progressive Form

37. Major purchases (e.g., car, boat, etc.)

If a general approach to any story was coded "3" (intermittently or *descriptions told intermittently*), determine the following and code up to four mentions.

1. Couple drifted back and forth from one story to another
2. A major event in a prior story is brought into telling a subsequent story without any major elaboration
3. A mismatch of couple on storytelling (e.g., one spouse gets ahead of the other on the storyboard)
4. Interviewer directs couple off track in telling their story, hurries couple through their story—High Priority
0. Inap: none of the above; no second, third, or fourth mention

Affective Coding Manual

Interviews conducted as a source of stories of newlywed couples' histories together—from their first meeting to their dreams of the future—are coded for affective themes. The rationale for such coding is that statements of feelings by storytellers are perhaps the most diagnostic motivational information we have about people's concerns in their lives. Much of the coding of thematic apperception for achievement, affiliation, and power motives ultimately rests on the presence of affective statements in one form or another. We use parallel ways of thinking about feelings occurring in a story about one's own marriage. We assume that the more often a given type of feeling or need is described in a person's marriage narrative, the more likely one can see that type of feeling as being particularly important to the person's construction of his or her marriage. Included as affective themes are direct and indirect statements of feelings and needs (goals, intentions). These are more fully described next.

Type of Affect

Statements of Feelings. These include direct affective statements such as feelings of attraction (liking, enjoying, caring, loving, is attracted to, interested in, etc.), repulsion (hating, disliking, etc.), and affective states (happy, sad, frustrating, being stressed, overwhelmed, content, angry, fearful, being excited, etc.). Conditional or future affects such as "would like" should be coded as statements of feeling although a good inference of need could be made as well.

One can code only certain indirect states of being for which affect can be easily inferred (it was nice, sweet, great, good, beautiful; times experienced as mellow, good, interesting, or fine; things turning out fine). Do not code a phrase or sentence for affect if the only basis for the coding is an adjective about a person's attributes (e.g., don't code "he was a depressed person"; but code "he was depressed"). Similarly, do not code a statement for affect if the only basis for coding is a positive or negative adjective about some discrete entity or object (e.g., the dress was lovely; the food was bad). These are probably simple descriptors, not necessarily implying an emotional response. However, affect can be inferred from more global positive or negative statements about a larger event or occasion (e.g., the wedding was beautiful; the trip was a disaster).

Explicit mentions of relationships from which one can easily infer positive affect (e.g., use of the word "friends" or "lovers") are also coded. In the mention of relationships, just the use of the word is insufficient. The coding of the statement of a relationship must be supported by the mention of a friendship activity (e.g., "we spent a lot of time together," "we helped each other often," or other such mentions of friends supporting or helping each other or simply seeing or visiting each other). The negation of statements of relationships, such as "I didn't really have friends to spend time with," should also be coded.

Actions that clearly imply a particular affect can be coded for that affect (e.g., laughter implies happiness, crying implies sadness, freezing up implies fear). In any of these indirect statements one must be able to infer easily that feelings exist. Be sure you can quickly infer that the person would easily say, "I was feeling good (or bad) about _____."

Statements of Need. These include any direct statement of hoping, wanting, wishing, needing, intending, or otherwise having certain specific goals; or any indirect statement of goals (having ideals; being determined about something, relying on, being committed to, or serious about something or somebody; having positive anticipations of future events or situations, such as looking forward to a wedding). "Trying," "planning," or "deciding" to do something is not to be used to infer a statement of need.

Elaboration of Identifying Affective Statements. Do not infer affect from being skeptical, doubting, or just thinking about something in general, such as "we were planning our trip" or "I thought we would be married within a year." Do not code general statements about affect, where affect is mentioned but no one in particular seems to "own" it (e.g., "Different people have different ideas about what happiness is"). Do not assume that the word "feel" always implies that an affect is present. Sometimes people say "I feel that" when all they really mean is "It is my opinion that" (e.g., "I feel that once you get married, your own family comes first"). Do not code statements that are heavily laden with sarcasm (e.g., "That was a lot of fun!" said in a very sarcastic tone), as it is difficult to know exactly what affect the speaker is conveying.

Code "nagging," "bugging," "bothering," and so on as affective statements. The person who is being nagged, bugged, or bothered is the one feeling the affect (source), the person doing the nagging, bugging, or bothering is the object of that affect. "Being tired" or "being sick" is not coded for affect, but being tired or sick of something is.

Do not code for mere agreement by one speaker of the other speaker's affect. For example, do not code wife's affect: "H: We love our house." "W: Yeah." But do code for the wife in the following: "H: We love our house." "W: Yes, it's a terrific place."

Statements of conditional affects (e.g., it would make one unhappy; spouse would have been so angry) or needs (e.g., if we move to Florida, I want to live by the water) should be coded. Affective statements in the form of questions—do you want something or are you upset about something—should also be coded. Denials of affect (e.g., husband: You were mad; wife: No, I wasn't) should not be coded (i.e., in the aforementioned case, do not code the wife's utterance).

If consecutive phrases or statements from the same speaker reiterate the same affect, the coder should not code the reiterations. If the initial phrase or sentence is interrupted by another thought, and then a repetition occurs, the repetition should be coded. What constitutes an interruption? If the interruption is by the other speaker or the interviewer and it is not just laughter, agreement, or a simple phrase, then the reiteration should be coded.

If the same affect is repeated in consecutive phrases or sentences, but the person to whom that affect is attributed shifts (I-statements to we or third person statements, or vice versa) then each affect should be coded. Similarly, if two speakers repeat the identical affect immediately following one another, each should be coded. For example, you would code "H: We loved our wedding. W: The wedding was wonderful" for two affects, one with the husband and one with the wife as speaker.

Moreover, if the same general affect is expressed in a sequence of utterances, but the object shifts (e.g., from the spouse to the relationship), then code the shift as another utterance with an additional affect code. However, if the specific person being referred to shifts but the category remains the same (i.e., the "other" category) do not code for two affective utterances. For example, code for two affects: "H: I was glad to see my wife; I was glad we were together." But code for only one affect: "H: I enjoyed meeting her brother and I liked meeting his wife."

Finally, if the object category remains the same within a sequence of utterances, but the topic shifts, then you should code the shift as another utterance. For example, "I was mainly concerned about the money, the job, and about getting a home or apartment" would be coded as three statements, with topics "finances," "work," and "housing," respectively. In summary, when the same general affect is expressed in a sequence of utterances, but the speaker, source, object, or topic of the statement changes, code the utterances separately.

In coding for the presence of an affective statement, the coder should indicate on which criterion the decision to code was based: either feeling or need statement.

> Code: 1. feeling
>   2. need

Direction of Affect

Is the affect or need positive, negative, or neutral? Only the negation of a negative affect (e.g., not unhappy, not bothered, not something bad) is coded as neutral. Affect that cannot be clearly identified as positive or negative (e.g., "surprised," when you cannot tell from context if being surprised is positive or negative) should be coded as a "9" (not ascertainable), not a "3" (neutral).

All needs are coded as positive unless a negative grammatical construction is used (e.g., I don't want a _____ or I want not to _____). Only the negation of the words "want" or "need" are coded as negative. The negation of more indirect statements of need, such as "She wasn't serious" or "we weren't committed to buying it," should not be coded.

> Code: 1. positive
>   2. negative
>   3. neutral
>   9. NA

Speaker of Affective Utterances

Is the person who voices the affective statement in the interview the husband or the wife?

Code: 1. Husband
         2. Wife

Source of Affect or Need(s)

In this coding, the coder indicates who is experiencing the affect according to the statement made. If the affect comes from an impersonal setting (e.g., "It was wonderful"), or the speaker uses the impersonal "you" (e.g., "You're going to get really mad when something like that happens"), code the speaker of the statement as the source. To aid reliability, this rule should be followed quite strictly, even when you could make a reasonable inference that the source of the affect is the couple (e.g., husband mentions "things you like to do together"—word "together" might make you think he means "things we like to do together"; however, not everyone would make the same inference, so stick to the speaker as the source.) The only exceptions to this rule (i.e., code the speaker as the source) are instances where the speaker mentions "us" (e.g., "It was really great for us"), "our" (e.g., "Our honeymoon was wonderful"), and so on. Those statements are coded with the couple as the source.

Code: 1. husband

         2. wife

         3. couple—most often noted in cases where "we" is used

         4. other person(s)

         9. NA

Object of Affect

This code asks who or what is the affective statement about. Who or what is inspiring the coded affect? Who or what is the affect directed toward? For example, the statement spoken by the wife "I was in love with him" is a statement in which she is the source of the affect but her husband is the object—he is what the affect is directed toward. The major distinctions coded are similar to those used with regard to the source (husband, wife, relationship, other person(s)/situation(s)). The category of situation includes references to housing, the wedding as an event or occasion, and political situations. At the end of this section, examples are given after each coding category.

    If it is not clear whether a person (or relationship) should be coded, or whether a situation should be coded, give priority to the person (relationship) as the object of the affect. For example, if the interviewer asks "How are things going now?" and the wife replies "Things are going great," it is not clear if she is talking about her life in general (i.e., the situation, code 4), or about the relationship (code 3). Unless context indicates otherwise, you should assume she is talking about the relationship.

Use the relationship code if you are unclear whether to code for a person or relationship. For example, code for relationship "I want things to go well" if it occurs in the context of describing a courtship.

Code: 1. Husband—(e.g., she loved me; my wife was unhappy with my smoking).
2. Wife—(e.g., I was attracted to her; I wanted her to go to school).
3. Couple relationship—(e.g., I like that we were similar; we have fun together).
4. Other Person/Relationship/Situation—(e.g., we were friends; my mom and I enjoyed preparing things; we had fun at our wedding; we fight a lot [when no specific cause is given in context]).

Marital Context

In this code, the coder dates the occurrence of the affect or need, in terms of the couple's relationship history.

Code: 1. Before knowing spouse
2. Early contact and courtship (including period living together)
3. Wedding (including wedding planning)
4. Initial time after marriage (honeymoon & initial weeks after wedding)
5. First couple of years [if applicable; Years 3 and 7 only]
6. Current marital life
7. Future marital life
9. NA

If the speaker mentions an emotion that occurred at some unspecified point in the past (e.g., "I used to be afraid of commitment") the context should be a 9.

Talk of hypothetical events (things that haven't happened yet, but might happen in the future; e.g., "If you ever left me, I'd feel lost") should be coded with a future context. Wishes for the future should also generally be put in a future context (e.g., "I hope I can get a better job"—although the emotion is being experienced now, it is about a future event, so code it for future).

Sometimes a speaker will mention an emotion that is being experienced now, but has also probably been experienced in all past contexts (e.g., "she is close to her family," "she enjoys her job"). If it is clear that emotion still holds true for the present, then code it in the "current marital life" context.

Specific Topic Focus

Certain problems or life conditions in connection with marital affects and need have been selected for special note in coding. If the statement can be coded for two or more of the topics listed, code the most dominant one.

Code: 1. housing, location of residence
2. children
3. work (education should not be coded in the work category)
4. finances
5. families or family member
9. NA

Motivational Basis for the Affect or Need

To code the motivational basis for the affect or need, the coder determines whether the affective statement is related to one of two motivational issues: agency or self-expression, or being connected or related to another person. These are defined by the following types of goal states:

1. *Agency or self-expression:* mastering an activity; performing on one's own; achieving a vocational or educational or other achievement goal; getting one's own way about something; having a voice in what is happening; liking the kind of person one is; having values expressed. A couple separating from others should be coded for self-expression motivation, even if the source is a couple rather than a single person. Code a husband's statement "We wanted a place of our own" as agency. Code statements that indicate failure of agency as agency (e.g., "I was upset because I didn't do well on a test").

2. *Being connected or related:* being loved; being friends; loving, supporting, helping another; loving one another; enjoying doing things together; enjoying being married; relying on another; being interested in someone; being involved with someone. Code statements that indicate a lack of con-

nection (without necessarily indicating a desire for agency—e.g., "we weren't very close at first") for connection motivation.

3. *Both agency and being connected motivations:* Elements of both motivations may be present in a given affective or need statement. Most apparent would be instances of "fighting" or "arguing," which is an objective condition from which affect can be inferred. Such statements have elements of both agency and being connected. Fighting implies self-assertiveness in the middle of disrupted mutual concern. Thus, code fighting (3) for motivation. Mentions of a lack of arguments (e.g., "we never argue") should be coded, and have a motivation of 3. Similarly, wanting a relationship to be a certain way with some emphasis on the person's own picture of the relationship would be coded (3). Wanting help from someone will be coded a (3), wanting a child or children should be coded (3) unless the person is explicit about the condition for having children. In that case, the focus on meeting self-expectations should be coded a (1). Being jealous should be coded (3).

9. *NA:* Some affective statements may not be codable in any of the aforementioned categories. For example, "It was very relaxing" is hard to code for a specific motivational concern. Being interested or liking an object does not fit well into either of the preceding categories, unless it fits a value-expression and should therefore be coded as agency; finding someone "interesting" is ambiguous; code as (9). All of the above would be coded (9) or nonascertainable.

A desire to separate can be coded either as a self-expression motivation or a negative relational motivation. Arbitrarily code it as agency.

Negative affective states are clearly codable in the appropriate category—for example, fear of failing under agency, fear of rejection under being connected.

Interaction Coding Manual

Sequencing of talk between the spouses is coded for interaction. Not all talk is coded, only the sequential links.

Collaboration, Conflict, Confirmation, and Laughter

Four major types of interactions are coded in listening to a couple's presentation of the story of their marriage: *collaboration, conflictful, confirming,* and *laughter.* The coder must listen to the quality of the sequences for husband and wife and vice versa, spontaneously generated by their own styles. That is, coders must pay special attention to the times when one spouse's utterances follows the other spouse's utterances, and then decide whether these sequential interactions indicate one of the following communicative messages:

- Collaborative—I wish to add and elaborate on what you said.
- Conflictful—I don't like what you said.
- Confirming—I like what you said.
- Laughter—I am amused by what you said.

The kinds of sequences that fit under each are presented next. Coders should attend only to the first phrase, idea, or sentence of the interaction. If a sequence contains more than one major idea, code only the first one. However, if the first phrase, idea, or sentence is an agreeing phrase (e.g., "Yes" or "That's right") and then the speaker goes on with a sentence or

217

phrase that could be coded as collaborative, the second phrase can also be incorporated, resulting in a code of *confirmation and collaboration.*

If a person continues a specific storyline that had been interrupted by his or her spouse's interaction, that continuation would not be coded for collaborative, conflictful, or confirming unless in some way this continuation was responsive to what the content of the interruption had been. It would be coded *continuing* or *nonresponse,* depending on whether or not one can infer that the continuation represents a clear rejection of what the spouse said. If there is even a slight shift in direction of the storyline, it should be coded as collaborative. If it is unclear whether the continuation is or is not responsive to the interruption, code it as continuation. Strive to keep the collaboration code "pure."

Collaborative Sequences

The following are the kinds of sequences that should be coded as collaborative:

1. Picking up words or ideas of the spouse and adding to them, extending the storyline, or qualifying a description or a point being made. However, if the coded qualification represents a clear disagreement, it should be coded as conflictful.
2. Questions of information that further the story. (N.B. These questions should be coded as collaborative interactions whenever they occur. They need not be first-sentence interruptions.)
3. Answers to questions that further the story. Those that do not should not be coded.
4. Continuation of storylines after interruption if the continuation reflects the interruption, as noted earlier.
5. Any foils for the spouse storyline (e.g., posing a question that enables the story to continue).

Conflictful Sequences

The following are the major interactive sequences that are coded as conflictful:

1. Disagreeing about facts; denial about events or timing. If the apparent disagreement is in the form of a question that is accepting of the spouse (e.g., "Was it the 24th of May or the 25th?" when the other spouse mentions the 24th as an important date in their lives), then it should be coded as collaborative.

2. Interrupting to tell a different point without open disagreement but without consideration of what had just been said. It may often be hard to distinguish interrupting from collaborating. A judgment of the tone of the speaker may be necessary. If the interruption is accepting, code as collaboration; if the interruption is hostile or at all negative, code it as conflictful. More significant might be a judgment of whether the narrative sequence was interdependent.

Confirming Sequences

The following are coded as confirming:

1. Any direct statement indication of agreement (yeah, yes, you're right, or repetition of the same words. If an elaboration of the person's ideas or words, code it as collaborative).
2. Um hums.

Answers to questions that confirm what spouse thought was happening are coded as collaborative rather than confirming.

Laughter Sequences

Code laughter only when it is the only "statement" made. Code laughter as a separate category. Any laughter that is interactive with a spouse should be coded. If the laughter clearly indicates an amused reaction, code as confirming within a subcategory of laughter. If this is unclear, code as other laughter.

1. Laughter indicating amusement coded as confirming.
2. Other.

Continuation and Nonresponsive Sequences

In addition to the four categories already discussed, there are four additional ones. *Nonresponse* is coded for all sequences where a person explicitly ignores the spouse's statement—either a collaborative or a conflicting one. These instances are when the spouse makes a statement that has to be taken into account logically but is rejected in the next utterance. There are instances of overlapping talk where this would not be coded as nonresponsive. Do not code over-talk if it is not intelligible. If a nonresponse is an interruption, code it as conflict.

Responses to interruptions that come as quick interjections without time for the spouse to respond should be coded under the category of *continuation*. This last category includes continuation of the narrative after an interruption, which is not directly responsive to the interruption as collaborative, conflicting, confirming, or explicitly nonresponsive. If it is unclear whether to code collaborative or continuation, code continuation.

Special note should be made of the interviews in which the husband or wife goes off the storytelling track into an ongoing interactional discussion concerning their current lives. Code these sequences even if they are not apparently storytelling. Often they are coded as *other*.

Interruptions by the interviewer should not figure into the coding of the interactions. Responses to interviewers' questions are not coded—no matter how long they are.

Other and Not Applicable (NA) Sequences

The two other categories available for coding discourse links are other and NA sequences, described next.

> *Other*. Process-oriented interaction and other reactions that are not codable under previously described categories.
>
> *NA*. Interaction unintelligible or difficult to code. If only a portion of the utterance is unintelligible, code the portion that is intelligible. If a coder codes one unit as NA and there is no other intervening discourse, the subsequent link is, by definition, also NA.

Marital Context

In this code, the coder dates the occurrences of the interactions in terms of the couple's relationship history.

1. Before knowing spouse.
2. Early contact and courtship (including period living together).
3. Wedding (including wedding planning).
4. Initial time after marriage (honeymoon and initial weeks after wedding).
5. First few years.
6. Current marital life.
7. Future marital life.
9. NA.

ADDENDUM TO INTERACTION CODING MANUAL

Clarification of Other and NA Sequences

Code an interaction as other (process-oriented interaction) if the speaker is clearly making a comment out of the story context. For example, "Do you want a glass of water?" or "Can you get the baby?" Code an interaction as collaborative if speaker is making a comment about storytelling; speaker is not out of story context as in previous examples. Some examples may be "Should we talk about the future now?" or "You can start the story."

Collaboration and Confirm Combination Code

Code *collab/confirm* (9) when the interaction represents a combination of both codes.

EXAMPLE:
H: We were busy preparing for the wedding.
W: Yeah, we had to devote a lot of time to preparations. (code collab/confirm)

EXAMPLE:
H: We really enjoyed our honeymoon.
W: We really enjoyed our honeymoon and needed the time alone together. (code collab/confirm)

SUMMARY OF CODES

Use coding manual for detailed explanation of each code.

System

1. affect
2. interaction

Speaker

1. husband
2. wife

Type

1. collaborative
2. confirm
3. conflict
4. continue
5. nonresponse
6. laugher (confirm)
7. laughter (other)
8. other
9. collab. & confirm
99. NA

Context

1. Before knowing spouse.
2. Early contact and courtship (including period living together).
3. Wedding (including wedding planning).
4. Initial time after marriage (honeymoon and initial weeks after wedding).
5. First few years. [If applicable; Years 3 and 7 only.]
6. Current marital life.
7. Future marital life.
9. NA.

GLOSSARY
Narrative Coding

Collaborative: Shared participation; echoing; dueting; use of "we" in the storytelling/narrative.

Directive Iwer: Iwer asks unnecessary questions and/or interrupts with questions or comments; changes or blocks the flow of the narrative.

Drama/dramatic content: (a) negative obstacles; (b) surprising change(s) in a turn of events; (c) suspense, meaning doubtful anticipation about the outcome; (d) a turning point (e.g., separation, pregnancy, death).
  Note: Pregnancy in the present/future is not coded as dramatic content unless it is described as a turning point, creating change in the relationship.
  Note: Dramatic content can mean many occurrences of the same thing (e.g., many obstacles, or multiple occurrences of a–c (e.g., negative obstacles + surprising change)). It can also mean one event of some magnitude in the relationship.

Drama/dramatic style: This aspect of the narrative coding refers to the storyteller's way of telling/describing what happened. It has to do with the way in which the storyteller expresses emotional feelings and/or liveliness of style.
  Note: Ways of determining dramatic style would include listening for emotional feelings/liveliness of style (vivacity, excitement, enthusiasm, articulateness, and elaboration in the narrative of the storyteller).
  Note: Elaboration also has to do with complexity in the story structure.

Episode: A story.

Inappropriate (Inap):   Inapplicable; providing no further information.

Intermittently (in general approach to the narrative):   A tendency to tell a story in a nonlinear way; drifting back and forth from one story to another; a major event in a prior story is brought into a subsequent story without elaboration; a mismatch of couples on storytelling (e.g., one gets ahead of the other on the storyboard).

Low priority code: This flag indicates that you should use this code only when other information is unavailable.

Narrative: Generalized talking with no specific beginning, middle, or ending; descriptions.

Not ascertained (NA):   Not mentioned or not discernible.

Progressive: A progressive narrative form indicates anticipatory increments in the relationship of a positive kind.

Regressive: A regressive narrative form indicates a negative outcome in the relationship.

Stable: A stable narrative form indicates no clear change or increment in the relationship.

Story: Talking with a specific beginning, middle, and ending; a subset of a narrative.

Tension: Negative obstacles in the story content; a sense of strain or opposing forces in the relationship of the couple and/or outside the relationship.
   Note: How much tension for each source can be measured in explicit or implicit expressions of affect and/or frequency of mentions about the tension. An event of great magnitude would not be coded as causing tension unless the couple perceived it that way.

Theme: A unifying subject or idea in the details of a story; the things and events that characterize particular features or qualities of a story. A theme organizes the telling of a story.

ADDENDUM—CODING NOTES (YEAR 1)

Physical separation can include break-ups.

Evolving out of contact can include growing up together without specific reference to friendship, always being around each other, and working in the same place.

Opportunity for family to be together and consolidate includes reunion themes.

General Approach to Narrative Task: Coding a narrative as category 3, a story or set of stories told intermittently, means deciding that a story exists, and any categories among 1–4 can apply. Only code the story that is out of sequence as being told intermittently. For example, if a couple told all of their stories in the order of the storyboard but their story ending returned to the courtship part, only the courtship story would be coded a 3; the future story is coded as applicable.

Coding a narrative for conventionalized continuity in response to questions means no story exists and the information you hear in the narrative, whether it is sequenced or not sequenced, is coded a 4.

Chronology of events: Planning the wedding is coded as part of the wedding story. Out-of-sequence information (e.g., courtship in wedding story; present in future story) is coded in appropriate story.

Amount of tension: A little tension may be coded when there is mention of a problem and no clear affect statement is made. *Some* tension may be coded when there is mention of a problem and clear affect is present, but no elaboration about the problem. *A lot* of tension may be coded when there is mention of a problem, clear affect, and some elaboration about the problem, or else very strong affect.

Source of tension: Code a source only once. If there are competing or overlapping tensions, make a judgment based on the emphasis given to the tension in the story or narrative.

Type of tension: If there is more than one type of tension for a source of tension, CARD and use code "97." Always give specific information about the type along with verbatim statements.

Prioritizing: Use high priority codes where applicable. When no high priority codes are applicable, code according to specification (e.g., in order of dominant aspect, or order of mention, or emphasis on couple). In instances of competing categories where neither of these rules apply, look for logic of the story content, e.g., *debt* vs. *work*: "We were in debt. Mike didn't have a job. During that time (we were in debt) he was unemployed and when he did work it was not regularly" would be coded for work (not debt) because the logic suggests the debt arose due to lack of work.

Other Do's:

1. Record tape counters for each story's beginning and submit card with records.
2. Record time for total hours spent coding a tape in the left margin of the code sheet.
3. Record check coding on a separate sheet and label as "check coding."
4. CARD any ambiguous information.
5. Take notes in your own style and feel free to submit these with your records.
6. Education/career may be coded when there is evidence of enhancement of skills or advancement, either laterally or vertically, in present or future job.

Author Index

Subject Index